AF471221

INSIDE SOCCER

INSIDE SOCCER

TONY WOODCOCK
WITH PETER BALL

Queen Anne Press

A *Queen Anne Press* BOOK

© Tony Woodcock 1985

First published in Great Britain in 1985 by
Queen Anne Press, Macdonald & Co (Publishers) Ltd,
Maxwell House, 74 Worship Street,
London EC2A 2EN

A BPCC plc company

British Library Cataloguing in Publication Data

Woodcock, Tony
  Inside soccer:
  1. Woodcock, Tony   2. Soccer players—England
  —Biography
  I. Title   II. Ball, Peter, *1943*-
  796.334′092′4   QV942.7.W6
  ISBN 0-356-10079-0

Typeset, printed and bound in Great Britain by
Hazell Watson & Viney Limited,
Member of the BPCC Group,
Aylesbury, Bucks

INTRODUCTION

This book is not the one Tony and I had originally hoped it would be. When it was first mooted, Tony's career seemed to be continuing on its extraordinarily successful path. He had won first division championship, League Cup and European Cup winners' medals with Nottingham Forest. Cologne had been less rewarding in terms of medals, but in his three years there he had broadened his footballing experience, and been widely regarded as one of Germany's most successful imports.

Although his return to England to join Arsenal in the summer of 1982 was still having its teething problems, he had entered the England team with striking success, coming on as substitute to claim England's one goal against West Germany in a friendly, and then getting two goals in their next game, the European Championship qualifying group match against Greece in Athens. After a long and frustrating wait, it seemed as if he had at last established himself as a regular international. Although Arsenal's League position left something to be desired, the League Cup was well enough under way for them to have real hopes of a trip to Wembley.

Of course, being a success as a player does not mean that you have anything to say, as countless football 'autobiographies' testify. It was quite clear from my first long talk with him, when I was doing a feature for *The Times*, that Tony did. He is a thoughtful and intelligent man, who thinks about his game and the game in general. He was also in the unique position of having played under Brian Clough and two of the greatest names in European coaching, Hennes Weisweiler and Rinus Michels, before joining one of the most respected in England, Don Howe. His list of striking partners contains England and Germany's best: Francis, Withe and Birtles for Nottingham Forest; Müller, Fischer, Allofs and Littbarski for Cologne; while Paul Mariner was a regular international partner before linking up with Tony at Arsenal. That alone meant that Tony had a perspective and authority few players can match, and ensured that there was a very good book in him. The decision to do it as a diary, and start it as soon as the idea was suggested rather than at the natural point of the opening of a season, may appear rather perverse.

Diaries always seem to me an ideal format – the perfect vehicle for revealing the day-to-day life and workings of a football club, which is still an area of great fascination in all the millions of words written about football every season. And they also have a loose enough structure to enable their writer to go off at interesting tangents.

There were pressing reasons for doing it at once. The most important as I talked to Tony was that he was still going through the process of reintegrating into English football; the difficulties he was experiencing had provoked some very revealing thoughts about the natures of the European and English games. Those, I thought, would not be as fresh with a whole English season already under his belt, and I also thought that the fact that a player of his calibre should experience and articulate those difficulties would open a few eyes. We hope it will do so.

The other reason for going ahead immediately was the prospect of having a Wembley appearance as the climax of the book. That did not happen, as Arsenal lost in two semi-finals, which was why this is not the book we had hoped for. With the end of the season ruined, as Tony was injured, we decided to carry it on into the new season.

Thus it is the diary of a calendar year rather than a football one. But that is how most of us live our lives, and the fact that it encompasses parts of two seasons rather than one whole has its compensations. It deals with the end of the 1982–83 season, and the beginning of the 1983–84 season, showing how – in spite of all the new hopes – the life and experience of most players at most clubs is unaltered, the same mistakes are repeated, the same hopes are dispelled by reality. It has also provided an added bonus in putting the sacking of Terry Neill into better perspective than starting the book at the beginning of the 1983–84 season would have done.

PETER BALL

1 JANUARY
Arsenal 2 Swansea City 1

It takes time to adjust to a new club. And when it is in a different country, with a different type of football, it takes even longer. I think a lot of people expected me to just slot back into it, because I am English, but for the last three years I have been playing in a totally contrasting game, and the first half of my first season back has been difficult. That has not surprised me. I didn't have any illusions that it would be easy, but I had forgotten some of the differences, and I had not really expected to find others. There are varying kinds of fitness. When I went to Germany I was used to playing a lot of games and I found the training hard. Now that I'm back, having been used to the training, I'm finding all the games hard.

And the game differs in many ways. At the moment, I am finding all my concentration is needed just to control the ball. In Cologne I never had to think about that. It was one touch and away. I knew how the passes were coming, and when they were coming. At Arsenal, at the moment, I don't.

I don't think I'm getting enough of the ball at present. Jon Holmes, my adviser, says that I've always complained about that wherever I've been. He said I did it in Cologne all the time. But I've been watching some videos of my games in Cologne, and in comparison I'm on the ball the whole time in them.

But I think most players, however good they are, find fitting in with a new team takes time. In my last year in Germany, Cologne bought Klaus Fischer and Klaus Allofs. When they first came they had a terrible time. The papers said, 'They are even playing worse than Woodcock when he had his bad spell.' And that opened a few people's eyes. Here were Klaus Fischer, 'Der Bomber' for the national team, and Klaus Allofs, who had been the top scorer in the 1980 European Championships, and suddenly they couldn't play. People began to say, 'What must it have been like for an Englishman to come over and try to fit in?' I still get the Cologne sports papers occasionally, and Fischer has settled in now, but Allofs still hasn't, even though he is a very good player.

By those comparisons I don't feel too unhappy. The team has not been doing too well. We have been very inconsistent, but beating Tottenham over Christmas was encouraging. And I am hoping that at last I am set for a proper run in the England team. It was something that used to disturb me when I was with Cologne. In my last year I was top scorer, and keeping two German internationals on the bench, yet I couldn't be sure of my place in the England squad sometimes, let alone the team. I hope under Bobby Robson that has changed. I've scored four goals in two games, plus ten minutes as sub, so I hope that this year I will at last make one of the strikers' spots my own.

At least I have begun the year with a goal, which is a good omen. Even more hopeful, in the light of what I've said about fitting in, is that it was made by Vladimir Petrovic, our Yugoslav international midfield player, who was making his debut after what must have been one of the most long-drawn-out transfers of all time. Obviously he found the game a bit strange, even though Swansea had their two Yugoslavs playing, but he did enough to suggest that he will give us the quality we have been lacking in midfield. He gave me the pass for the goal, and it was the sort of pass I haven't seen much of since I came back to England. I cut inside, gave it to him and carried on running, and all of a sudden it came over the defender's head and dropped into my path. I caught it on the half-volley, and that was that.

Arsenal signed Vlad before the World Cup. But then Yugoslavia did so badly their association put up all sorts of blocks on their players moving abroad, as a punishment. Several times it seemed as if he wouldn't be coming, but they finally relented and we got him just a week ago. A lot of transfers, particularly international ones, seem to have their difficulties, with an element of cloak and dagger about them, not to say broad farce. My move from Forest to Cologne certainly had both. It began at Heathrow. We had been playing in a tournament in Bilbao, which we won. I hadn't signed a new contract, so I was getting some flak from Brian Clough.

We were in the baggage area waiting for our luggage when this reporter came up to me and said, 'There's a gentleman outside, a foreign gentleman, a friend of Kevin Keegan's, and he would like to see you.' There had been a lot of speculation about me going abroad, so I thought, 'Hallo, there could be something going on here.' I got a piece of paper, put my name, address and telephone number on it, and the reporter led me out the back way so that I didn't have to go through customs. And there was this little bloke standing there. 'I want to speak with you. I am friend of Kevin's.'

I was expecting Cloughie to appear at any moment, so I just stuffed the bit of paper into his top pocket and left it at that. A few of the lads had noticed something was up, but Cloughie didn't seem to have noticed anything so I just said, 'Tell you later', and we got the coach back to Nottingham.

That evening I got the phone call. The man said his name was Felix. He is Gyula Pasztor's runner. Pasztor is a big European agent, a Hungarian who looks like a 1930s gangster, and he had taken Kevin to Hamburg.

Felix came up to Nottingham the next day. I met him at the station and took him home and he said, 'I have something very interesting for you. A West German club wants to sign you. Are you interested?' I said I was, so he produced a sheaf of papers and said, 'Sign this'. They gave him permission to work on my behalf. I looked a bit doubtful so he said, 'Phone Kevin'. I did and said, 'Felix wants me to sign this paper' so Kevin said, 'See how it is worded and say that they can only act for you with Cologne.' Otherwise he could have touted me all over Europe.

So I signed. The next stage was a series of telephone calls, and then I was visited a couple of times by Pasztor's lawyer, a man called Viktor Wieme from Brussels. He wanted to know how much I wanted. I told him and he said, 'Not possible. Only Rummenigge and Breitner get that in Germany.' So I just said, 'That's what I want,' because I had spoken to Kevin and got a few tips – although he did contradict himself a bit.

The negotiations just dragged on, so in the end Jon and I said that we wanted to talk direct to the people in Cologne. I said, 'I want to meet the president because it is ridiculous to keep going through you.' They weren't happy about that, but finally it was agreed that we should go over to Cologne; that brought the cloak and dagger and farcical elements into full play.

Jon and I drove down to Gatwick one Saturday after we had played Leeds at the City Ground. We couldn't get a flight direct to Cologne, that would have been too simple – we had to go to Brussels to meet Viktor and go on from there. So we stayed the night and were flying off in the morning. We were getting an eight o'clock flight, and at about 7.30 we were walking towards the departure lounge when suddenly we ran into one of the Forest committeemen, Mr Macpherson, who is now the chairman.

'What are you doing here?'

'Oh,' I said, 'I've just come to meet a friend, then I'm joining up with the England squad.' Which I was – but at seven a.m.? And he had seen me just about to enter a departure lounge but he didn't think anything of it. He still doesn't know what I was there for.

We waited until he moved off then went through and got the flight. We met Viktor and Gyula Pasztor at the airport and they drove us to Cologne. The journey was a farce. We constantly thought the car was going to break down, but it made it. Then we discovered there was a time difference of an hour, which Viktor had not realized, so we were an hour early.

We met the president, Peter Weiand, at his penthouse, with the manager Karl-Heinz Thielen. The discussions between the agents and Thielen just went round in circles, and in the end Jon nodded to Thielen that they should meet in the toilet. So they both slipped off and began to sort things out.

It turned out that the agents had told me several misleading things, and we realized we should have spoken directly to Cologne in the first place. Jon and Thielen sorted things out, and then we went to the training ground, which I was a bit worried about, because I thought people might recognize me. But I had this toe infection and I couldn't walk; I couldn't keep up with Jon, and it was a really funny sight. Here they were trying to sign this two-million-Deutschmark player and he was hobbling across the car park like a cripple.

Then when we were walking past a group of Germans Viktor suddenly started talking to me in German. So I said, 'What's this?' and he explained, 'Just an act so that those fans would think you were German'. Cloak and dagger to the last.

But even though Macpherson didn't twig, of course Cloughie found out sooner or later. Carole decided to take German evening classes. She went down to sign on, and saw John McGovern's girlfriend in the queue, so she ducked out quickly, and had to sign up for a different class. Even then it didn't make any difference. Cloughie said one morning, 'I hear Carole is learning German. Thinking of joining a German club are you?'

Cloughie was incredible. He knew everything that was going on. Once, when I had got into the team, I was going past a garage and I thought I'd go in and see if I could get a sponsored car. So I went in and asked to see the manager. It turned out that he knew who I was – he was a keen Forest fan – and he immediately said yes. I thought I'd better clear it with Cloughie, so I went to see him. I'd got a couple of things to see him about, and I brought up the other thing first. Before I could ask him about the car he said, 'By the way, I think it was brilliant you going into that garage.' He had known all about it within a couple of hours.

Kevin did give me one useful tip. He said, 'If they ask you what religion you are, say "nothing", because you have to pay five per cent of your earnings to the Church.' That was the best piece of advice he ever gave me. When we got to Cologne they asked, 'What religion are you?' Carole had just got 'Chu . . .' out when I interrupted her hastily, 'Nothing, nothing at all.'

Coming to Arsenal was much more straightforward, because foreign teams let you speak to anyone even while you are under contract. The year before I left Cologne I'd spoken to both Manchester United and Liverpool, but I really wanted to play for Arsenal.

In fact two summers ago, before my last season with Cologne, I had been on holiday in Portugal with my old Nottingham Forest team mate John Robertson. Jon and Larry Lloyd were there too, and one day we had a game of tennis. Afterwards we were sitting around having a beer, and they were asking what I was going to do. I said I didn't know, so Robbo said:

'Well, who would you like to play for? Will you go back to Forest? Liverpool? United?'

So I said, 'I've always fancied Arsenal. I fancy a London club.'

'Do you mean to say you don't want to play for Liverpool?'

I answered, 'Not really. If everything was equal I'd sooner go to Arsenal.'

Robbo was incensed. 'You'd snatch their hand off if Liverpool came in for you,' he said.

But I was serious. I said to Jon when we were talking about it that going to Cologne had been an adventure, and going to London meant the adventure was continuing. Going to Liverpool or Manchester would have meant that the adventure was over. Playing for Liverpool would be exciting, playing for United in front of 50,000 every week would be exciting – but there would be nothing exciting about living in Manchester.

London is different. I've always liked it since we used to come down for weekends. Everything happens here. There is something special about the place. I shall live in London when I stop playing. It is funny, because when I was at Forest I used to read about London or Southern players who would refuse a move because it meant leaving London or the South. I could never understand it at the time. I used to say, 'You have got no choice, you go where the job takes you.' But I can understand it now. I love the place. I love the theatre and the choice of films, and the restaurants, and when we have got our own house it will be almost perfect. At the moment we are living in a club house in Radlett, which is all right – a lot better than being in hotels with a small baby, which we had to for a time – but it is not the same as having your own house. We think we have found somewhere in Totteridge, however, which was our final choice of area.

3 JANUARY

One of the most difficult things about adjusting back to life in England is a very small thing – hand-shaking. In Germany everyone shakes hands with everyone. When I first went out there, I couldn't believe the amount of hand-shaking that went on. I thought of it again when I went downstairs in the hotel this morning. In Germany you went down for breakfast and the coach, Hennes Weisweiler, would be sitting there, and you had to go and shake his hand – and the president and manager if they were there too. For the players you just came in said, 'Good morning' and knocked on the table, which meant it was for everyone. But you had to walk round and shake the coach, manager and president by the hand. If they came in late they would go round the table shaking hands with everyone. It was the same in training. Every morning when you went in you shook hands with the trainer. I can imagine what Don would think if we all did that. But I can't get used to not doing it – now I never know whether to put my hand out or not.

Liverpool 3 Arsenal 1

We were a bit naïve. Our good little run over Christmas had made us feel quite buoyant. We came up here thinking we were going to attack them! Well, we did get a good goal near the end. Brian Talbot played a one-two then volleyed it in, but it was all over by then. We caught them on a good day, and we were penned in for ninety minutes. It felt like they had fourteen men.

Petrovic couldn't believe the pace. He was very impressed by them. He had seen them on TV, and played against them some years ago in a European Cup tie, but this was his first real taste, and he couldn't stop talking about them. He kept saying they must be the best team in Europe. He was a bit overwhelmed by the pace. Every time he got the ball there was someone on top of him. And they weren't just hustling him, they were really clattering into him. He just couldn't grasp the physical dimension of the game at all. The thing is that they do work very hard. They have eleven very good players who all work very hard. They tackle and chase back and give everything they've got. Even when they are on top, people like Ian Rush will still chase what Don would call a 'lost cause', and get his tackle in.

4 JANUARY

Yesterday was our fourth game in eight days. What a difference to Christmas in Germany where they have a month's winter break. What Rainer Bonhof and Berndt Cullmann and the others would say about it I can't imagine. Well, no, I can. When we had two games in a week they would all complain. We'd play on Wednesday and Saturday and they would say, 'Oh, this English week really takes it out of you.' It became a big joke when they knew I was coming back to England.

And it certainly does take it out of you. I was really stiff this morning. I'm shattered already, because although we don't train as hard as in Germany, playing all these games requires a different type of fitness. There are different attitudes to fitness too. Here if you haven't trained all week they'll patch you up and send you out on the Saturday. In Cologne if you didn't train until the Friday they wouldn't let you play on the Saturday. I remember the first time that happened to me. We had this game in Dusseldorf, and I was playing well and raring to go – and I was fit. I didn't train until the Friday because I'd had a knock, but it was only a bruise. Rinus Michels, who was coach at the time, just said, 'No. You can't play on Saturday if you haven't trained all week.' We go to the other extreme. You spend all week on the table, get off the table to play and then get back on the table on Monday.

Against Birmingham early in the season Noel Blake and I went up for a ball together, and he came down on my foot. He must weigh about fifteen stone, and he came down right on my toe. It was lucky I wear big heavy boots or he would have broken it. I couldn't walk or get my shoe on for a week. Yet on the Saturday at Luton they wanted me to play. I shouldn't even have tried. They had my boot on a brush handle in the changing room banging it down to try and make a bit more room in it. Then Terry got Luton's doctor out of the hospitality room to give me an injection, and he plunged it straight down and I hit the roof. Anyway, they froze my toe and I got my boot on and played the game.

I came off and got the boot off somehow. On the Tuesday we

went up to Liverpool to play Everton in the Milk Cup. I couldn't even get the boot on for training. We trained up there on the Wednesday morning, but I couldn't even get a shoe on. Yet in the evening before the game I went in to have an injection from the Everton doctor, and told him what had happened with the one at Luton; he said that had probably bruised the bone. He pushed it in sideways so it was all right and I hobbled out onto the pitch. I was hobbling around, and after fifteen or twenty minutes Alan Sunderland said, 'I've got to go off.'

'Why?'

'My hamstring's just gone.'

I thought, 'Oh God!' and Sundy hobbled off and I played the rest of the game walking on the side of my foot.

That went on for another two or three weeks until finally I was wearing one of Brian Talbot's boots, a size nine, and because it was a different weight and style to my usual ones, I got a calf strain. I should have just said, 'Look, I can't get my boot on, I'm not going to play' instead of going out for four or five games with a really swollen and bruised toe – but they were allowing me to do it.

Goodness knows what would have been said in Cologne about pushing broom handles into the soles of boots. There they would just have said, 'You're not fit, and that's it.' They wouldn't even have allowed me to train.

The Germans go too far the other way. I suppose there are arguments for and against both ways. It's really down to the player. A lot of German players would think that if they hadn't trained hard they wouldn't have the stamina to last the ninety minutes, and that they wouldn't be mentally alert. It would affect them psychologically, whereas the English pro tends to take what comes and get out there and play.

The Germans are much more scientific though. They are very weight conscious. We are weighed every week at Arsenal and your weight is written down, but if a player was found to be a couple of kilos over in Germany, there would be a real palaver about it.

They think English players are fat. They used to laugh about how much English players eat. During the European Championships in Italy we stayed just outside Turin in a sport school at Asti. They gave us loads of food – bowls of spaghetti and everything. We were there for ten days. Germany stayed there for one night and could not believe how much food they were given. And when they heard we had stayed there for eight or ten days they said, 'You've no chance!'

14

They were never allowed to drink Coca-Cola or orange squash or anything like that, just mineral water. They think the others are bad for you. I don't think it matters, although it probably would to a German player, because if he drank a lot of coke it would prey on his mind, where English lads wouldn't even think about it, they'd just knock them back and go out to play. A German player would think, 'I've eaten too much, or drunk something I shouldn't have done, I'm not going to perform very well today because I can't do things at my peak.'

8 JANUARY
Arsenal 2 Bolton Wanderers 1 FA Cup Third Round
We started brilliantly. For the first ten minutes Bolton just couldn't get out of their penalty area, and we were unlucky not to be four up in that time. Of course it slowed down a bit after that, but we were never in any danger, although we made heavy weather of it late on.

One of the nice things about being back in England is that you can go off and have a relaxed drink after a game. In Cologne after home games we all had to eat together – the players, the president, manager and trainer back at the training ground. There were these three long tables, a top table and two going down from each end of it, and you only sat round the outside. If we'd been beaten it was a disaster. We all just sat there looking at each other, and spent two hours just wanting to get away, to get home.

We once asked if we could have small tables so we could sit and chat. That happened for a couple of weeks, then the next week it was back to the long tables again; all we could do was sit and watch the TV with the clips from the other games on. At the end the president would get up and make his speech – either 'Congratulations' or 'We've got to do better next week'. And that would be it, apart from shaking hands with everyone.

It's a bit different at Highbury. Most Saturdays Graham Rix and his wife and Carole and I go out with a couple of friends for dinner, and then probably on to a club. Immediately after the game Graham and I go to this pub, The Green Man at Turnpike Lane, which is run by a friend of Graham who used to have a pub in Southgate. So if we are all going in to town we meet there. It gives us an hour with Jack to discuss the game. Because the pub is always empty at that stage it gives us the chance for a quiet drink.

The pre-match rituals are different too. When I was at Nottingham Forest we just used to have a bit of fish or chicken or a steak. In Germany when I first went there under Hennes Weisweiler we used to have to be down for breakfast at 9.30 – we always stayed out at this hotel in the forest the night before a home game – and we all had to have eggs in some form. Then you would have lunch again at 11.45 or 12.00 for a 3.30 kick off. There would be spaghetti on the tables, potatoes, virtually a normal meal – things which English clubs would consider far too heavy to have before a game. And there would always be a thick cream cake or a piece of cheesecake with plenty of cream to finish up with. That seems excessive, particularly given what I said about German players saying the English eat too much, but they had this theory about a high intake of starchy and sweet things before intense physical effort – I think it's one that a lot of athletes follow now.

Towards the end of my stay in Cologne I'd just have breakfast. If I had lunch, especially if it was steak, at three o'clock I'd feel a bit heavy, so I cut it out. Feeling hungry at three was better than feeling full. At Arsenal we go to the South Herts Golf Club before a game. I miss breakfast and just have a pre-match meal of poached eggs on toast.

10 JANUARY

We've got another home draw in the Cup – against Leeds United; and we are in the quarter-finals of the League Cup, against Sheffield Wednesday. So although we obviously aren't going to win the League this year, we can hope to get to Wembley, which would be a nice way to celebrate my return. I've never played in an F.A. Cup Final, but with Forest we got to the League Cup Final twice.

12 JANUARY

We have got a clear week this week, so we are doing some heavy training – although not compared with Rinus Michels in Cologne. It is interesting to compare how different top coaches are. I've been fortunate in my career in that I've played for some of the great names in management and coaching: Brian Clough, Hennes Weisweiler and Michels, who are two of the biggest names in European football, and now Don Howe.

Cloughie of course was a one-off. He wasn't a coach, and you couldn't compare him to the others. Once he decided I could play he did a lot for me in terms of giving me confidence. Yet even though he was a forward himself, and a very good goal-scorer, he never talked about the techniques or passed on tips.

Don is more like a continental coach. He wants to work with players, wants to help them, to work on their good points and their bad points, and really wants to pull it out of you. Don is closer to the players too. If you go away, you sit and have a drink and a chat with him.

You couldn't do that with Michels. He was much more formal, shaking hands every morning. Michels was also the hardest trainer I have ever known. When he first arrived in Cologne he literally ran us into the ground, and he carried on doing it for two years. It got to the point where even Rainer Bonhof complained – and that really is something. Bonhof is really dedicated, and loves training. And when he says, as he did, 'I've had enough of this', it must be extreme. Some people think that continental players don't do the heavy physical training that we do. But contrary to legend, the training in Germany is heavy – it isn't all ball work. Michels was the hardest, but the training was always more strenuous than in England.

There was one occasion under Michels when we had not done particularly well on the Saturday and we did not see the ball until Wednesday afternoon. It was just running, running, running. Then on the Wednesday afternoon Michels was on pitch number six, which was a ten-minute walk away, sitting waiting for us to come. The training was so hard that at one stage we had a meeting and asked him in and said, 'Look, can we do a bit more shooting, a bit more football? This is killing us.' He said, 'Who is stopping you? You can always do it after training. You can get a ball out and do some shooting by yourselves before or after training.' He said he wouldn't change his ways. It was the way he did things, the way he'd been successful. He had done it like that for ten years now, and he was set on doing it his way.

Sometimes he had us running on the day before a game. I was probably the biggest moaner there. We would come out of the changing room, and instead of starting with stretches, as with an English club, we would go straight into a fifteen-minute run round this big lake. They would all swear in English, 'Fucking running again,' but by the end of the session I'd have really got into it and I would finish up with the front runners, getting some good times. They couldn't understand why I moaned so much when I came out, and then ran like that at the end.

But I must admit that under Michels' regimen I did feel fit.

During the World Cup Finals last summer I was not match fit; I had played for England against Holland at the end of the season, but then there was a six-week gap before I played against Spain. But as far as training in Cologne went I was in peak condition – I felt really strong, much stronger than I do now.

Michels was very strict, and the players just did as they were told. There was a classic example of his way of going on when we went to Munich to play Bayern early last season. He called a meeting for one o'clock in our hotel. We sat in reception waiting, because he had not told us where it was. He came walking through the lobby and went down the stairs to the basement, and we just went on sitting there. He didn't reappear, and after about fifteen minutes we thought we had better go and have a look for him. He was sitting waiting for us with his blackboard out. And as we went in he said, 'You are all fined one hundred Deutschmarks' (or whatever it was) 'for being late.' So we said, 'That's stupid. Why didn't you tell us where it was when you walked by?' And he said, 'You should use your own initiative.' That made me giggle, because it sounded a bit like Cloughie, but it really put some players' backs up.

If you enjoyed playing football, Weisweiler was tremendous to work with. It was hard at times, but at least everything was to do with playing football. If you had to run, you would be running with a ball. Most days you would go out in three or four different groups and work in different areas of the field, but everything was related to what would happen in an actual game. One group might be crossing and heading. Another group would be having a five-against-five keep-ball session. There would be lots of one-on-one situations: an attacker against a defender with a goalkeeper in. You would have six attempts to beat the defender and get your shot in; then we would change round. So you were getting all your physical training, except for one session on a Tuesday morning, done with a ball. We did that sort of thing every other day. Weisweiler had a great reputation as a tactician. When I first went there I found it difficult to understand him, because his English was not that good, but I thought his strength really was a tremendous common sense about the game. I liked him a lot. When you first meet him he seems a real grump, very miserable. He is a typical Kölnsher – a bit rough and ready. On Friday nights we would go to the training camp, and I used to sit next to him at the dinner table and we would chat a lot. He always used to say I was a continental footballer, not an English one. I remember soon after I had joined he said, 'These stupid journalists keep asking me why you are fitting in so easily. Are they daft? Can't they see you are a continental footballer, not an English kick and rush one?' He said that from the first day right to the end. I used to say, 'Well, Forest beat Cologne.'

On those Friday nights I used to room with Berndt Cullmann. We could hear Weisweiler singing, as he used to have a few beers and champagne to build up for the game. One night I woke up and thought I was dreaming: I could hear someone singing, and of course it was Weisweiler. Cully got his shoe and banged on the ceiling, and he quietened down for a bit. Half an hour later he started up again. . . .

14 JANUARY

It's a standing joke at Highbury that if I've got the ball anywhere around the edge of the box while we're training, no one will get a pass. I do love scoring, and in training I love smashing it into the back of the net. In the World Cup I got the nickname Lasher because of that. But they should have seen Dieter Müller. I have never played with anyone who had the lust for goals which he had. Fischer, Allofs, Birtles, Withe, Francis, Sundy, all the forwards I've played with love scoring like I do, but Dieter was something else. If we played an amateur team, he'd still show no mercy. If he got one, he'd want two, then three, and so on; he was insatiable and didn't mind how they went in. I've seen him dive for a ball and hand it in when it looks as if he has headed it. He would rather have a stinking game and score than a good game and not. It used to worry him if he wasn't scoring. Some games he would play really well and not score, and he didn't like it. If I said, 'You played well, Dieter', he wouldn't understand it. 'Ja, but I did not score.'

What you noticed about Dieter was that although he wasn't powerful, he always kept his shots down, and was rarely off target. He had a low back lift, and he would just stab it in. The number of times you thought, 'God, that's not going to go in', and it would just trickle over the line. In the penalty box you have always got more time than you think. I used to rush shots because I was frightened that if I didn't get a shot in quickly I might lose the chance. I don't think I do that now. Dieter, though, never rushed. He wasn't a quick type of player, or at least he didn't look a quick type of player, which might have had something to do with it.

He wasn't fully appreciated at Cologne. He used to get a terrible press if he wasn't scoring, and for someone who scored so many goals the club handled him badly. Players from other teams thought so too. When you were having a chat after the match they would say, 'Dieter's leaving this year then?' And I would say, 'Well, it looks like it.' I don't think Michels fancied him particularly. And they would say, 'It is ridiculous. He has scored so many goals over the last eight years he should be a hero, not knocked when he doesn't score.' I think he was hounded out of Cologne.

He is in France now, and still scoring lots of goals. He will do that for anybody providing you show confidence in him. I think in the 1976 European Championships he got a hat-trick in his first game. One of the things which made me sign for Cologne was that I wanted to play with him, and in my first season we had a tremendous partnership. We were called 'The Dream Duo' and all that sort of thing in the papers, and they compared us to famous partnerships of the past in Germany.

At the time we were playing up front together, with Pierre Littbarski, who was just coming through, breaking forward on the right from midfield. I was playing really well – I wasn't getting that many goals, but I was getting a few, and I was setting Dieter up with so many. Anytime I got the ball anywhere around the box I'd get in a cross and he would be on the end of it. But when the team wasn't playing so well we had our disagreements, because Dieter wanted to stay in the centre. He didn't think he should move out of that position. He felt he was there to score goals and he should just stay in there, and that I shouldn't come across and get in his way. We used to discuss this a lot when we saw one another in the evenings. It was just as well we were friends because otherwise I think it could have got a bit heated and caused antagonism.

'It's best for me,' he said, 'if you play out left and get some good crosses in for me.' I wanted him to go out wide sometimes so we could share it. And when he moved on, that was the way things worked out with Fischer.

15 JANUARY
Arsenal 3 Stoke City 0
We played quite well, made Stoke look a bad side, yet as they've been getting some good results, it was quite encouraging.

Vlad is still finding the pace a bit much, but he scored a great goal. A real continental free kick. It was on the left side of the box, and he chipped it over the wall and into the top corner.

18 JANUARY
Arsenal 1 Sheffield Wednesday 0

19 JANUARY
Highbury was like a wind tunnel. It was an awful game, the ball was up in the air the whole time, flying over our heads. It was one of those light ones; I don't mind them because if you get a good strike on goal they really fly in, which is an advantage for forwards. But when the ball is in the air all the time in the wind they do swerve all over the shop.

But really it's down to control, and playing controlled football: we just didn't do that. Wednesday have got this huge back four, who Sundy and I could probably get in amongst on the ground – but we got nothing, everything was fifty-yard balls flying around in the air.

According to the papers, though, Jack Charlton said my goal was a fluke. I don't know what he means by that: I thought it was about the one bit of football we played on the night. Petrovic played a one-two on the right to get to the by-line and crossed. I came in at the back post, and the ball bounced up and as it was skidding away from me I hooked it in. I thought it was a good strike – it certainly wasn't a fluke. The only thing I can think of is that a defender mis-kicked the cross as it came in.

Jon Holmes came to the game and we had quite a late night of it. Jon has handled me since my days at Forest. He started off with Peter Shilton, which was a great advertisement for him in my eyes. I looked at what Peter had got and what he did with himself and thought, 'That can't be bad.' When I first met Jon I was always asking him questions, and went to see him several times. And finally he said, 'You'll do, I'll work with you.' At that time he was working for a company, and doing the agent's work as a sideline. When we first did some deals I said, 'I'd like to pay you, not the company you are a director of.' He said, 'No, I work for the company, pay them', which indicated how straight he is. Then he had a bust up with them, and didn't know what to do. A lot of people had said they thought he would be successful by himself, so Peter and I got together and said we would like to back him. So we formed a company, basically a sports promotion company, although to keep it going during the early years he carried on with his insurance and finance work. So instead of paying an agent fees to do work, we were basically paying them back to ourselves.

He is not the usual kind of agent who is just after his ten or twenty per cent. You don't sign a contract with him, and although he helps you, unless you want to help yourself he is no good to you. He is more a financial adviser than an agent and is very knowledgeable on financial matters. Arsenal consult him on players' financial and tax matters, and that indicates how good he is; whereas a lot of these so-called agents just haven't got a clue. All they are interested in is getting as much money as possible. If someone wants you to go and pose nude on top of a building, they'll say, 'Yes, go and do it' as long as they are getting their cut. Jon would say, 'I don't think much of that idea, what do you think?'

He is very straight, and won't do anything illegal. Sometimes with boot contracts and things like that you can get offered cash. Jon won't have anything to do with that. He says, 'If you take it, don't let me know.'

Peter and I keep him on his toes. I've come up with loads of schemes on tax and investment and things. And he says, 'Well, you could do that. And if you get away with it, great. But you could also end up in gaol, or you could lose the lot.'

I've often had discussions with him when we have a contract to do promotional work. I'll say, 'Go for as much as you can', whereas John tends to say, 'Don't skin the rabbit, leave a bit on to let it grow again.' When we do the deal I'll have a little moan and say, 'We could have got more for that.' And we could. But he thinks that if you have done a deal and you are reasonably happy with the money but haven't bled them white, they'll come back. I'm not sure. I don't always agree with that.

He and Cloughie don't get on too well, although I think Cloughie must respect him. Jon always makes everything watertight in contracts, and I think the contract he got for Peter didn't please Cloughie too much. So when I was talking to Cologne, he wouldn't let Jon into the ground; we had to sit in the car in the car park to tie a few details up. It was ridiculous. Fortunately Jon gets on very well with Ken Friar, the Arsenal secretary, so we don't have that problem at Highbury.

21 JANUARY

Well, at least we avoided Liverpool in the League Cup semi-finals. They've got Burnley. We have drawn Manchester United. Obviously they are a good team, but we played them off the park at Old Trafford earlier this season, and it was 0–0 only because we missed our chances. Of course we'd have preferred Burnley, although after the way they won at Tottenham on Wednesday I'm not even sure about that.

22 JANUARY
Notts County 1 Arsenal 0
We really didn't play. Not for the first time Don went spare afterwards. You couldn't blame him, because we never looked like doing anything. The service was dreadful: I'm just not getting the type of passes I want. And the game just passed Vlad by – he still hasn't come to terms with the physical side, having people crashing into him as soon as he gets the ball.

29 JANUARY
Arsenal 1 Leeds United 1 FA Cup Fourth Round
We had a struggle. We had been doing quite all right, when they got this breakaway goal. We were attacking, and someone tonked it out of defence, setting Connor free. Peter Nicholas went steaming back, just got his foot in and sent it flying past Pat.

So then it was really difficult. It was getting near time, and you could feel the buzz of dissatisfaction growing when Sundy nipped in for the equalizer. So at least it has given us another chance, but it is really disappointing against a second division team when you don't win on your own ground. They aren't a bad team, but you just shouldn't have that sort of problem with them.

2 FEBRUARY
Leeds United 1 Arsenal 1 FA Cup Fourth Round Replay

3 FEBRUARY
We scraped a draw in the last minute after having an awful lot of the ball. Graham Rix hit in a free-kick from thirty yards at the near post which asked a few questions about their keeper.

As soon as we got inside the dressing room all hell broke loose. Don said some players weren't brave enough, they weren't putting their heads onto crosses. Whether he meant us or not I didn't know, but my automatic reaction was that he meant Sundy and me, because when they won't name names you are bound to think they mean the forwards. Sundy believes they do. He argues with them more than I do, because he thinks that whatever happens at Arsenal the forwards get the blame. They've only got to say something slightly off-key and he will be straight in. When I first joined he always seemed to be moaning. He seemed to hold a grudge against them, and I used to say, 'Shut up, Alan, forget it.' But now I can see what he was on about.

This time I dived straight in. I said, 'That's wrong. I put my head in for balls whether it's going to be kicked or not, and Sundy is the same.' And I said that the reason we didn't get in there was because when players get into crossing positions we're not sure if the ball *is* going to come in. You make three or four near-post runs and they check it back onto their right foot so you are dead. The next time they get to the line you think, 'Well, they are going to check out because that's what they've done the last three times' and they cross it instead. That's why you don't really know what is going to happen in certain positions.

Alan and I have a lot of arguments about this. We say, 'Get the ball into the box. If we don't get on the end of it then you can have a go at us about it. But you can't have a go at us for not being there if you haven't crossed it.'

They say, 'Well, we haven't crossed it because no one's there.' But that's our responsibility. If the balls are coming in it's up to us to get on the end of them. But if they aren't, then we can say, 'Look, get them in the box.' I think sometimes our problem is we want to be perfectionists. We try to do too much, players try to pick someone out; we've got so many good footballers in the team they want to do it in the right way. They get to the by-line. 'Is there anybody there?' But by the time they've looked up, sometimes it's too late. Instead, they should get there and say, 'Okay, I can see a space. I'm going to hammer it in there and hope that one of the lads is going to get on the end of it.'

On this occasion it had been crossed, and Don said, 'Well, so-and-so didn't put his head in.' And I said, 'Well, you should name names.' If people don't put their heads in Terry and Don should go and tell them, 'If you don't do it next time you are out of the team.'

They should put people on the spot. And then if they don't do what's needed, they should be out of the team. I think that could be done a little more. There's not the same pressure here as at Forest and Cologne. People like Graham Rix, David O'Leary, Kenny Sansom, Sundy and I are virtually guaranteed to go on playing even if we have a bad game. There's not the feeling that you'll be left out if you are not doing it. Early in the season, when we were giving away a lot of goals, Kenny said in one team meeting, 'Don, you can talk about tactics and everything, but whoever is not "doing it" should be out'; but it took about three or four weeks and a few more battles before it actually happened.

It was different at Forest and Cologne. Of course at Cologne where we had four internationals vying for two forward places there was a lot of pressure. With Rinus Michels, if you hadn't been in the game in the first half hour you knew the big card was going to come out and you'd be off the field. That created a tremendous amount of pressure, but you knew you had got to go out there and do it, you couldn't go out and think, 'Ah, my touch is not quite right today' and be a bit lackadaisical. You knew you'd got to overcome that quickly or you would be off the field, and the next thing was you might be out of the team. It was difficult for Michels, of course, because if he played Woodcock and Littbarski up front and things weren't happening, everyone would say, 'Why haven't you got Fischer and Allofs on? What are those two internationals doing sitting on the bench?'

You might think that kind of pressure was counter-productive, but I was top scorer for Cologne that year.

Of course Don would say, 'Yes, but we don't have internationals sitting in the reserves. Who should I put in? Because I'd rather have X in the team than Y, even if he is playing badly, because I might get more out of him.' I can understand that argument, but I still think you need to know that if you aren't doing it then your place is in danger, because otherwise players get complacent. That was always true at Forest – you were always aware you were playing for your place. If a player wasn't doing it at Forest, Cloughie would have no hesitation, he'd play an 'A' team player if necessary, if the first teamer wasn't giving him one hundred per cent. Cloughie used to point the finger and say, 'You, You and You' whereas at Arsenal they tend to say, 'The players know who we're talking about', so you might think 'He means me', but he doesn't come out and say, 'It's you' in front of everyone. I think you should name names.

Last night's draw means that our Milk Cup semi-finals with Manchester United have been put back a week, because the FA Cup replay takes precedence. That means I shall miss the England v Wales match – which is just what I didn't want to do. I've played in the last three games, and I'd like to think I've earned myself a run in the team now. I thought the partnership I had with Paul Mariner in

Greece was very promising, although it was also a good team performance.

Paul got a lot of stick after that game – very unnecessarily I thought, because he played well. He missed a chance when he tried to lob the goalkeeper, and put it wide, and once he should have pulled one back for me. All he had to do was square it and I was in. But for fighting, knocking the ball down, and really putting himself about he did a great job – but that seems to pass unnoticed. One paper said, 'He has not got the class to play for England.' How they can say that when we've won 3–0 in Greece, played some really good football, in spite of being kicked quite a lot, is beyond me. And it makes you feel vulnerable the whole time. I've had twenty-odd internationals now, but I've never had a proper run in the team; because you are always looking over your shoulder you don't like to miss a game. And at the moment I'm finding international football much easier and much more enjoyable than club football. Of course you can't really count Luxembourg, but the international game is more like the football I've been playing for the last three years; there's more passing, and less chasing and battling. I really enjoyed the game in Greece; I thought we played very well – and I can't say I've enjoyed many League games this season.

4 FEBRUARY

I've got flu, so I didn't train today, and I don't know whether I shall play tomorrow.

5 FEBRUARY

I didn't play. I went to the Golf Club and they asked how I felt. I said, 'Well, I feel a bit rough, but I'll go to Highbury and see how I feel when I've got my kit on.' But by the time I'd driven to Highbury I felt dreadful, so I went in and said it was no use me even trying to play. I went straight home to bed.

There was one consolation in missing the game. It meant avoiding Jimmy Case. He is frightening, and is certainly the hardest – or whatever you want to call it – player in the country. When we played down there this year I knew he was coming to do me and I jumped – a scissors jump. I got so high I thought he had no chance of catching me, but he *still* caught me. I couldn't believe it.

9 FEBRUARY
Arsenal 2 Leeds 1 FA Cup Fourth Round Second Replay

10 FEBRUARY

Terry Burton, the reserve team coach, was doing the team talk because Don was away sick, and he said, 'Anything around the box get it in to Woody, get it into his feet, just give it to him': music!

In the first half Kenny Sansom knocked me a ball, and came rushing at me before I had it under control, wanting me to lay it back so he could have a shot. At half time I said to him, 'Ken, when you knock the ball into me, stay out of it and see if I'm going to turn the player first. I might get round him, I might get a penalty. And if I can't do anything I know you are still there and then I can give it to you.'

He said, 'Yeah, but I was coming in at pace and I thought I could get in a shot.'

So we went out for the second half and the ball was knocked in to me and this time people stayed out of the way; a quick turn and it was in the back of the net. Kenny rushed up and said, 'Point taken. I thought you were wrong during the first half, but now I can see you were quite right. I can't argue with that – you've shut me up.'

Kenny is such a good footballer, but he says he doesn't get forward as much as he used to or would like to; he feels more restricted at Arsenal. He's very difficult to get by as a left-back, but I wonder whether he would be more effective in midfield for us, because he is fast and can go past people.

Sometimes he is too good a footballer for our good – or at least for mine. I've played with people like Frank Gray and Frank Clark at full-back on my side. Frank Gray would do a little bit, but Frank Clark just used to do the simple things. He'd get it and give it to John Robertson, who'd give it to me, either into space or to my feet. That would be the first thing they'd look to do and if it was on it was 'Here it is, have it'. Kenny, however, looks at me sometimes and thinks, 'Well, I can't give it to him there, I'll look over there, then I'll look back'; it might be better for me sometimes if I was playing with someone with less ability who would give it straight away without thinking about it. Kenny does think too much about whether my marker is going to come round in front of me and nick it off me if he plays it. But I like playing against a man-to-man marker – I like to feel him there and I keep saying, 'You don't have to worry about me, Ken, just get it up there and I'll take care of it' but, because he's such a good player and thinks so much about his game, he's reluctant to do that.

Man-for-man marking has never bothered me. Even at Forest when we first really came up against it in the European Cup we didn't let it interfere with our game. We never used to bother about the other team, we just went out and played our game; and Forest players would give me the ball even when I was tightly marked because we had so much belief in the way we played.

After being at Cologne, I actually like being marked man-for-man. I know where the defender is, and I'm sure I can get a yard. When I first went there it was very tight. I've got a photograph of my first game in which the defender could be stuck to me he is so tight; the ball is nowhere near. We are just watching play and he is looking over my shoulder. It was Tenhagen, who is supposed to be pretty good, and he stuck that close for ninety minutes.

Weisweiler used to say, 'When Tony is in the penalty box, just give it to him. It doesn't matter if he is tightly marked, give it to him. He'll decide what to do then.' That came up because to start with I'd take up lots of positions but the ball wouldn't come. So he asked the team, 'Why didn't you give it to him?' and they said that I was so tightly marked whenever they looked for me that they thought they shouldn't give the ball to me, or that I didn't want it.

One of the most important things I learned in Germany was about movement. When I first went there I'd be moving all the time. I'd show up on the left-hand side, and then when it was switched across, which often happened because German football is not all that direct, I'd be over there on the right shouting, 'Give it me.' And it would go back across again and I'd go back to the left still shouting 'Give it me.' I think the crowd loved it, and there were all these lines like 'Woodcock always moving', 'Woodcock always in action'. But they kept telling me, 'You can't have it all the time. Don't move for it. Don't show for it all the time, because then your marker knows that wherever the ball is going, you are going to follow it and you are going to be wanting it.' I didn't know whether they were right or not, but I thought I should give it a try, and learned that I should hold my ground and wait, and then go when I thought I should have it. I'd pretend I wasn't interested, and see the ball played to someone else and react for his ball. It was wait until something is on, then go, and take your marker by surprise rather than running all over the place shouting 'give it me.' But in England it seems to be all hurry-scurry.

28

11 FEBRUARY

Chris Whyte, our young centre-half, has a problem with his hair. He's getting a bald patch – it's coming out in clumps. He is very sensitive about it, and gets a lot of ribbing. Every month Rixy tells him, 'Chris, I've got something for your hair.' And every time Chris falls for it.

'Oh, what?'

'A matchbox to keep it in.'

12 FEBRUARY

Our game at West Ham was called off because of the weather. We've suddenly hit a cold spell after thinking we'd got away with it. It makes you wonder a bit about having a mid-season break, because we played perfectly well through it in January, and now in the middle of February, when we would be starting back again, we're ice and snow-bound.

15 FEBRUARY

Arsenal 2 Manchester United 4 League Cup Semi-Final First Leg

16 FEBRUARY

We gave ourselves a chance in the last couple of minutes. I got one and Nicho (Peter Nicholas) got one, so from being completely dead we've still got a little bit of hope when we go up there.

The pitch was all against us. It was frozen hard – impossible to play on really – and very difficult for the home team which has to try and create something. They could just sit back and soak it up and then catch us on the break; but having said that, they were very aggressive, very positive, and seemed very hungry for it. We tried to play pretty pretty football, which was hopeless on that pitch, and they got stuck into us, knocked it forward and chased after it. They put us under pressure the whole time, and they were surprisingly physical. Moses and Nicho had a bit of a go, but they were all really crunching in and winning the ball.

It could have been a disaster, but those two late goals have given us a bit of hope – and the result didn't please them.

18 FEBRUARY

Jon and I had dinner with Graham Taylor last night. I played for him for a month at Lincoln when I went there on loan from Forest. We had a good talk – he understood what I was saying about the type of balls I think I should get played to me. I wish it was as easy to convince Don. I introduced them because Graham had spoken to me while I was in Cologne. It was quite funny. One afternoon I had this phone call from the *Cologne Express*, which is the Cologne scandal sheet. 'It's Siegfried Drach here – Elton John's manager has just rung up for your telephone number. Is it true you are going to Watford?'

I said, 'No, I think it's his concert in Dusseldorf; he probably wondered if I wanted a ticket.'

Half an hour later the phone rang again and this voice said, 'Hello, it's Elton here.' If I hadn't had the previous phone call I'd have thought someone was winding me up. He seemed a bit nervous but asked, 'Would you be interested in coming to Watford?' I had to say that really I wanted to join a bigger club, but I thanked him for asking and said I'd phone Graham for a chat. I did, and Graham said that in the future he hoped that he would be signing international players and foreign players and could I give him some pointers? So I suggested that the best thing he could do was to pick Jon's brains, and it seemed to work quite well.

The dinner had some unfortunate repercussions though. I ate some stuffed mushrooms, and they seemed a bit greasy at the time. Today on the train up to Middlesbrough I felt really sick, and I went to bed as soon as we got to the hotel.

My going to Lincoln was what the loan system is really all about. I was a young player with no chance of first team football at Forest, and it gave me a chance to go down and get some first team experience at a lower level. I think that is a good idea, but it does seem to be abused now. Established first division players going on loan to another first division club seems ridiculous.

19 FEBRUARY
Middlesbrough 1 Arsenal 1
Yet again this season we gave it away. We took an early lead with another goal from Rixy, and we soaked up all their pressure until the last couple of minutes. Don went crackers again, because it was such a silly goal to give away. Kenny thought Pat was coming and he left it. Pat had shouted to Kenny to knock it away, but he didn't, and the fellow came in behind Kenny and put it away.

Because of that I got fired at as well. Before the game I'd still felt a bit queasy, but I'd said, 'Well, I'm fit enough to play – there's no question of me not playing – but I don't feel a hundred per cent; I feel a bit sick', and they didn't say anything. Afterwards, though, Terry and Don had a go, saying I shouldn't go to these foreign restaurants and eat stuffed garlic mushrooms a couple of days before a big game. I should know better and watch what I was eating. I said, 'What a load of rubbish. Just because someone has made a mistake at the back and let a goal in', and Kenny Sansom came up and backed me up.

People keep on getting Graham and I mixed up. Malcolm Allison did so today. I was walking along the corridor when he said, 'Hello, Graham, how are you?'. I didn't correct him, I just said, 'Fine, thanks.' It must be the hairstyles.

22 FEBRUARY

On paper the prospect of going to Old Trafford already two goals down from the first leg looks like an impossible task – but I'm always optimistic. If you can get an early goal it changes things completely, because they are likely to get rattled and you are then only one goal behind, making a completely different game. In the League Cup, unlike in European competitions, the away goals don't count double, so losing 2–4 at home was no worse than being beaten 0–2, which is another advantage.

This might all sound like whistling in the dark, but I can still vividly remember a game we had at Forest. We played Leeds in the League Cup semi-finals, and we won 3–1 at Elland Road, so our home leg looked a formality. But they got an early goal, and suddenly it was a different game. We equalized, but then they went in front again. When it was 2–1 Tony Currie hit the bar, just before half-time. As it was, we hung on, but if that had gone in. . . .

And I'm not sure about United. I think if we can get an early goal we could do it, because then we will only need one to tie it up, and if we get that anything could happen. They would be really tense, particularly in front of their own crowd.

23 FEBRUARY
Manchester United 2 Arsenal 1 League Cup Semi-Final Second Leg

24 FEBRUARY

We battled ever so hard, competed for everything. We didn't get the early chance, but it finally came in the second half. Chris Whyte got up for this header. He should perhaps have done better, because he was close in, but he really thumped it and it bounced away off the post. Five minutes later they broke away and Steve Coppell shot. It went through Kenny's legs and Pat was unsighted. And that was that. If that header had gone in all hell would have broken loose.

It got a bit nasty. They were really steaming in again. In fact Bryan Robson was stretchered off. He had been crashing in and this time he came in and trod on the ball. That was an accident. Noddy Talbot was butted in the face by Moses and that wasn't.

We don't think the scores were a fair reflection of the difference between us. We think they were flattered. Coming back the lads were saying, 'We'll save them for the FA Cup Final.' We do think we can beat them next time.

Wilf Dixon did not do well with United. He gives us our run-down on the opposition. It's quite an event. He has their names up on a blackboard and goes through them, with their weight alongside. Sundy sometimes has tears running down his face he is in such hysterics at some of the things Wilf says. He has to sit there with his head down and his hand shielding his face so that no one can see.

The classic was against Spartak. He had all these names written up which meant nothing to us and he can't pronounce, and he was telling us all these things about them which were meaningless. 'There's Lermontov at centre-forward, and Sholokhov at outside-right, but the bloke you really have to watch is Yevtuschenko.'

Before the first United game, though, he told Kenny, 'You don't have to worry about Steve Coppell – he's gone. His legs have gone, he can't run any more.' Coppell was possibly their best player in the first game, and he got the crucial goal last night.

26 FEBRUARY
West Bromwich Albion 0 Arsenal 0

It was Pat's 1000th game in first-class football, which is a phenomenal achievement. It was probably one of his easiest too. Everyone lined up and applauded him onto the field at the start and that was the last thing worth clapping in the game. It was very heavy, and we were very tired.

Don and Terry, though, seemed reasonably satisfied afterwards. I mean, they weren't jumping up and down with joy, but they didn't have a go at us either. Presumably they thought a point and a clean sheet was quietly satisfactory.

Sammy Chapman's dad came up to me before the game. 'Sammy sent me – am I all right for a ticket?'; it is becoming a ritual whenever we play in the Midlands. There were only 13,000 there, so it was quite easy to oblige.

Sammy Chapman is something of a folk hero in Nottingham. Even though he was there before the success, if we go into the town now and mention his name everyone knows who he is. He was a real character, a bit of a hot-head sometimes, who played for the club in the second division days in the seventies. He was club captain for a time, and was always expected to move on to the first division with somebody. Unfortunately, he was one of those good pros who never really got the break at the right time, although he was still there when Cloughie arrived.

I've only been here six months, so I don't know Pat that well. He is quiet, like his image. When we have one of our periodic crisis meetings he will come in and say a little, and it is very much to the point. He will just say, 'We have got to do this' and that's it, and he is very firm about it. Once he was worried that the back four were letting the ball bounce – no one was going and attacking it – making him insecure as a result. So he just said, 'We've got to attack the ball; the centre-half has got to attack the ball or it is going to put us in trouble. It has got to be done.' You can be misled by his quiet image though. When you sit down and talk to him he is fascinating, with lots of stories about Watford and Tottenham, and the things he has learned from being in the game so long. I can listen to him for hours.

He is intelligent, and I think he is very strong. He knows what he wants and I think he will generally get it because he knows how to go about things. He doesn't go shouting his mouth off, but you can sense his determination – there is a quiet strength about him.

I would not want to cross him. I suspect if anyone did, that would be that. I don't know that anyone ever has, but I don't think you would get a chance to do it a second time: he is rock hard.

Pat is a great goalkeeper. He is a master at using his whole body, and was probably the first British goalkeeper to use his feet as a major part of his technique. He is wonderfully agile, and those great hands of his are like buckets. His trademark, the one-handed catch, is really inspiring to his own team. But I think his greatest virtue is his calmness. There can be twenty men in the penalty box and nothing will ruffle him. He will kick a ball out. If he parries a shot, he doesn't look as if he is scrambling to get after it, but seems to collect it as if nothing had happened. You see some goalkeepers, even good ones, who parry a shot and are then scrambling and rushing around to get the second shot. But he will knock it down and almost amble after it.

He seems always to be in the right position, which is a good sign. You don't see him diving around that much. Someone comes into our box, and our defenders are panicking because he is going to get a shot in. It flies through a ruck of players and Pat will be standing there, and he just knocks it down. It so often happens that he is in the right place when everything is hectic in front of him that you can't say it is only luck.

28 FEBRUARY
Arsenal 3 Middlesbrough 2 FA Cup Fifth Round Replay

1 MARCH
We still might get to Wembley after all. We've got Villa at Highbury in the sixth round, and they seem to have a thing about Highbury. We stuffed them comprehensively in the League before Christmas, and Tony Barton said afterwards that they always get done at Highbury.

Middlesbrough played some really good football last night, but then everyone seems to be against us at the moment. We changed tactics and had Rixy down the right because Don thought Malcolm Allison might overload the left to combat Kenny, Rixy and me. It worked a treat. We got a goal in the first ten minutes. Rixy pinged over a cross with his right, and I came in at the far post for a header.

They really came back well though, and were probably a bit unlucky not to get a draw.

3 MARCH

We are really having a light week after playing those three games in six days. Today we just went for a walk round London Colney which is where our training ground is, up into Shenley and back, and finished for the day. Petrovic couldn't understand it. 'What's going on here? A walk!'

Of course footballers are never satisfied. We were walking along and the wind was blowing and it was quite cold, so everyone was complaining. 'We're freezing. It'd be nice if we could run.' If we have a hard morning we never want to do anything, and if we have a light morning we want to do some heavy work. I quite enjoyed it though. I thought, 'This is not bad. It's back to the Forest days is this.' Cloughie was a great man for walks. He used to take us up to Scarborough. Whenever he got a couple of days to play with it was up to Scarborough.

We used to have this walk down to the sea front and then up round the back of the town. The first time we did it we didn't know what we were letting ourselves in for. I think it was before the League Cup Final replay with Liverpool, so it was around this time of the year. Scarborough was deserted and, as you can imagine, a bit windy. We went for a two-hour walk along the sea front; it was spitting with rain and really windy, and we were all huddling deep into our clothes. There were a few choice comments floating around on the wind.

Even when we went to Spain for a mid-season break it would be compulsory to go for a walk on the beach. We'd put our training kit on and then he'd say, 'We're not training, we're going for a walk on the beach.' Even though it wasn't really warm he'd say, 'Right, everyone's shoes and socks off. In for a paddle.' And you would have to paddle up and down the beach. On one occasion when he'd told us there would be a walk beforehand, we all put our tracksuits on except Peter Shilton and David Needham. They turned up as if they were going out for the day, wearing nice slacks and casual shirts. And he said, 'Look at those two idiots. I'll put a stop to their little game. Everyone on the beach, we're all going for a paddle.' We didn't mind, because we'd got our tracksuits on, but Shilts and David had to roll their trousers up.

A walk was part of our Saturday morning ritual at Forest for away matches. We always had to meet at eleven a.m. to stretch our legs and get a bit of fresh air. It didn't matter what the weather was doing. I remember once being in Manchester and it was throwing it down. We were staying at this motel with a main building surrounded by chalets, which had a small plastic cover over them, and we walked up and down under that.

We used to go for pre-game walks in Cologne too, on the day before a game. We always went to the same hotel in the forest the night before a game. Germans tend to get fixed into a routine, and every time we went along this same twenty-minute walk. The path was circular, and I got fed up with it so I said, 'Why don't we go the other way round for a change?' They all said, 'No. No. You can't. We go this way round.' That changed when Rhinus Michels took over. Then we started going on different walks. He obviously liked them, because we would go for an hour, even one-and-a-half hour walks. And everyone was saying, 'Is he mad? Two-hour walks!!'

4 MARCH

Again we had a light morning. We just had a bit of a warm up. Don even said, 'If you want a five-a-side have one; if you don't, don't,' which is really unusual, because Friday five-a-sides are a big thing at Arsenal. Everyone was saying yesterday we will have to beat Forest now, because if we don't next week's training will be murder after not doing much this week.

Tomorrow will be interesting, if only to see what Garry Birtles is wearing. When we were at Forest he always used to wear what he would call the latest fashion – which was not the word most people used. He appeared in all sorts of things. At Forest he was into the baggy look: baggy woolly trousers and jackets. I used to call him Charlie Chaplin. One of the most memorable things in Italy during the European Championships was our last match, against Spain. We'd beaten them 2–1, but we were out of the competition by then and spent the evening in the hotel discotheque. There were a few residents there, but it was mainly the England party; most of us were still in our England suits because it was after the match. Garry went up to get changed, and he came down in this yellow and black striped sports shirt, which he was wearing with a tie. When he came walking in everyone fell about.

We thought that was bad enough, but the next morning when we went to leave he capped it. It was fairly hot and we had been told 'smart casual' to travel in, so we were all in our England casual shirts and slacks. Then Garry made his appearance in this heavy tweed and wool suit with a shirt and dicky bow on. He must have been sweating buckets and the lads just couldn't believe it. But it seemed that the more comments he got, the more outrageous he seemed to get.

Garry is a very good player though, and I rate him very highly. He has got nearly everything. He scores goals, and although he isn't really a pace-man he's quick. He's very good for his size in the air. He can hold the ball, he can turn with it, and he can run at defenders. Once his confidence is there he is as good as anyone in the country. And he'll work all day for you. I've played with a lot of big names up front and he certainly ranks among them: I can't think of anyone better.

When he first came into the Forest side, though, it made my life difficult; still, looking back I think it helped me. We'd been used to playing with Peter Withe as our target man. Then he went and Steve Elliott came in. He was a good player, a good honest player with good skill, and a good finisher. But he was unlucky because he came into the team at the start of the season after we'd won the League, and for the first two or three games we just weren't playing well. We got a draw at Coventry and Steve hit this great shot on the turn which hit the post. That would have been our winner, but it didn't go in. We just weren't getting it together, and although he was doing quite well, he wasn't getting any goals. So things had to be changed and as he was the young lad who had come in, he went out and Garry was given his chance. And he took it with both hands.

His first goal was in the European Cup against Liverpool in only his second game. He'd come in on the Saturday – against Arsenal funnily enough – and he'd played well, done a lot of running and showed good control. So he stayed in against Liverpool and got a goal. He and Larry Lloyd put me through and Ray Clemence came out. I saw this red shirt out of the corner of my eye – I didn't know it was Garry – so I knocked it past Ray and he just tucked it in.

Then for the second goal he went down the line and crossed. I headed it back down to Colin Barrett, who scored probably the best-ever Forest goal in our three years. It was a great move and a fantastic volley to finish. That was it, the team were playing better and Garry was in, and for the next three years everything was fantastic for him.

It changed my game a bit though. I'd been used to playing with Peter Withe. Everything was knocked into him, and he would knock it down for me to finish off or run at players and get crosses in. But when Garry came into the team he wanted to do that, and when you get a new member in the team you expect them to do their own thing initially. He had bags of enthusiasm and just did what he wanted really. And he was running into the spaces I used to occupy, so I found myself taking more of Peter Withe's role than I really wanted to. I was having to play as target man with my back to goal and lay things off, but the team was still tuned in to the way we had played with Peter there, and the rest were saying, 'We need you up there and you've just got to do the best you can.' The result was I didn't get so many goals that season, but Garry got a hatful – something like twenty-seven I think. So it was a hard season for me but in the long run it probably added something to my game, being forced to play up there and do that.

As we worked things out we both exploited the space down the left which John Robertson created. His first season in the first division he played as an out and out left-winger, but he got such a reputation that there would be two or three players on him. So what he did was drop very deep to get the ball, leaving a space up the left touch line. He knew we'd both be running there – and he could knock it blind. You don't have to look up if there's a space, and he knew Garry and/or I would be running out there.

If both of us were out there already he had two options. He could either hit the first man or by-pass him and hit the second. Then the former could spin and get it off the front man. It was simple, given that you had players with Robertson's talent, but it was so hard to stop and that made it the most dangerous thing about our team. Yet no matter what other teams used to do to try and stop us we would still carry on. Of course it all depended on Robbo's talent, and there aren't many players like him about. But Muhren does much the same, and I keep telling Graham Rix he ought to try it. He wants to be more involved.

When I left Forest Garry seemed to have everything going for him. I remember Brian Talbot had seen him and Paul Mariner play in a 'B' International and Brian raved about him. He said, 'He's in a different class. There's no way he won't play for England.' But when he did it all started to go wrong gradually. He was thrown in at the deep end against Italy in Turin. At the time I was quite pleased because I had been in Cologne for just six months, and I was still settling in there, and looked forward to joining up with him again. The previous season, before I left for Cologne, I think we had finally hit it off. We each really knew what the other was doing without thinking, and it began to pay dividends that season. I was sure we had something special, and I didn't think we could have lost it over six months.

But after I'd left he had had a fantastically hard season. He'd just played against Hamburg in the European Cup Final, and he had been on his own up front. He must have run I don't know how many miles – he'd played about eighty games and he was shattered. After that he was never given a real chance. It is strange with the international situation sometimes, because you work hard for your chance, then you get it and maybe after one game – if you haven't done it – you are out. You've got to take your chance when it comes, but in international football you do need some kind of run to establish yourself. If you are good enough to get picked in the first place, if the manager has got enough confidence in you to pick you, then you should be good enough to get a few games. The manager should be able to say, 'This is who I want to play up front, and it doesn't matter if he has a bad game, he is going to play in the next game – it doesn't matter what the press say.' That's what happens in Germany.

But it didn't happen to Garry. Maybe also it is down to Paul Mariner being that much more geared up when his opportunity came, saying to himself, 'This is my chance; now I've got to take it.'

I don't know, but I think that has a lot to do with it in football. A lot of top players have had to struggle. When you become a footballer you have to really want to succeed badly enough. I had to fight against Brian Clough at seventeen or eighteen years of age. I went to see him and said, 'Look, I want to play centre-forward, I'll score some goals and create some goals, and if you aren't going to play me then let me go on loan somewhere.' That took a lot of doing because I was terrified of the guy.

With Garry there wasn't quite that much determination. He drifted out of school, he got his job, earned his money and spent it enjoying his weekends, and got into football and won all these trophies. His first three years everything was fantastic for him, but he hadn't come through the hard school of wanting desperately to be a professional footballer, and do things, only to have someone say, 'You can't do it' and having to fight against that.

I remember going back to Nottingham from Cologne one Christmas. Garry was at Old Trafford by then, but he always came back to Nottingham whenever he could, and we were in this night club together with John Robertson, Viv Anderson and our wives or girlfriends. We were all sitting at a table having a few drinks, and we got on to football pretty late in the evening.

Garry said that he didn't really enjoy playing football. He must have been in his barren spell, or just out of it. He was saying he could go back to carpet laying without any regrets at all, and it wouldn't bother him not earning footballer's wages. So of course we said, 'Why don't you?' Now whether it was the drink or not I don't know, but he said that as he had been given this gift as a footballer it was his duty to use it. He said he was a good player, and lots of kids would love to be footballers but have not got the ability, and he thought if you have the ability you should use it, not waste it. We argued and argued for hours. We were still in the club about 3.30 a.m. when everyone else had gone home. I'm sure not playing wouldn't worry him. I think he appreciates the money, but probably not as much as the rest of us at that table. And although he does enjoy playing, he doesn't enjoy the rigmarole of being a professional footballer.

I think he might have lacked that little extra determination to make things happen when he went to United. I don't think the style suited him; still, the style at Arsenal doesn't really suit me at the moment, but you have to keep battling on. I was with him for a couple of evenings when all the turmoil around his transfer to United was going on, and he was wondering, 'Am I moving or aren't I?' and it was upsetting him. But when he did move to United I got the impression he expected everything just to slot into place, like it had at Forest. When he had that long spell he gave interviews saying, 'There are more important things than scoring goals. It'll come right, it doesn't worry me.' I'm sure it didn't, not as much as it would some players anyway. But generally I think he thought it was going to make itself happen, that he didn't have to do anything to help it along – it would just come right in its own good time.

But when you go to a new club, even though you know you are a good player and you are joining other good players, you have to work doubly hard to make sure things happen.

When I came to Arsenal I wanted to be a huge success and was determined to make it happen. I didn't come thinking 'Everything's just going to fall into place', because I knew it wouldn't. I've been proved right!

Of course everyone at Forest had the attitude that things fell into place of their own accord to some extent. If you were having a bad spell you didn't work on things. You were more likely to be given three days off than brought back to work extra hard, and when you have won things that way you tend to think that is the way to do it. I'm the same. I think Cloughie is great. I look back to the days when he used to come in at 2.45 p.m. and really gee us up to go out, and that's what I need at the moment. I haven't seen much of Garry playing since I came back, but I'm sure that he is benefiting from that now he is back at Forest.

I've continually said to Graham Rix that he ought to play as John Robertson did. Muhren's a similar type, or at least he was at Ipswich. What they both have, and it is a sign of a good player, is that they do the right thing at the right time. When there are three players in front of them they knock it. When there is only one, they take him on. It's simple. But I've been with Clough, Weisweiler and Michels now, and they say that the most difficult thing in football is to play it simply. The easy ball is the most difficult ball. Look at Muhren. He gets the ball and with one touch in it goes. That is the first thing he looks for every time. He gets the ball and it's 'Is there anyone down that left side?' and 'Can I just dink it into the box?' He looks. If it's not on he doesn't try and force it. He'll send it somewhere else. But then he gets it back and it *is* on. He notices it straightaway, and 'bang' in it goes. Graham wants to be involved all the time. He wants to show what he can do on the ball, which is fair enough, but he races all over the place. He agrees with me; but he wants the ball all the time, and says, 'If I hang out on the left, who is going to give me the ball?' He probably would get less of the ball if he played out there. But what he did with it in ninety minutes could be much more effective and beneficial to the team. If he was doing his stuff, which he is quite capable of, he would have a much better chance of getting in the England team in that position, and a much better chance of going abroad – which he wants – because there aren't that many left-sided players around.

I am biased, because he is a good friend, but I think he is a good player, and when I look at his ability to go past players and put balls in, and then I see him down in the left-back spot I have to say it is not right. There aren't many players who can do what he can do, so what is he doing back there?

5 MARCH
Arsenal 0 Nottingham Forest 0

For the spectator it was probably the worst game I've ever been in, and it was pretty terrible to play in too. No one said much afterwards; we all realized it had been diabolical. I think afterwards all the players felt sorry for the supporters, but at the time we couldn't do anything about it. Well – perhaps we could have. No one blatantly wasn't trying, but I think if we had all dug deep down into ourselves after the game we would have said, 'I could have given a bit more.' There was no enthusiasm, no drive. And the trouble at Arsenal at the moment is that we haven't got anyone to get a grip and make things happen, someone we can all rally round, someone to say, 'Come on, let's get together and make it work.' But there wasn't that sort of bite, and we couldn't snap out of it.

It was the kind of situation which the Forest team when I was there would have overcome. Larry Lloyd would get hold of things at the back. Archie Gemmill would definitely get things going in midfield. If Archie had been playing on Saturday, he would still have been running round at a hundred miles an hour, tackling and shouting. And if you see someone like that giving one hundred per cent themselves you've got to respond when he tells you to do something.

But there was no one like that on the field. We've got a young team at Arsenal now, so perhaps that's why – there's no Pat Rice or Sammy Nelson or Willie Young any longer – and John Hollins doesn't give people rollickings. If I shoot when I should have squared it, he'll say, 'Hard luck, son, keep trying,' rather than blasting me.

As it was there were a million mistakes. On the rare occasions the ball did come forward we were that bad we couldn't control it. The service was bad anyway. But normally when a ball is knocked in it sticks as you turn; this time it would bounce a yard off you, and it was such a tight game, with so many bodies about, that if you knocked it off a yard someone got a foot in and sent it away from you. This was happening to every player on the field. Someone would knock it off your toe and it would go to a Forest player. He'd give it straight to an Arsenal player, who'd give it straight back and so it went on. You get periods like that in football matches, but this one went on for eighty of the ninety minutes. Yet their Wilson might have had a hat-trick in the first quarter of an hour; and I could have sneaked it at the end, but the goalkeeper made a great save.

I said to some journalists afterwards that the fans ought to be given their money back. I said that because of our experience during the week when we went to see 'Song and Dance'. When Gemma Craven had had to give up, her understudy took over, and afterwards she came out with Andrew Lloyd-Webber, and he said, 'Anyone who saved their tickets can come back on another night, because you've got to hear Miss Craven sing.' If they do that in the theatre, I don't see why we shouldn't try it in football. You could let them in free to one of our less glamorous games where we're only going to get 20,000 anyway, and it might boost the attendance a bit. But I can't really imagine football clubs trying it.

7 MARCH

Predictably we had a hard morning at Highbury, for a Monday anyway. We played a bit of football in the gym, then into the weight room, then onto the track.

8 MARCH

Another hard morning, but a good one. We played five-a-side, then did doggies. It was a really good blow out, short and sharp but exhausting. After we'd finished the doggies all the lads collapsed. Still, we have a day off tomorrow.

10 MARCH

Another hard day! Whether this is a result of Saturday's performance against Forest I don't know, but we did look sluggish against them. It looks as if this week has been geared to put a bit of sharpness back into us.

11 MARCH

The usual Friday five-a-side. Terry didn't announce the team, but it looks as if Vlad will be back in. He's been playing on the right-hand side of midfield in the little bits of work we've been doing this week on formations and shooting practices. There's no indication who will step down for him though.

My old Forest partners seem to be coming one after the other at the moment. Tomorrow it is Peter Withe, who was my first partner in the Forest team. I've believed in instant partnerships being formed ever since, because we hit it off so well from the start. When he came to Forest he played his first game in the reserves, along with me. I don't think he had played for a few weeks so they wanted to give him some match practice, and I was his first partner up front. I can't remember who it was against, but we won 1–0 and I got the winner. Temporarily that was a parting of the ways, because I went off on loan to Doncaster the next day, and he went into the first team.

A month later I came back and played in the reserves against Liverpool at the City Ground. We drew 3–3, and because I'd been playing in the fourth division I was full of confidence and I played really well. So they brought me in for a mid-week Anglo-Scottish cup match. Larry Lloyd had been signed in the meantime, so he didn't know who I was; when he saw me in the dressing room he thought they had gone out and bought another new player. It worked instantly: Peter got the first, I got the second, and generally we caused havoc that night. We just hit it off straight away. Ironically, since after the first game in the reserves I'd left the club on loan, we played together for two years.

Needless to say I like him as a player. I think he is very good. He has come on in leaps and bounds since he arrived at Forest. When he first joined us in the second division his control was not that great. His first touch has probably improved one hundred per cent since then, and now it is not bad at all. I think Peter's improvement came because he worked very hard at it. He is one of the best trainers I have ever seen; he never grumbles at all. If you have a hard morning he will be out there leading the pack, and really going at it. At the end of that first season we went out to Majorca before we knew whether we had won promotion or not; when we landed we got a phone call through to say we had. You can imagine what it was like. There we were for a ten-day holiday and we heard that we'd won promotion. So all the lads were out having a few beers, guzzling champagne, really celebrating. But every morning Peter would go for a run on the beach. He was a fitness fanatic, just like Garry Birtles.

After training in normal weeks you would always find him there having a bit of shooting practice, or practising control. But there was also the fact that we were a good team at the time as well. The team was getting better and better, and confidence grew as a result. Confidence has a lot to do with most things. You win a couple of games, and all of a sudden you find the ball sticking to you, and I think he felt that, because most of his career had been with teams in trouble.

Sometimes now he will try things because of the confidence he has gained, 'Fancy Dan' things, as Cloughie would say, back-headers and delicate little flicks which don't come off; but mostly he realizes his limitations, and also realizes why he is in the team. Basically he is a good, honest centre-forward, an old-fashioned battling type, very good in the air. He is great to play with, because he is always up there, he takes all the knocks, takes all the bashes, knocks people around in his turn; you just need someone there to pick up the pieces after he has gone through the brick wall.

When we were having that very good run, he was outstanding. He is a very, very good target man. In fact he probably plays more with his chest than with his head or his feet. It became a bit of a standing joke at Forest that he didn't use his head or his feet. Virtually everything was knocked up onto his chest, and he would spring it back accurately, passing sometimes about ten yards off his chest. He could also handle it on the floor, and that is even more true now, as well as battling for everything in the air. He is very good, very unselfish: he'll knock things down in the six-yard box when some people would go for a header at goal.

Apart from the few over-ambitious tricks which creep in now and again, he does play within his limitations. He knows what he has got. He doesn't try to beat players, he doesn't go at them and try to go past them – he gets it under control, lays it off and makes a new position so you can find him again. He is a very chirpy character. Some people have said bordering on the insane! I wouldn't want to say that. I don't like to say he gets on your nerves, but he does. He does some daft things. Once at Forest someone brought a tray of chocolate eclairs in and had a bet that Peter could eat the lot. He scoffed about twenty-three of them. He is the biggest eater I have ever seen: he will finish his own meal and if you aren't careful will then be on to your plate as well.

He used to have these sayings at Forest, which drove people crazy. 'Oh no, I did' or 'Oh yes, it isn't.' You would ask quite innocently, 'Did you get that goal last week?' and he'd say, 'Oh no, I did.' And he started it with referees. They would blow the whistle and he'd go, 'Oh, no, I did,' and start laughing. He was always arguing with referees, moaning all the time. I don't know how many times he got booked.

Cloughie and he were always arguing too. I think they respected each other, and you don't have to like each other as long as there is respect. But there was an awful lot of mickey-taking between them, and because Brian used to be a centre-forward there was a lot of toing and froing. I remember once Peter scored four against Ipswich when we were top of the first division. He wanted the ball afterwards, and Cloughie said, 'You are not having that. I'll give you a ball when you can play football.' And he wouldn't give it to him.

I never knew why Cloughie sold him though. They had had a few rows, and this time they were arguing over the contract. I don't know whether this is true or not, but I heard that the difference between them was only twenty pounds. It certainly was not worth all the upheaval if it was as little as that.

Still, all credit to Peter. Possibly at Forest they thought they had seen the best of him, and he went down into the second division with Newcastle. But he has come back and really proved them wrong. He has been a great buy for Villa. There are rumours at the moment they might let him go at the end of the season, but if they do, he'll be a tremendous buy again for whoever is lucky enough to get him.

12 MARCH
Arsenal 2 Aston Villa 0
After the game Tony Morley said to Graham Rix, 'You must fancy your chances of going all the way, now.'

Graham said, 'Well yes, if we get a good draw.'

Then Morley said, 'You were probably confident before when you heard you'd got us at home.' Graham said, 'What do you mean?'

'Well,' said Morley. 'Our lads said, "Oh, here we go, in for another hiding at Highbury" as soon as we heard the draw.'

That would explain something, because they seemed a bit subdued, and perhaps there was that little doubt in their minds.

Even though I got the first goal, I didn't enjoy the game. I haven't enjoyed a game really for a few weeks. I don't enjoy a game unless I'm getting a lot of the ball, and even when we're on top I'm not getting that amount. And when I do get it, I'm not getting it where I really want it. They aren't tuned in yet to the areas where I need the ball. I'd like the first thought for everyone in midfield to be, 'Can I play it forward to Woody on the edge of the box?' Sundy would like the same, but I don't think they are that way inclined. We just have things tossed up to us and we get the occasional flick on, but if I don't read it off Sundy there's no one else to pick it up.

It was a funny game. In our pre-match meeting Don told Sundy to play where Rossi had for Juventus, because he thought he'd spotted a weakness down the Villa right flank – he felt it had been very exposed. I thought it was only a weakness because of bad play rather than a general thing. This seemed especially true for the first goal – there were three men marking Rossi and he got in front of all of them.

That was beside the point though. Don had got the idea that there was this weakness, so the whole team talk was directed to how we should react to it. After being with Cloughie, I don't think you need all that, especially for a cup-tie. I think you just have to get people in the right frame of mind, and then if you are good enough players your football is going to come through.

But Don went on and on. Sundy and I looked at each other. When he'd finished Sundy started talking Italian, and I asked him if he thought we were going to play in black and white shirts instead of red ones.

Then of course we went out and we were two up by half time; the cross for my goal came from our left, and we did produce most of our threats down that side. But then we are primarily a left-sided team, with Kenny and Graham Rix and I all favouring that side. If we were usually a right-sided team and it had happened then you would have to hold your hand up and say, 'Right. That's great. It worked.' But in our team when we play well that's where it will come from anyway.

The real problem is that we just don't play with much confidence. We're not sure enough about our jobs to push a back-four player into midfield so a midfield player can push up and make an extra forward. We seem to say keep it tight and wait for someone to produce a bit of magic and stick one in for us.

But within those limitations, which meant it didn't flow particularly well up front, we did quite well. The crucial thing was we stopped Villa in midfield in the first half. Peter Nicholas did very, very well. We were biting very early with tackles, and we were picking the second ball up. I always think it's a very good sign if you are picking up everything that's going spare. And everyone was getting tackles in, and if anyone did miss there was someone else there in support straight away.

We were really keyed up, and I had a couple of rows with Rixy, and one with the bench. These were small things, but they were a good example of the problems and disagreements we're having at the moment. Peter Nicholas knocked a ball up the wing. Both Sundy and I had just made a run out there, and as we were both coming back we were caught flat-footed when it was knocked forward. Nico could have played an easy ball inside and changed the play, but he just tanked it forward. And Terry and Don were shouting, 'Get running, you lazy bastard.' So we got the blame for not chasing a bad pass. It was the same old argument again, because in the last three years in Germany it's been drummed into me that you don't chase lost causes, and that was a lost cause. In Germany it's the person who has played the ball who is responsible. It's his bad pass, not my bad running that created the problem.

But I was wound up because of that, and a few minutes later the ball went out wide and I chased across and clobbered the Villa player who was there: he went over the touchline and hit the boards. He caught his arm and he was really in pain. I apologized, saying, 'OK, I caught you, but I didn't mean to hurt you, it was just one of those things.' I thought the referee would give a foul, but he gave us a throw-in. I was bending over the guy and Rixy wanted to take the throw in so he shouted at me to get back on the pitch. As I walked past him he pushed me. Toni Schumacher used to do that in Cologne and I think it's terrible, it looks really bad especially in front of 40,000 people. So I turned to Rixy and said, 'You don't have to push me in front of 40,000 people. Don't you ever do that again.'

Then a few minutes later it started again. Someone flicked one on on the left side of the field. I'd just run forty yards and I collected it, but then knocked it too far ahead and a defender came across and took it out to the corner flag, and I didn't chase him. I thought if I cut off the goalkeeper someone else could go into the corner and block him there because it's better for me to be in the box. But then Rixy started shouting at me to get out and get chasing because no one else had gone out there; he had a bit of time to turn and whack it clear. So I shouted back, 'Look, I've just run forty yards to pick the ball up. Someone else can push up in there.'

Then two minutes later I got the goal, and Rixy was racing over and jumping on my back, and I gave the bench a little wave to say, 'How about that?' I said to Rixy afterwards, 'If you hadn't come over and congratulated me there would have been big trouble.' He said, 'Oh, I'd have been over quicker, but I was a bit tired,' and we laughed about it, which is another difference from Germany, because in Cologne he wouldn't have come and congratulated me. In Germany when you have a really heated argument on the pitch it could often carry on for two or three days of not speaking. Here we just seem to forget about it. You never go over things said in the heat of the moment with Don and Terry either, but I'm not sure sometimes whether that's a good thing.

Afterwards Brian Talbot said, 'Great finish', and several other people thought I'd taken my goal really well. I felt that it was a fairly easy chance. Kenny went to the by-line and I thought I'd just hold back a bit because if he screwed it back I might get a half-volley or something. But he knocked it a little bit inside to Sundy, Sundy missed it, and I came in behind him and moved onto it. I knew Evans and the keeper were both coming in and I really concentrated – it was just a question of getting there first and shooting high to miss all the legs and bodies which would be flying around. The main thing was to hit the roof of the net, and to hit it as hard as possible. Two or three bodies came in as I hit it and I went over the top of them.

It wasn't a special goal, but it was a good time to score, because too often we've pressed teams this season in the first half, gone in 0–0 at half time and then lost it. This time the pressure paid off. Then Vlad got a second, and that really was a great goal, because it was a very good dummy by Sundy, with Vlad finishing it beautifully.

It was great for Vlad. He is happy enough. He likes it here, and is happy with all the players – it's just a question of him getting settled in. He finds two games a week tiring, but then I do too. People say he has got to fit in with the English game, to adapt to the English style, but they don't realize that it's the same for me. The biggest problem for him is that in Yugoslavia he was the superstar, and there was a slower build up in play with everyone giving him the ball the whole time. It was, 'Give it to Vlad and he'll set things going.' Here they don't give him the ball because they don't have that much time to pick him out. And then when he does get it there are always people charging at him, and he's not used to that. But when he's got that little bit of time he can pick you out, and the pace he puts on the ball is perfect. There was one occasion in the second half when he was surrounded by players, but he picked out Alan Sunderland and set him free. Unfortunately Paul Davis missed the cross.

Sometimes when we are playing, and even in training, he'll find you when you don't think he can. Because I'm not used to playing with him yet, there have been occasions when I've seen something and thought 'That ball's on', but then haven't gone there because I didn't think we had anyone good enough to play it in, and Vlad has done so. It's my fault not his, because I don't react. You've got to be alert and expect the unexpected from him, because he's aware of what's going on even when things are tight around him. Even if he's not looking at you, or even in your direction, he knows you are there and if you make a run he'll find you, because he sees things other players wouldn't see. And in tight situations around the box he knows when to make the pass.

It's really just a question of us getting him into the game more, of giving him a lot more of the ball. I'm sure if he played for Liverpool or Manchester United or anyone in Europe he'd get a lot more of it. Obviously if we were a better team it'd be easier, but I'm sure too that if we perhaps had a better system he could be more involved, and he'd be a great buy for us. It's like Arnold Muhren. He's not a great tackler, he doesn't run all over the place – although he can get back and nick the ball away when necessary – but he plays those lovely balls in. And nobody talks about him not being physical enough. If you've got someone there who can compensate for that, that's all you need. I think it's wrong to judge Vlad on just a few games.

I couldn't have trapped a medicine ball. You get games like that. You get games where the ball feels like a lead weight when it comes to you and you know it's going to stick every time – it's under control straight away. Other games it takes its time to come and you wonder, 'Is it coming?' Then you try and cushion it and it flies off you. You can't explain it, it just happens. And then you really concentrate on controlling it, and you control it so well that it sticks between your legs. Other days the ball is played up and you can turn in one, maybe lose a defender in the process, and it's as if the ball was tied to your bootlace. It's strange.

I might have ended up with two goals for the first time this season. It was another example of our not getting our crosses in early enough. We didn't play well in the second half, but we might have scored on a couple of occasions. Paul Davis went on this mazy past about three players; all he had to do was hammer it in to the near post and I would have been there. But he knocked it, and he knocked it again and again, and when he finally came to cross it he clipped it in. There had been a good space by the near post, but by the time he'd done all that and then clipped rather than hammered it, we had to wait for it to come; by then there were two or three players waiting for it. Perhaps if he had smashed it in at the first opportunity I'd have been in there first and there's a good chance it would have been a goal.

50

Chris Whyte and Stewart Robson had outstanding games in the centre of defence. We said afterwards that Peter Withe hadn't put himself about as much as usual. How much of that was down to them I couldn't tell. Usually you expect him to belt a couple of people whether he was having a bad game or not; perhaps if he is on his game he puts himself about, if he isn't, he doesn't. But maybe they got on top of him so much he couldn't get into it. Was it Peter Withe's failings or their achievement? I thought they were outstanding.

13 MARCH

So we are in the semi-finals, and as long as we avoid Manchester United, we will be quite confident. We want to save them for Wembley. On the coach coming home from Old Trafford after the semi-final of the Milk Cup, we said, 'We'll get them in the FA Cup Final.' We were very disappointed with the way we played in the first leg, but we thought things could have worked out a bit differently with luck in the second. But we would really fancy ourselves against Brighton or whoever wins the Sheffield Wednesday v Burnley tie.

United obviously want to avoid us too. I went to the television centre for a recording of *A Question of Sport* and Gordon McQueen was there with Graeme Souness for another edition of the programme. He said they'd sooner save us till Wembley!

14 MARCH

FA Cup Semi-Final Draw:
Arsenal v Manchester United (at Aston Villa)
Brighton v Sheffield Wednesday (at Highbury)

So it was not to be. Before the draw all the lads were saying, 'We wonder if they will fix it,' because United v Arsenal would have been a classic Cup Final. It's unfortunate the draw didn't go that way. The semi-final will be like the final now. It'll be a great atmosphere. We're not frightened of them, although we certainly don't relish the thought of playing against them.

A friend we go out with, David Dein, who is a real Arsenal fanatic, rang up after the draw and said, 'Don't worry, we'll beat them.' Then he said, because it must have been in the papers that I hadn't played in an FA Cup semi-final before, 'I hadn't realized this was your first FA Cup semi-final. There you are you see, when you come to Arsenal you keep getting all these new things. It's great for you, isn't it?'

'I said, 'Yes, and I haven't played in the second division yet either,' which when you look at the League table is a possibility. That soon shut him up, that did. It didn't go down at all well.

Of course I have. What I should have said was, 'I haven't been fighting relegation before.' I mean I like new experiences, but not this kind. The Cup Final would be great. That's if we can score. If we score the first goal then we've got a chance.

15 MARCH
Birmingham City 2 Arsenal 1

16 MARCH
It was terrible. It was typical of our whole season really. We'd done very well against Villa, and then we went up to Birmingham and played terribly. We are just not positive enough. We could have sneaked it – we had a couple of chances when it was 1–1; then I probably wouldn't be saying such bad things about the match.

We worry about other teams too much. All Don's pre-game talk was about Harford and how we were going to cope with him. But we shouldn't be so concerned about teams like Birmingham – we should just go out there and steamroller them.

Still, perhaps I've got an over-inflated sense of our ability because we are Arsenal. I think of Arsenal as The Club, but we are down near the bottom of the table. All right, we are having a good cup run, but then so are Brighton. Why should I be so confident? We have got all these good players. We are a good team, and we ought to start thinking we are a good team. It's about time people started telling us, 'Come on, unless you pull your fingers out you are not the team you think you are. You've got the potential to be a good team, but until you start doing it you're just one of the also-rans.' And we are just not doing it. It was the best pitch we've played on for months. I went out before the start and thought, 'This will really suit us. We'll be able to knock it around, push and run, push and run, there will be no problems.' But it just didn't happen. I don't think we played freely enough – we were a bit cramped.

Because we keep changing our style to adapt to our opponents the understanding isn't there. There's such a gap between midfield and us in some games that we've got no chance. Sundy and I are expected to get up there and flick it on and then go and pick up the flick on too. It means you are having to make sixty-yard rather than twenty-yard runs. And Arsenal never really pen another team in; we never hold people in around the last third of the field. It's very rare with us that you get balls flying across our opponent's box to give a bit of excitement with people diving in and missing them and the ball coming back in and someone getting his head to it. If we get in an attack it might end with us getting a shot in, but it's just as likely to end going straight down to our end and them getting a shot in. We never put people under sustained pressure. It's partly a question of confidence, of being positive and thinking, 'We can beat these,' so players press up in support.

'It's also a question of how we play. If we built it up more, played it around and played in to people who could then hold it and knock it off and go for the return, we might put more pressure on teams. But instead we have all these thirty–forty yard balls knocked up, and you are scrambling to get them all the time.

Don likes balls knocked into space. That's fair enough if you've got someone who can knock a good long ball. They keep on to me to come short and then check and spin and go long for the ball played into the channel between the centre-half and the full-back. That's fine if you've got Hoddle or Muhren or someone with a really delicate touch who can knock those balls; but with us it's got to be a hell of a ball, and I don't think we have anyone to play them except perhaps Vlad – and he just wasn't involved again. We've tried those runs and not many have come off. The ball goes floating over you. Don likes Kenny Sansom, for example, to play the ball over the full backs . . . but then why don't we start talking in team meetings about getting the front players out behind the full-backs? Because of the things that are said about doing all these runs, I'm not sure whether I should be coming short to pick the ball up or what.

They think I want the ball to feet too often, but I've had to have passes to my feet for the last three years, because there's always been someone right at my back all the time. Playing into space more may be right, but because the understanding isn't there, if I come for the ball to feet on one occasion, then on the next feint to do that and check and go the other way I'm as likely to have given my own player the wrong idea as the opponent. It's hard to develop that understanding, and I don't think it's there because we are changing all the time.

On one occasion the ball was played up to me, and I could see Paul Davis coming up. The defender was really tight on me, so I just played it back three feet with my studs. I was hoping Paul would just clip it and play me in. The marker didn't know whether to go for the ball or not, so I'd lost him, but Paul went racing past me, into the box, and the ball went back into no-man's land. He didn't grasp the situation, didn't realize that I want someone just behind me so I can knock it back. He was going on for a ball, whether from me or someone else I just don't know, which wasn't on. And I think if a front player gets a certain type of ball knocked up to him the midfield player should be able to read what's on.

In spite of the team talk, we didn't cope with Harford. They had quite a few chances really, because he was glancing the ball down and their midfield players were running through onto them. There was one fellow through on Pat all by himself three times, and their first goal came that way. Then we gave the winner away in the last minute.

Last night was really depressing. If we're going to play like that against Manchester United we might as well not bother to turn up. I think we ought to attack them, because I don't think they've got the best defence. But the way we play with the ball being knocked up to us plays into their hands – they just go bang, bang, bang. We play back four; midfield; front; and very rarely do we move from it. I keep saying to Paul Davis that at goalkicks he could push up in front of me sometimes and I'd come in behind him just to get a bit of variety. If he gets stuck up there I'll drop back and fill in for him just for the sake of changing it around sometimes.

Terry said in the Sunday papers after we'd beaten Villa that it was a good performance, but we'd now set a standard and if we didn't do that at Birmingham he'd have something to say – inconsistency wouldn't be acceptable. I wonder about them though. At St. Andrews the atmosphere wasn't right in the changing room before the game. It was really light-hearted – a laughing, joking sort of atmosphere. I was part of it too. Terry and Don are the kind of people who join in with the lads, they aren't the strict type. I sometimes have a massage before a game, and I said, 'I'll have a rub.' Terry was giving it to me, and as I'd got a bruise I said half-joking, 'Oh, not too rough.' Everybody latched onto it, and Terry joined in. And I just don't think it's the right sort of atmosphere before a game, because even if you don't want to take it out on the pitch with you I'm sure you do. Against Villa – and earlier against Spurs and United or any other big game – it was nice and quiet and serious beforehand. There weren't any jokes then, no one said very much.

Again at Arsenal there's music on the coach, and the lads play cards. But Cloughie used to take the cards from the players at lunchtime. When you left the hotel on the way to the stadium it would be, 'No cards, no music on the coach. Get your minds on this game.' And it would be the same in the changing room; when things reached a certain stage Cloughie would say, 'Come on, get your minds on this game.'

I think it's Terry and Don's job to sort that out. They would probably say it was up to the individual, that each player should be big enough to sort that out for himself. But when you are in a group and things are starting to sway it's easy to get caught up in it all. I agree you should try and pull yourself out of it and really say, 'Come on, let's have a go,' but they should make the effort as well, not put all the onus on the players. The players should do it, but if they aren't, the management have got to take that responsibility.

It's really part of the whole question about our motivation at the moment. I think players should be able to motivate themselves. Players know when they are not doing it, and they should sort it out themselves – they have got to take some responsibility – but if they aren't then Terry and Don should get the whip out.

Cloughie judged his moments for relaxing things though. When we went to Anfield in the European Cup, we travelled down in the morning, and as we were on the coach going along the motorway, a crate of beer suddenly appeared. 'Come on lads, let's have a beer together.' Bottles were opened and we all had a bottle of beer. In fact some lads had two or three! Then we got to the hotel, sat down for lunch, and there were bottles of wine on the table. 'Have a few glasses of red wine lads, it'll help you to sleep this afternoon.' So we had a few glasses each then went off to bed. We got onto the coach just after six p.m. The kick off was 7.30, and usually you get there an hour beforehand. At 6.15 we were still sitting outside the hotel waiting for Cloughie. Peter Taylor was panicking more than anyone. 'Well, where is he? Where the heck is he? It's diabolical is this, it's a quarter past six and he's not here. We've got to get to the stadium yet.' The police escort was there, but no Cloughie. Eventually he came out. 'Sorry lads, but it's only ten minutes to the ground, and you don't want to be sitting around in that dressing room. It'll be packed in there already, anyway, so we'll have missed the traffic.'

We got there just before seven. And we went out and won the tie,

55

and afterwards it was, 'Right everyone back on the coach straight away. You don't want to go gloating in their players' room do you? Get on the coach and we'll go back and have a beer.'

He was a great one for that sort of thing. When we played West Brom in the FA Cup quarter-finals I was in my bedroom in the hotel. I'd just been watching *The Professionals* when there was a knock on the door. It was just after ten, so I thought it was one of the lads messing about; I said, 'Yeah, what do you want?'

'It's the boss!'

I opened the door quickly, and he said, 'I'd like you down in the bar in five minutes. Get changed and come down.' So we went down and it was 'beers all round'. We all wanted to get to bed. So Archie Gemmill, who was always having rows with Cloughie, always rebelling against him, said, 'John Robertson's here and he doesn't like beer.'

'OK, what does he want then?'

'A dry martini and lemonade.'

'Right, bring a couple of dry martini and lemonades. Now what are you having Archie?'

'Nothing.'

'Have a dry martini.'

'No, I don't want anything. I want to go to me bed.'

'You're having a drink before you go to bed. What are you having?'

'I only drink champagne,' said Archie, who really doesn't drink.

'Waiter! Bring us a couple of bottles of champagne.'

And Cloughie opened the champagne, got some orange juice and we were there until about one a.m.

That was par for the course. When I went back to Cologne to sign for them I stayed at the hotel we'd used when we played them in the European Cup. And all the waiters were saying, 'We thought you had no chance. We told everyone in Cologne that you were boozing the night before.' They couldn't believe it.

18 MARCH

We had a 'clear-the-air' meeting, in which I came in for a lot of stick. It started with the five-a-side – which are still very competitive – the youngest six against the rest. They are very close, very hard fought, because no one likes to lose. But having won the bib for 1982's worst player in just three months; three months into 1983 I'm already well on the way to retaining it. It gets spread out quite a bit. Alan

Sunderland always votes for Paul Davis, whether he plays brilliantly or not; that's a standing joke, so Paul gets one vote every week. But today was a bit disappointing, because they only went through half the votes, my team and two of the others, and I got six of them. So I can tell what my own team mates think of me, and that's a bit disappointing.

It goes back to Forest. On a Friday at Forest you never did five-a-sides. It was twenty minutes on the track and finish. You would be itching to get a ball out and they would say, 'No ball, nothing more' – and we had success that way. It was the same if we had a bad game. There they were more likely to say have three days off; here after a bad performance you are more likely to be in for three extra afternoons.

I don't know which is right, but you always go back to the way you do things when you are successful, so I think of what Cloughie did. I'm not sure that a forty-five minutes blood and thunder five-a-side on a Friday is a good preparation for Saturday. If I'm going to be doing it on the Saturday I don't feel I need to be dashing around and fighting for every ball on the Friday. Graham Rix will fight for everything, chases everything and moans all the time on Friday morning.

Then we had this meeting. Maybe because I'm a new player who cost a bit of money they wanted to show that no one could escape having a bit of stick given to them, but I came in for it. Terry Neill said I wasn't brave enough against Birmingham. I disagreed with him. Then all the players started chipping in, saying, 'What's the matter?' We said we don't give one another enough rollickings on the pitch, and that we don't accept them properly. If you shout at someone in our team he is likely to turn round and say, 'You get on with your own job.' That's what it has been like this season. Alan Sunderland and I shout at one another and I think we accept it, but when someone else gets on to us we tend to resent it. So we said we've all got to get it together, and if anyone says anything it's got to be backed up by the whole team. If one player isn't doing it, the whole team has got to get on to him.

Then Don came in and said, 'It's all down to attitude. Why is Graham Rix always moaning at Tony Woodcock in five-a-sides? Because Tony doesn't want to do them and Graham does.' So then I started getting stick from Don because I'm not the best five-a-side player in the world, and because my attitude isn't right.

19 MARCH

Arsenal 4 Luton 1

Leading up to the game in the morning I didn't say anything to anyone – I was really trying to get tuned in to playing against Luton, and was determined to do well. I think I put my head in anyway, but I was thinking, 'I'll start putting my head in there.' I didn't agree with Don, but maybe on a couple of occasions against Birmingham he was right, I don't really know.

I don't think I ran around or challenged any differently to the way I had the week before. It was just that I got the chances and put them away – well, maybe against Birmingham I could have scored once or twice. There was one occasion when I probably should have stuck it in the net myself instead of trying to set it up for someone else, but the chances didn't really come in that game. Getting a hat-trick was nice after getting all the stick before the game.

I thought it was a good hat-trick too. We bossed them in midfield from the start, got our tackles in early and were winning the second ball which is always a good sign. We started off at a hundred mph, and that shook them back a little bit. And after the first two goals it was all over. Sundy and I always had that extra yard whether we were going long or dropping off short because the whole team was going well, and we hit them so early they didn't really know what day it was. The centre-half Elliott is a big, strong lad and he was coping with the high balls all right, but was a bit lacking on the floor, so we took him there.

The first was a clearance which went really high and came down on the edge of the box. It was one of those where you are looking up at it thinking, 'Is anyone running in behind me? Should I volley it, should I try and control it?' If it was in practice you'd try and control it, and you'd push it on and score, but in a match your control has to be spot on, you've got to concentrate on the ball. I was pretty pleased, because I stayed calm while I was waiting for it to come down, brought it down with my left and hit it very early with my right and it flew into the corner.

The second was a great move. Sundy put Noddy Talbot clear with a great forty-yard ball from left to right, and he hammered it back into the middle. I don't know whether it was a shot or a cross. I was slightly ahead of the ball so I controlled it with my right knee and hit it on the turn – a good finish.

For the third Rixy gave a nice little chip into the box. I took my time again; it was a bouncing ball and I controlled it, waited for it to rise off the ground and did him on his near post. It was the opposite of what it should be really, because when I brought it down I thought, 'I'll squeeze this in at the near post,' but when it went in I thought, 'How have I done it? You shouldn't let them go in at your near post.' I am always suspicious of scoring goals at the near post, because goalkeepers shouldn't be beaten there. Maybe it's coming from Germany where they do everything so precisely, and everything you do has to be right. And if you go down the left and get into the box they'll always say, 'Hit the far post', because if the goalkeeper parries it there will be someone else coming in. So there's just this nagging little question mark against this one. I don't know whether it would have beaten Peter Shilton.

Noddy was brought back for Vlad. Terry brought a programme in to the dressing room, held it up and said, 'The team's on the programme.' Well of course you can't see what's printed on a programme across the room, so it took Vlad a minute or two to realize what was happening; then he just walked out of the changing room.

When we went two-up, the friends who were with Carole in the stand said, 'That's it, you've won.' And she said, 'Oh, I wouldn't say that.' She says at Arsenal she can't relax unless we are three-up with five minutes to go. It was the same in Cologne. Even when we were three-up there she couldn't relax until the final whistle. Whereas at Forest as soon as we went one-up she thought, 'That's it, they've won. Game over.'

My Dad was down as well. Afterwards he said, 'That must be the best pitch in football.' I said, 'You must be joking. It's as bumpy as anything, and you don't know what's going to happen when the ball comes to you.' He shook his head knowingly and said, 'Well, I reckon it must be one of the best.' I was a bit cross. I said, 'Crikey, how many times have you played on it?' It was a mess.

My father was a great help to me, and I know he is proud of me, but he is deliberately perverse sometimes. The first time I played at Wembley, which should have been a great occasion for him, all he said afterwards was, 'It could do with a lick of paint.' And when we won the European Cup against Malmö, I took him to the ground the next day and took him inside and gave him the European Cup to hold. Trevor Francis came in and I introduced them, and all he could talk about for the next month was meeting Trevor.

21 MARCH

We had the hardest session. We were in three groups and we did a weight circuit, and then went into the gym with a football. It was really hard – a very good session – but unusual the day before a game.

22 MARCH
Arsenal 2 Ipswich 2

I got up this morning and I couldn't walk, I was so stiff after our weight session yesterday, and I was really in pain. My stomach muscles were in agony – which really makes you wonder about the wisdom of doing that sort of session the day before a game. If you are doing it right through the season, okay, but in a one-off situation like this it was a bit heavy; it doesn't really seem very wise.

I couldn't move during the game. We had a good warm up before it in the gym, and we really needed it. I couldn't move a leg, and it took me half an hour to get into my normal stride. But by the second half I was starting to get a little bit cold again, and feeling stiff.

I wasn't involved in the game – I didn't do much at all – but I could have had another hat-trick. I should have scored with a header in the second half. I thought, 'If I connect with this it's in the back of the net,' but I headed it straight at Cooper. And when the rebound came out I tried to lob it over him into the net – as casual as you like – and it just clipped the bar. It was the same as the Villa goal; I thought, 'Over his head and into the net,' against the coaching manuals which tell you to shoot low, but this time it went over rather than under.

And in the first half when Sundy hit the bar I could have scored. I'd gone in for the keeper parrying it, but it came back so quickly off the bar that it was virtually past me before I controlled it. I think I did the hardest part by actually stopping the ball without it running away, but then as I pushed it on to get my shot in I pushed it too far. Terry Butcher got a tackle in; as it spun up in the air I got in a header over Cooper but there was someone on the line.

Russell Osman caught me in the first five minutes. He and Butcher are both very hard, they both crunch you and knock you about a bit – you get a couple of bruises playing against them. If you are playing balls up in the air or you get a ball which is played a bit short for you, there's no doubt you'll be hit. This time Russell caught me with his elbow on the side of my upper arm. It wasn't really my ball, but the way he went for it, steaming in with his arms out! I couldn't move my arm, I was in such pain I couldn't lift it. He must have hit a nerve, and throughout the game I had such an ache.

I don't mind playing against them though. I know them quite well and we always have a good chat. When we played at Ipswich earlier in the season I scored a scrappy winner.

We have this running joke because they think I eat quite a lot. I don't know where they get it from; they keep saying, 'You can eat, you can. You really like your food,' at England meetings. And at Ipswich before the kick off Russell called me over to the half-way line, puts his hand down his shorts, says, 'I thought you'd like this before the game,' and pulls out a pork pie. Then he ran off; I had to give it to someone, so I gave it to Terry Butcher and said, 'Get rid of this for me.' I don't know how long it had been in Russell's jockstrap, but he gave it to their trainer who scoffed it during the match.

I'm not one of those players who notice opponents though. Sometimes if you are playing against a player or a team someone has played with or knows, they'll come up to you and pass on tips. 'He likes to dwell on the ball too long so maybe you'll get a chance to nick it off him;' 'He's not very good on his right;' 'He might go to sleep a bit.' Some players like to be told that sort of thing in advance, but it doesn't bother me. I just go out and play, and I don't take too much notice of what they are doing. Unless someone hadn't let me have a kick, I couldn't tell you how they played. In fact afterwards when people say 'so-and-so played well,' I never know whether they have or not unless it's an opposition forward, because I can see them from where I'm standing at the other end.

When you are 2–0 up you shouldn't throw it away. Even if we didn't deserve to be 2–0 up – because there were chances on both sides – you shouldn't lose a two-goal lead, no matter how you are playing. Even if you are playing terribly and sneak two lucky goals you shouldn't throw them away. But that's the way things have been this year. We've done this four or five times now – got a lead and then squandered it.

The worst thing about it was that we had the ball on both occasions when they scored, but didn't clear it quickly or far enough. And there wasn't *one* red shirt in there, there were several. Perhaps that's the problem, everyone leaving it to one another. 'He's got it, it's all right, no he's got it. Oh, I've got it, maybe I should kick it. No, he'll kick it,' when one of them should have bossed the other out of the way and put it into the stand somewhere. That happened twice and we lost two goals through not being positive and attacking the ball.

The most remarkable thing, though, was the time we didn't concede a goal. Burley took off from the right-back position when they had a free kick on the half-way line. I saw him go, and the next thing I knew he was in our box to gather the free kick with no one within twenty yards of him; a great run, someone said. It was diabolical marking. Okay, all credit to him for going, but he ran a hell of a long way and he must have gone past a few red shirts on the way – someone should have picked him up. Fortunately Chrissie Whyte scrambled it off the line after his shot hit the bar.

The wind didn't help matters. It was gale force, and Highbury yet again was like a wind tunnel; and when it is windy with a very hard pitch playing is difficult.

The crowd didn't help either. If we are winning they get behind us, but they are quick to have a go. George Wood, who came in because Pat's got a foot injury, got a lot of stick, which was really uncalled for. He looked a bit jittery, but the defence in front of him was a bit jittery too. And if you haven't got a centre-half in front of you who is going to attack everything, it's bound to put you a bit on edge, not knowing whether to come or who is going to take it. With a makeshift central defence, with John Hollins and Chris Whyte, it was difficult – they were letting the ball bounce, and that made it hard for George.

In a way we missed Robbo more than David O'Leary for that reason, because Dave doesn't challenge for everything, whereas with Robbo you know he will. He's going to put his head in everywhere. Even when he shouldn't you know he is going to challenge for it, you know he is going to do the positive thing.

That probably cost us the two points. If we'd won tonight and beaten Birmingham, as we should have done, we'd be in the top six.

23 MARCH
Although it was a day off, most of us went to Highbury at lunchtime to give Pat Jennings a bit of moral support for the launch of his autobiography. Pat asked us to go, so we went. It was about all I was capable of doing, because after last night and even more that training session on Monday, I couldn't move. I looked at my chest and stomach muscles and I really thought they had swollen up.

I've only skimmed through the book, but I was quite surprised by bits of it. I thought, 'I didn't think Pat would say that, or go into that', because there were bits about money and his treatment by Tottenham where I didn't expect him to be so revealing.

24 MARCH

Even though I couldn't move, it was a great training day. We had two teams in a finishing exercise. There were two of us in the middle and the rest of your team crossing. You got three minutes to see how many goals you scored, and then when you finished you went to the back of the line. We also changed formations – near post crosses, far post crosses. It was really good, and competitive. We lost by one goal on the day, but it was really enjoyable, a great morning. It was interesting coming in at all different angles and trying to get your shots in, particularly as you were against the clock and the other team was going to be scoring too. Pat, George and Rhys Wilmot took turns in goal. Rhys was absolutely fantastic, gave a brilliant display of goalkeeping.

25 MARCH

We had our football session in the gym, a five-a-side which ended up 2–2. It was a real blood and thunder game, not so much with the tackling, but both teams wanted to win and we got a really good sweat on.

It was such a close game that we didn't have a vote for the yellow bib. So for once I escaped getting it, because I have to be really keyed up to play five-a-side on a Friday. On some Saturdays, the less we've done on a Friday, the better I feel. I still don't know whether it is right to work quite so hard on a Friday.

Vlad is staying amazingly cheerful. He trains hard, and has good spirit, when you could forgive him if he said, 'I've had enough of this.' Obviously he wants to know whether he is going to be given a contract or not, because if he isn't he's got to find a new club. He wants to stay. He likes the club, and he likes London – he's made some good friends here – but if they don't want him they ought to tell him now and save him hanging on in suspense.

If they *are* going to sign him, they've got to play him, because the only way he will adapt is through playing games. It doesn't matter if he has two or three bad games, because playing is the only way he will overcome his settling-in problems. At the moment he's in and out and the lads feel a bit sorry for him. He's been unfortunate in that when he's played we haven't done that well, and it's usually been a hectic game, a cup-tie or something, so that it's been that much quicker and more physical. The game against Luton when we were comfortable would have been an ideal opportunity for him to show what he could do. We were well on top and had that extra yard, so I think we would have seen the best of him there.

Of course you can't tell what a game is going to be like beforehand, but you can have some idea. And this little run of league games before the semi-final would have been a good time to settle in. Ipswich would also have been okay – you know who is going to let you play football. Maybe they've made their minds up already. But they keep bringing him back, so perhaps they are a little unsure. In training you can see he's tackling a bit more – he's a bit more fiery, more aggressive. What he really needs is to get a bit more confidence when he's playing for the first team, and the only way he's going to get that is by playing.

26 MARCH
Everton 2 Arsenal 3
Before the game Alan Sunderland said, 'A couple of years ago, if we'd been 2–0 up that would have been it. We'd have shut up shop and no one would have got through us.' Which is right. It was the same at Forest. When you score a goal you do tend to relax a little bit, but with us it's extreme. So we said, 'Right, if – when – we get a goal today, everyone gees one another up, and for the next ten minutes we've got to make it doubly hard for them.' It was a pity we didn't do it in the first minute, because we were 1–0 down then! But when we went 2–1 ahead we said, 'Right, that's it', and gave one another the nod. We proved that we can do it, because we were really tight, we were all in it together, and they had no chance.

The first half was a shambles though. They were shouting at me on the bench. I was waiting for the ball to be played over the top, and they were shouting for me to get into the space before the ball. If it's played there I'll go after it, but they wanted me to go there first. They've got their opinion, which they think is right, and I've got mine, which I think is right.

In the first half we gave a hell of a lot of balls away in midfield. The service was terrible I thought. But whenever things are going wrong, the front players get the blame. And when we came in at half-time, it was our fault, because we kept coming off our defenders and wanted the ball played to feet. To say something like that – that

Chris Whyte races to congratulate a triumphant Woodcock after Arsenal's first goal against Aston Villa in their 2-0 1983 F.A. Cup Quarter-Final win.

Cloughie, Peter Taylor and squash racquet, once his two inseparable companions — now there's only the squash racquet.

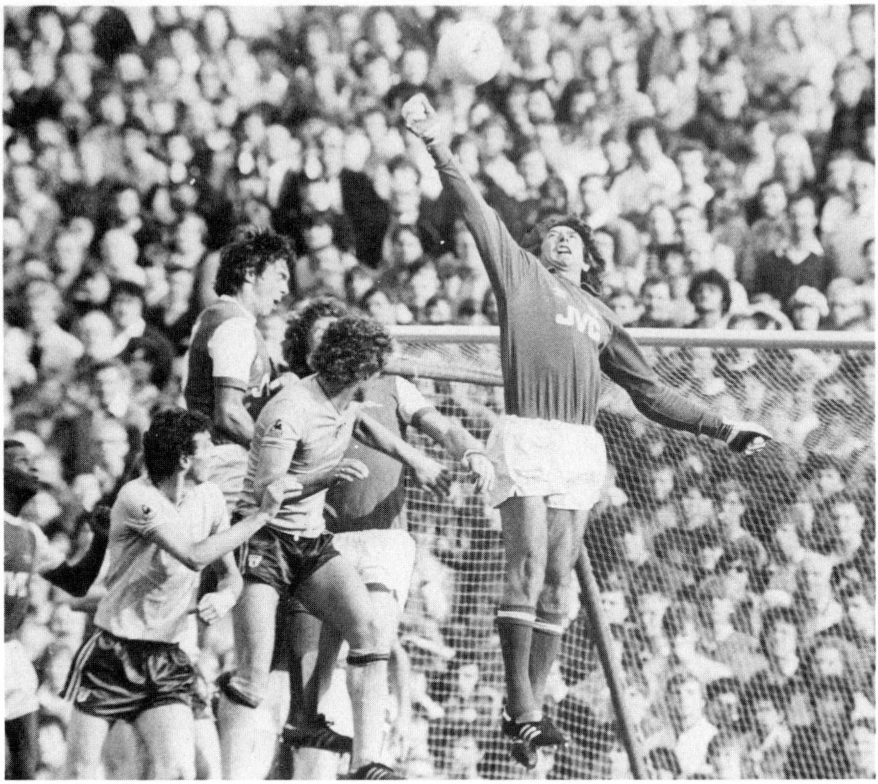

COLORSPORT

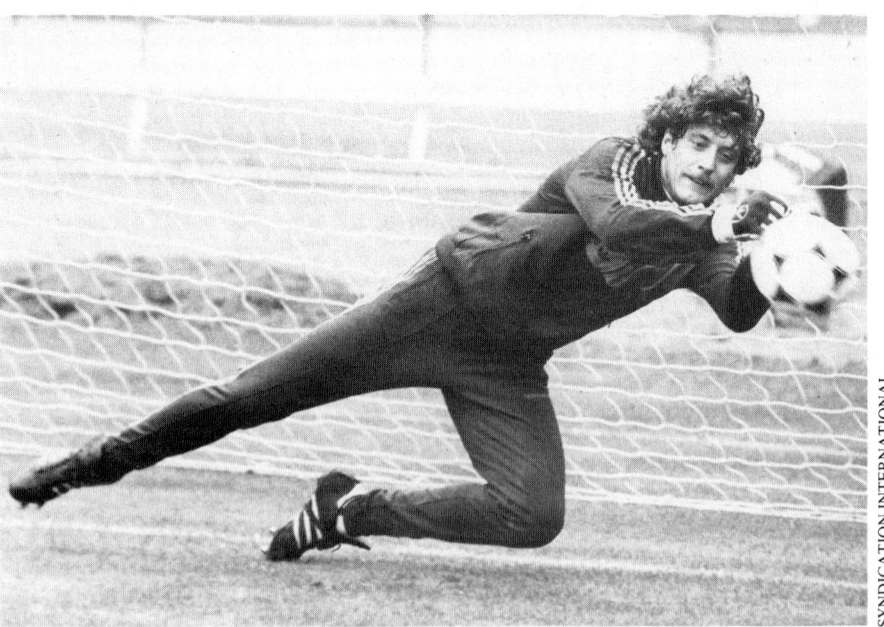

Pat Jennings in control above the hurly-burly. A one-handed catch like this instills the team with confidence.

SYNDICATION INTERNATIONAL

Harald Schumacher punching his way to success.

we're giving the ball away because the forwards aren't making the right kind of runs – is rubbish. So Sundy and I started arguing with them again. Then Sundy said, 'Forget it. We'll stick together during the second half and see if we can work it out between us.'

Whether we started making the correct kind of runs in the second half I don't know, but I don't think so. Journalists asked afterwards about a change in tactics, but I think it was more a change in attitude. The first goal was quite a good one. I pulled it back for Robbo. The second was a bit of magic from Sundy, the kind of individual flash of brilliance we rely on too much for our goals. And the third I put away.

We never looked in that much danger. We controlled the second half, which makes you think, because on paper they've been doing well. They held Liverpool, held Manchester United. And the reports said they'd outplayed Manchester United in the cup-tie before losing in the last minute.

27 MARCH

We, the England party, that is, reported to West Lodge Park for Wednesday's game against Greece in the European Championships. There was a big thing a few months ago about us not going there again because luxury hotels make us soft, so in future we were meant to be going to the National Sports Centre at Bisham Abbey. That was booked up this time though, so we are back to the hotel.

It's a lovely place. I don't think you can blame the setting. It was just that under Ron Greenwood, to my way of thinking, things were a little slack. Possibly I thought that because I was coming back from West Germany, where things were very rigid and there was lots of discipline, but at Forest too it was much tighter. It got better when Don was brought in, but before he came it was too relaxed. I approve of a bit of freedom, but it went too far.

Some of the lads would go to the dogs on a Monday night. Well, that's fine, you need a couple of hours off. But they were also going on Tuesday nights, and not just going but eating there as well. There were people shooting off in all different directions.

Even in training it was a bit slack. Ron Greenwood would call everybody together and you'd gather round and all of a sudden you'd see Kevin Keegan and Trevor Brooking still knocking a ball around or shooting at someone, and he'd say, 'Just wait a second until they've finished', things like that. And Trevor Francis, Viv Anderson and I would look at each other and say, 'Can you imagine Cloughie standing for some of the things that go off here?'

When Don was brought in that sort of thing changed, particularly in training. We used to have five-a-sides, and if you ask any of the Arsenal lads they were a joke. You'd have twenty-one players playing on a small pitch, running around laughing and joking. You could have a bit of fun, but I hated playing them. Don got things organized. You could still have fun with Ray Clemence playing as a striker, but it was everyone really trying in a serious, competitive game, which can be equally enjoyable.

Another thing the Forest lads used to question under Greenwood was that there used to be about fifty people in the dressing room at Wembley before an international. Cloughie used to throw everyone out, directors, everyone. But at Wembley you've got the fellow who opens the first door into the changing room, another who opens the second door, the one who puts the tea bags in the pot and the one who puts the milk in your tea, the bloke who brought you to Wembley on his motor bike and another who has just got off his horse and is in collecting autographs – all this an hour before kick-off. And that's wrong. Even the two fellows who do the tea shouldn't be there. Then at half-time there would sometimes be a lot of people around. That was at its worst in the European Championships in Italy when there were all these coaches around.

In Italy there were always loads of coaches around, asking what I did differently in Germany, that sort of thing. Particularly in the Italy game when I took a lot of stick, a lot of tackles from behind. They asked if I was taking the ball wrongly, inviting them to hammer me. And I said, well, with the type of balls I was getting there wasn't any other way I could take them; we kept playing the ball around at the back and then after it had been right across the back four and back again it was just humped forward. I must admit Kevin Keegan backed me up one hundred per cent on that. He said, 'You want to get out there. The balls we are getting aren't ones you roll onto and can turn on, they are being hammered at you so you have to hold them and then "Bang" you get hit from behind. It's no good saying we should be doing this or that. They are dictating how we play because of the type of balls coming forward.' Which was right; I quite enjoyed it even though I got hit a lot. I don't think Gentile won the ball off me fairly once, which I take as quite a compliment. He pulled me back loads of times. I did him, and he pulled me back to stop me getting away.

When I went back to Cologne the manager called me in and said, 'Do you fancy going to Italy?' And I said, 'No. I'm never going there. Why?' So he said, 'We've had a bid in from an Italian club.' I answered, 'I don't even want to know who it is.' About a week later I thought, 'I wonder who it was', so I went in and asked him. He said if I'd shown any interest in going he wouldn't have told me, but it was Juventus. That was flattering, and I wondered if Gentile had had anything to do with it. They must have asked him what he thought of me. I only hope he didn't say, 'He can't play, but he can take a real thumping.'

In the evening we went to the PFA dinner. I'd been really looking forward to it, because it was the first one I'd been to since I got the Young Player of the Year award in 1978. The following year Cloughie wouldn't let us go because we had some game coming up, and then of course I was away in Germany. But with the game on Wednesday there was a damper on the night for us. We sat at an England table, so we didn't get much chance to see our guests, and we left at 11.30 p.m.

Bob Paisley's speech was very funny though. When we glanced at the menu and saw he was guest of honour we thought, 'Crikey, that's going to be a stumbling sort of speech', but he made a real impression on everyone. He was funny about tactics, telling us that he couldn't understand modern sayings. He said 'getting in round the back' sounded like advice you give to burglars, and the first time he heard a coach talking about 'positive and negative' he thought he was talking to an electrician. He was knocking all the words so-called good coaches use. I wondered what Don was thinking, and Kenny Sansom said he was watching Malcolm Allison while it was going on and he didn't smile once. And when Paisley said, 'Right, we'll get down to something serious now', Malcolm gave several claps.

28 MARCH

I love to beat Shilts in training. We were shooting this morning and I said, 'I'll be knocking a few in', and he said, 'Oh, they'll all be flying over into the car park will they? I'll be tipping them over there.' It is satisfying to beat him because you know he will be trying for everything. This morning he did this fantastic save. He blocked the first shot, and then how he got across to the follow up to tip it round the post I just don't know. It was determination more than anything.

It is interesting being with the England team and comparing Ray

Clemence and Peter. Peter is a perfectionist, does everything correctly, works very hard the whole time. Clem is a different character – he's not a hard trainer. If he thinks he needs a session he'll do it, but he'll knock one away with his arm or head it out where Shilts does everything properly all the time. They are both great goalkeepers on a Saturday afternoon though.

I've been fortunate that I've been with three really good goalkeepers, Peter, Toni Schumacher and now Pat. Peter was in the Forest team when I got into it, and I compare everyone with him. Schumacher matched up to it, and obviously Pat does. It's almost impossible really to say who is the best. You would have to line the three of them up alongside one another and take your pick.

After training Trevor and I were collared by these photographers for a photograph together. They put us on a motor bike, which belonged to one of them. It made a change from them putting us on a putting green, or playing table tennis, or standing with a ball between our foreheads. So we thought we could just see tomorrow's captions – 'Revving to go', or whatever. 'Trevor Francis just arriving from Italy' was my suggestion.

I assume – or at least I hope – that Trevor Francis and I will play together at the front. Even if Paul Mariner had been fit, there would still have been a lot of talk that Trevor and I would be the partnership. It's clear from the way Bobby Robson talks about Trevor that he will play; Robson obviously likes him. The rest of us don't really know. We've had two team meetings already and it's only Monday afternoon, so there will probably be another one before the day is out.

I think I deserve to play though. I've had to wait a long time to get a place, and I missed the last game because of our Milk Cup semi-final, but I feel I did well enough in the previous matches to deserve to be considered a first choice. If I didn't get in I'd be very upset.

Ever since Spain I've roomed with Trevor Francis. I've got to know him pretty well now, although he was quite quiet at first. We are happy to sit in our room for a couple of nights and chat and watch TV. We watched the programme about Bobby Robson, which didn't tell us very much, and chatted a bit about the Chester Report which was published today. Of course we haven't had a chance to read it, but the initial impact was not very strong.

I can't really see that cutting the League down by two clubs will make any difference at all. If you are going to do something you should be decisive and stand by it. In Germany when I first went there, there was a second division North and a second division South. And suddenly, half way through the season, they said, 'There are too many teams. We are going to make a national second division, and the top nine from the North and the top nine from the South will form it.' And that was that. It was desperate for some people who were playing there and saw their livelihoods being taken away, but that was it. End of story. There was no trying to phase it in over a couple of years, with two being dropped this year, two more next and so on.

Of course it is easy for me to say this because I'm with Arsenal, and as we would be in a Super League if one came in, we'd be all right whatever happened. If I was with a second or third division team I would probably think differently.

Scrapping two teams is just not going to make a difference. There are eighteen teams in the Bundesliga. There's only one cup competition, and you get a mid-winter break. I played quite a few friendlies for Cologne last season, but I played only thirty league games – I wasn't picked for the first game, and I missed three through injury – and you seemed to just coast through a season. When we got to Spain in the summer I was still feeling fresh, feeling very, very strong. And I trained hard there too because I wasn't playing in the games. But coming back and playing two games a week I don't feel strong, I feel jaded – and there's still nearly two months to go. Most English players feel like that.

I was quite surprised when Trevor went to Italy. He used to ask me a lot about Germany, and he always said, 'I could never do that. I couldn't be bothered with all the hassle, with learning the language, all that sort of thing.' So when he went to Sampdoria it was a bit of a shock – but then he told me the contract he had negotiated. I think living abroad will be good for him. It is bound to help a person develop. Some people think he is a bit soft-centred, but he has fought back from some bad injuries, and at Forest he took some real stick from Cloughie. He kept coming back, so I think there is some toughness there.

I wouldn't say he is difficult to play with, but it is not easy for him to fit into a formation where he is told, 'You've got to do this for us today, Trevor', because he likes roaming where the fancy takes him.

A lot of players do that, but in Germany that wouldn't be possible because there are set things to do out there.

He didn't like being played wide on the right at Forest because it restricted him to a certain area and set him specific tasks. But we've discussed it since, and I think he recognizes that it was the best for the team while I was there anyway. Garry and I were up front, with Trevor on the right. His presence kept Garry and I on our toes because if one of us was not doing it Trevor could be pushed up front. In fact when they first bought him, Garry, Martin O'Neill and I were all in the team, and we said, 'We've got to watch ourselves now.'

Trevor is obviously a good player. He has got pace, he finishes well, and when he is fit he works hard. He keeps moving and showing for the ball. But he is instinctive, and you generally don't know what his performance is going to be like. When he has a bad game you can't say that he will keep doing the same things. He isn't like Klaus Fischer, for example, who will go on trying to do the things he does every week. You know where Fischer is going to go, and what he is going to try and do whether it is coming off or not. He is always up there for you. But Trevor is all over the place, and he is not going to be up there for you all the time, so it makes life a bit more difficult for his team mates.

It will be interesting to see how much playing in Italy affects him. When I was younger I used to receive balls like he does. I wanted everything on the run, and I would try and do people with pace, kicking the ball round them. Now I like to feel my defender there and be strong enough to hold him off. In the game nowadays, in international football and on the continent, it is all man-to-man marking and there is a lot of physical contact, a lot of nudging, and you have to be strong enough to resist challenges.

At the moment Trevor has this thing that when he is tackled he goes down with a spin. Sometimes he gets away with it and sometimes he doesn't. There are times when I think that if he had resisted the challenge he would have been in a better position. Other times he has gone down and got a free kick and you think, 'Oh, he shouldn't have had that one', and you've benefited. He probably could resist challenges more, but I am a lot stockier than him, and when he is at full pace he only needs a touch. But perhaps playing in Italy will bring that into his game.

29 MARCH

Bobby Robson announced the team.

In the team meeting the emphasis was on the lads at the back hitting long balls up to us as quickly as possible. Trevor and I looked at each other at that. It's not really what we want. And then we went out to play in a practice game, with five players from Spurs making up the numbers.

We started off, and all of a sudden Sammy Lee whacked two long balls and we just couldn't get them. They were hit way over our heads; he said, 'Sorry, lads, but in the meeting they were telling me to knock forty-yard balls so I'm knocking them. I know it's not on.' But at least it meant Sammy recognized that, and then we started to play a bit. Trevor and I got our partnership going and they just couldn't stop us. We won only 1–0. I got the goal, but I should have scored a couple more, and he should have put one in too. We were playing and moving, playing and going, and it really went well. But I don't know what sort of preparation it will be for tomorrow, because I expect that we'll be up against a very defensive team whereas we weren't today. But I've always thought we could play together very effectively, and today confirmed it.

Trevor said he could only remember one game of those we had played together, and today reminded him of it. He said, 'Do you remember which one it was?' and I said, 'Yes. Aston Villa.' We absolutely destroyed them between us. It got so bad in the second half that at one stage we had to say, 'Hang on. Let's take a two-minute breather', because we were getting the ball and playing one-twos and cutting them apart every time. That was a really exceptional night, when we did really well together. We won 4–0, and we both scored.

I like Trevor, I get on well with him, but I have to admit that I do resent the treatment he gets sometimes. Perhaps it was because he came through as a wonderboy at sixteen with Birmingham, but I think if *he* had got the two goals I got in Greece it would have made a much bigger impact. That's okay, there's nothing that can be done about that, but I do find Robson going on about him a bit much. It was discouraging to Paul Mariner and me, when I thought we'd done really well together in Greece, to have the manager talking about 'when we get Trevor back' and saying what a great player he is.

I can't help comparing it with the treatment I received when I was in Germany. I'd come back and play in the odd game, but I never really got a run. No one bothered to come over to Germany to see me play when I was playing on a regular basis in a settled team in Cologne, and I thought I was playing well. Everyone said at that time that West German football is the strongest in Europe, if not the world. They were European Champions in 1980, and World Cup Finalists in 1982, and I was playing in the top team, keeping two German internationals on the bench. Yet I was struggling to get in the England squad, let alone the team. They'd get me over occasionally if Cologne would release me and say, 'Well, we'll have a quick look at him,' but it didn't seem to matter how I played – I knew I wouldn't play in the next game. It was a bit frustrating.

Just before the World Cup we played Holland. I knew that was make or break for me, and that if I didn't do it I might find myself out of the squad. We beat Holland 2–0 and I had quite a good game, so I thought I'd probably clinched my place in the squad, but they weren't going to keep me in the team just because I'd done reasonably well.

Hopefully that is going to change now. I've played in the last two European games, and I'm now playing in this one. My goal now is to stay in until the European Championships. Barring injury I'm in possession now, and I can't see my place being taken off me. I shall certainly do my best to see that I keep it.

It still seems strange not having Kevin Keegan along. I think Mr Robson started off as if he wanted the first squad he picked to be around for two years. Although I'm sure Kevin could still do a good job at the moment, I think he was looking ahead eighteen months and wondering if Kevin would still be around then. He might and he might not, but that was Robson's biggest decision – it wasn't that Kevin wasn't good enough at the time. People say he had lost a bit of his sharpness, and his pace. But I think the problem was that he wanted to do everything. He was a bit like Graham Rix, wanting to be involved the whole time. All good players want the ball a lot, but if you are playing up front you've got to stay there, the midfield players need you there. But Kevin wanted the ball so much that he wanted to pick it up off the back four and give it to the midfield; get it off the midfield and get it to the other front player; then get it back off him and put it into the net. He wanted to do everything instead of sticking to one job. But maybe that was down to Ron Greenwood to work out. Perhaps Greenwood should have told him, 'I want you up front, I want your sharpness in and around the box, not back in midfield.'

I'm sure Kevin has still got his sharpness around the box. He might not run fifty or sixty yards as quickly as he did at Liverpool – or not do it as many times – but what counts is sharpness. They talk about players reaching thirty-three and say, 'Oh, he's not quick enough', but they are quick enough in the head and over twenty or thirty yards, and that's all you need. In international football especially, you don't see players running fifty or sixty yards at full pace towards goal. It's nice and slow and controlled until you are around the box, then you just need a yard to get a clear shot or a cross in.

30 MARCH (afternoon)
We trained a little bit this morning, running through corners and free-kicks. We have quite a good near-post routine, but they said that in the Under 21 game last night Greece had coped with those quite well but looked exposed on the back post, so to be aware of that option. This afternoon we will sleep.

England 0 Greece 0
A bitter disappointment. I was substituted twenty minutes from the end. What I really resented was that it was on the cards from before the kick off. If we don't score it is always a forward who is going to come off, although why that is I don't really know; after all he'd said about Trevor in the papers over the last few days there was no way he was going to bring him off. So as soon as I saw Luther Blissett warming up I thought 'Here goes'.

I wasn't involved in the game that much – but the way we played I had no chance, with the ball being tossed up in the air from forty yards. It's a gift for defenders. But I did put in a lot of work people didn't see – I was moving around looking for the ball. I was trying to show, making positions for people to give it to me. Whether the ball was good or not, I was still making the positions. So I was disappointed, but it was not unexpected. I don't think it would have made any difference who was taken off. It wasn't going to improve things. When you are playing at home and don't create a chance all night. . . .

Don said afterwards I should have moved around more, maybe moved back into midfield for a bit. I don't mind doing that, but when

I tried to drop back at the start of the second half to pick balls up and go at them, I would look up and there would be Trevor on his own up there. There was no one moving forward to fill my place. We seemed very static the way we played: back four; midfield; front two. And if I dropped back it was back four; five in midfield; and one standing on his own up there, instead of rotating.

I tried to go back to lose my marker, tried to create new situations. But all we were looking for was this forward ball the whole time, and I thought if I'm not there to try and get it, no one will be.

The balls were coming up from forty yards, and it is the easiest thing in the world for a defender to watch the ball like that. A forward can only move so much. You can move around when you are knocking it about and a lot of shorter balls are being played and people are moving off the ball. That's playing football. But when they are coming from forty yards you aren't moving, and defenders are with you, just waiting. You get the ball and bang! You've been clattered from behind. And if you don't get hit, if you are holding them off, there's such a gap between where the ball has come from and a forward that there is no one near you to give support. So you are holding the defender off as best you can, and they are clambering all over you – you know what they are – and you are having to wait literally a second, which is a hell of a long time on the field, for support to arrive. And by that time there is not just your marker but other people coming round as well, so you are being totally outnumbered.

The partnership with Trevor didn't really work. It couldn't in the circumstances, but it did bring out all the problems about playing with him. If we are going to be the two central strikers we have got to stay close together, playing one-twos, playing football. He says he doesn't like playing wide, but when he is playing as a central striker he drifts out there a lot, and it was hopeless him going wide and crossing for me to try and out-jump five big defenders to head it in. Okay, he was trying desperately hard to impress and do well, and if he isn't getting much of the ball he's got to go looking for it – but that left me isolated.

And he just doesn't think sometimes. There were a couple of occasions when I'd made a move to get the ball and it came, and then he'd go flying into the space I'd wanted to go into. And I had to say, 'Look! Stay out of it! Don't come into the space because all you are

74

doing is bringing another defender into it with you.' It's something I've been very conscious of after being in Germany, but at Arsenal we talk about that sort of thing as well, we think about the game, but Trevor just does everything out of instinct.

But in the circumstances we had no chance. Someone after the match said up in the bar, 'I'm a Sunday League player and even my team know that when I'm playing up front they don't toss in high balls. So when we've got you and Trevor up front, how come England do it?' There's no answer to that. Well, there is. Our football is a bit brainless sometimes. I remember the first England game I played after moving to Germany was against Eire. I'd been in Germany about four months. And Rob Hughes, then of the *Sunday Times*, came out to do a piece about me the following weekend. The German lads had read the reports of the game and they kept asking, 'But why are they tossing in high balls when you are playing? Why do they do that?' I was playing really well at the time, and they just couldn't understand it. 'You are playing well over here. And we know we haven't got to keep hammering it into the box because you are not that type of player.' They kept asking Rob Hughes why as well, and he couldn't provide an answer.

I did get some headed goals in Cologne. But not because they were tossed in high – because we didn't have anyone big. They were angled in or knocked in to the near post.

31 MARCH

I woke up this morning feeling depressed, and reading the papers didn't help. Whenever you get a 0–0, it is always the forwards who get the blame, yet there wasn't a chance created all night.

It's amazing how quickly things turn round – our press is so fickle. Before the game there was talk of us winnning 5–0, which was ridiculous, although the manager encouraged that sort of talk, and now it's a disaster and we are going to be struggling to qualify. It was a bad performance, but how can they say that? If we'd drawn 0–0 in Greece and won 3–0 at Wembley, we'd have the same number of points, and yet everybody would be happy. Struggling to qualify! Hungary's got to come to Wembley, they've got to play Denmark, they've got to go to Greece. They might have the games in hand, but it has been proved in the League Championship that having games in hand is not the same thing as having the points in the bag. So I think we are in quite a healthy position.

But talk of us winning 5–0 didn't help. People should have learnt from past results. Even in the World Cup Finals, Algeria beat West Germany. There aren't any easy international games any more. And it was fairly obvious after the way we played in Greece that they were going to come here and play with nine back, because they were rather impressed with us over there.

When I went to Germany, whenever Weisweiler or the players wanted to wind me up, they used to say, 'English football is just kick and rush', and I defended it like mad. I'm beginning to wonder. There was just no thought about it yesterday. Tossing balls in from the back is futile with Trevor and me up front. If they are going to do that they should play Peter Withe and Paul Mariner up there. If they want to play football and play it around, then put Trevor and me in. It was the same a couple of years ago against Rumania when we drew 0–0 at Wembley.

Ominously Bobby Robson said exactly the same thing as Ron Greenwood said after that game. 'We needed a big fellow in there to head the ball.' That makes me so sick. If he's going to play that way, why didn't he realize that beforehand? But that's not the only way to play.

I might be biased, and I know I'm always making comparisons with West Germany. But when I was there they were the giants of European football, and teams always came there to get behind the ball and defend. It was all they did because teams were frightened to death of them. I used to watch their international matches and I never saw West Germany panicking and just tossing the ball in. All the players were confident to have the ball. They'd say, 'Give me the ball. Hang on, I can't get in there. Have it back, play it around.' But we get the ball and we seem to go a bit hectic, trying to force things, trying to make openings which aren't there instead of saying, 'Well, we'll knock it around and it's going to appear somewhere.' Mind, then we would have to be sharp enough to see it and play the ball in when the opening appears. Against packed defences which are letting us have the ball on the half-way line, we might need a bit more craft in midfield. Sammy Lee and Gary Mabbutt are very good players, there's no doubt about that. Sammy is great to play with, he gives you the ball very early and things like that, but what we do with it is very important. It's vital in international football these days that even centre-halves can do something on the ball. They've got to come up and make an extra man. And we need midfield players to come up in close support and play one-twos or have the craft to take people on, because if they take someone out then the next defender thinks 'Shall I go to him or shall I stick with my man', and things open up. But we just don't have that sorted out at the moment.

We are all right away from home, or if teams come to attack us, but if we've got to break them down we struggle. It's not just a question of having a schemer in midfield – everyone has got to have the confidence to get the ball, and hold it and look, and if there is nothing on, play it again. Whether it is not being patient enough I don't know, but we seem to get it into the box and just hope for a break.

1 APRIL

The trouble with internationals is that the post-mortems go on for days. And if yesterday's papers were depressing this morning's were even worse. According to them Bobby Robson said yesterday that only three players had given one hundred per cent effort and could be satisfied. He criticized Alan Devonshire, said he had looked 'meek', and he said the forwards 'lacked aggression'.

If *that's* what he has taken away from the game, that worries me, because I thought there were much bigger, more important issues than that. He said only Peter Shilton, Terry Butcher and Sammy Lee came away with any credit. But Shilton didn't have a shot to save all night. Terry stood on the half-way line just tonking balls forward. Never once did he push forward and try to make something happen by coming up as a free man and playing one-twos. And Sammy. I know he was busy, but it just wasn't his game. In that situation where it's very tight you need someone who can go past a player, or play a one-two and create something, not toss it in and hope that something is going to happen.

Everyone tried: it was just that it was a brainless performance. We didn't play a single one-two around the box in the ninety minutes. We didn't commit anyone, and against these packed defences you need people to open things up a bit. If Alan Devonshire had been more in the middle, he could perhaps have done that. But look where they played him and Steve Coppell: stuck out wide waiting for someone to give them the ball. Robson said to them, 'When you get it I want you to run at players.' So they'd get the ball and run at them, and it just got tighter and tighter. Steve would get past one and there would be another coming in who would tackle him, or he'd poke it a yard too far ahead and it would get knocked out. And it doesn't take a genius to see that will happen. Dev's played three games for England now on the left, and he hasn't had a kick yet.

Mr Robson said beforehand that we were playing four-two-four and all the papers jumped on that, and said, 'Hallelujah, we're playing with wingers.' You can't. You can't have two men just standing out there waiting for the ball. And it means you've denuded your midfield, which is where you need to be strong and create things if you are going to break down packed defences. We've got this thing in England that a lot of continental teams play with wingers. They don't. They keep saying Rummenigge is a winger: he isn't. They keep saying Littbarski is a winger: he isn't. They think this because they might see them on the flanks, and they might hit in a cross or two, but that doesn't mean they are wingers. They say Italy play with a winger, but they don't. Trevor Francis was saying that in their league he hasn't seen a winger all season. They never come up against one.

What does Robson mean about lacking aggression? Not getting on the end of high balls? If there were good balls being knocked in to the near post, where you can get in front of the defender and do something, and it wasn't being done, then you could say that. That's what I think being aggressive is, and I think I *am* aggressive. But when they are tossed in, and not from the by-line but from deep positions from the half-way line even, then we want a six-footer who is going to elbow people and that.

Maybe that's it – someone said after the European Championships game against Italy in Turin that Garry and I were too nice, and that the only way to deal with Gentile was to give him some of his own medicine, to let him have an elbow in the teeth in the first five minutes. What good would that do? That really makes me mad. It's been said before, and maybe I should do it, but I'm not that way inclined. I push and things like that, but I wouldn't leave my foot there deliberately to hurt someone, and I wouldn't elbow someone in the face – I'm not that kind of person. What do they want? What is football these days when people say you should do that? It's not who can punch someone the hardest. If that was the case you'd go out every week and when the ref wasn't looking put one on someone. 'Okay, you know I'm about. You come and get the ball off me and you'll get another one of these.' That's not football. Sometimes I think maybe I should elbow a few more people, but what are referees for?

Of course you do need protection from the referees. On Wednesday he started booking people ten minutes from time, which is no good at all. But even if you say elbowing is justified because referees aren't protecting you, I'm not sure it would work. If I'd let Gentile have one in the mouth it might have given me a bit of satisfaction, but it wouldn't have stopped him tackling me. In fact I'd probably have been carried off on a stretcher after the next tackle came in. Sometimes I hear people say that I should do it and I think they might be right, but then you sit and think about it and wonder if it is going to do any good?

People say, 'Oh, defenders don't like playing against Peter Withe or Joe Jordan because they know they'll hand it out', but I'm sure defenders don't like playing against me either. They are all worried about pace and sharpness, about someone doing them with the ball and going past them. That's another type of fear, the fear of being shown up. Peter Withe can't start throwing his elbows about except when the ball is up in the air – unless he's going to risk being sent off. I can't instil my kind of fear in them unless I'm on my game and given the right kind of service. But that was where we came in.

I keep going back to elbowing people – it really annoys me. When we won the European Cup with Forest we were always up against those tight defences. We didn't resort to that sort of thing. And we scored a lot of goals. And you don't see Rummenigge giving someone a punch or an elbow. If you look at West German football in general I don't think there's a single player who would do that. Not one. Definitely not Fischer – you could say he is worse than me, he's such a mild-tempered man. He fights hard for the ball and holds people off, but he would never dream of kicking anyone or going up with his elbows. And they are saying that's what we need. It's nonsense.

I did catch Gentile a couple of times anyway, going in late. And the ref came up and said, 'That's enough of that. Once more and you're off.' The classic example was in Karlsruhe. They had this man who used to mark me every time. He was just there to put me out of the game. And on this occasion I was really on form, and he just couldn't stop me. I was by him every time, and every single time I was brought down. We were getting free-kick after free-kick, and looking fairly dangerous from them, but it was getting frustrating. We were 1–0 up at half-time, and we came out for the second half and immediately it was bang, bang, bang. Three on the trot. The third time I snapped, turned round and kicked him. And I got sent off.

Forwards are always the ones who get caught in that situation. Suppose I had kicked one of the Greek defenders who was kicking me on Wednesday night and got sent off after twenty minutes. What would everyone have said then? 'What a stupid thing to do', is what they would have said. It would be interesting to ask defenders about it, but I'm sure if a defender keeps fouling you and you keep going back at him he thinks, 'What have I got to do here?'

I didn't train. My groin was a bit sore again – it has been on and off since January – and with the knocks I got against Greece I just had a rub. It was what I needed, to relax and get over it.

2 APRIL
Arsenal 0 Southampton 0
It has been a terrible week. I picked up the *Daily Mail* in the morning and found, 'First Division footballer charged with rape' inside. It said Holloway Road, Islington and I thought, 'Crikey, that's around Arsenal, it's got to be Arsenal.' I got to the Golf Club – I hadn't seen the *Sun* or the *Mirror*, both of which had it splashed on the front page – and the lads said, 'It's Raph.' (Raphael Meade, our young reserve forward.)

Then we had this awful game. I was absolutely shattered. People don't realize how much it takes out of you getting kicked the whole time, and we were kicked a lot against Greece. Brian Clough used to understand because he was a forward. He used to say, 'I know what it's like to keep getting kicked and having to keep on picking yourself up again. It takes it out of you.' But most people don't think about that. I've got a bruise on the back of my thigh the size of a plate from a tackle on Wednesday, and stud marks on my other leg. And then two days later you have to go out and play against Southampton on a windswept day where you are up against Chris Nicholl and Mark Wright, who are both six feet two or three, and they are tossing the ball fifty feet up in the air for you to challenge for. I almost couldn't put one foot in front of the other – well, I could, but I had no change of pace, no bite, no sharpness. I just felt physically drained.

We had been due to report tomorrow night at the King's Cross Hotel at nine p.m. – they are taking us away for the night before the Tottenham game – but after the game they changed it and we are now reporting to Highbury at seven p.m. But not much else was said.

3 APRIL

One paper said this morning, 'Rix had a bit of thigh trouble and Woodcock was still sunk in post-Wembley depression', which was probably right really. But as another paper said, the ball was coming down with snow on it. And of course after the internationals the papers have a field day. It was, 'Withe: Bang in form for England'; 'Mariner: Bang in form for England'. It seems that anyone who is over six feet and has a good game, gets a couple of goals or something, is 'Bang in form for England'.

Of course the best possible answer would have been for me to have stuck a couple in myself, but I just couldn't put one leg in front of the other. The bruises from Wembley are still coming out now. I admit I had a bad game, I could probably have done more, but you need some help somewhere. It's a windy day and you are up against two big men and all you get is balls tossed up hopefully in the air and think, 'Am I going to be silly and start charging around everywhere?' As far as I'm concerned all it needs is a bit of thoughtfulness. I haven't played that type of football for a few years now, and I think people forget I've been away that long. They've got sympathy for Vlad, they say he's got to get used to English football, but they think I'm going to fall back into it just like that. As I've said, it's equally hard for me to settle down at a new club.

We went to Highbury, did a little training then went to the Royal Scot Hotel at King's Cross. Don and I had a chat about the Greece game, and about tossing long balls in, in particular. And Don was saying he couldn't understand why it was happening. That really surprised me, because I thought he had more of a say in things than that. As coach I assumed he would have a fairly big say, but from what he was saying he thought much the same as I do about it, which suggests that he doesn't have much influence on what tactics we play, contrary to what most people think – and I'd always thought, too.

4 APRIL
Spurs 5 Arsenal 0

When you are trying to recover from a 3–0 deficit after fifteen minutes it is a bit disheartening. Funnily enough, in terms of running and movement I felt reasonably sharp. I thought I covered a lot of ground, without achieving that much. Two were really bad goals – they both came from our mistakes, but you've got to give credit for the second, which was a volley. They just kept tanking balls up into the middle of our defence and we just couldn't cope with them at all. They just kept going through and scoring.

Sundy started arguing with Terry at half-time. He'd gone in hard for a tackle – kicked somebody or something – and Terry said he shouldn't have done that. Sundy blew up. 'We've given away three goals, we are 3–0 down, and all you can go on about is me tackling that ****!'

That was nothing to the rows afterwards. Don's first words afterwards were to point to me and Kenny Sansom and say, 'Him and him. They didn't want to play on Saturday!' We'd just been stuffed 5–0 by Tottenham and that was the first thing he came out with. Why didn't he say that after the match on Saturday? And we had this really fierce argument, Sundy and I, Terry and Don. The rest didn't say much. We were furious. We'd just been beaten 5–0, with a lot of bad goals, and all they wanted to talk about was the forwards and the runs we'd made. According to Don yet again it was down to the forwards – how many times Sundy came back from offside positions. I'd been caught offside a couple of times, too, and that and our runs were the big talking point. According to them the reason the ball kept being given away was that the forwards weren't making the right kind of runs. We said the reason we kept getting caught offside might have had something to do with the service we were getting.

But Don never seems to be in the wrong. You can't explain anything to him. Even if you say things to him he'll go, 'Yes, yes', very quickly, and it's as if he is telling you to shut up – at least that's the impression I get sometimes. I was so heated that I even shouted, 'Well, you might as well sell me at the end of the season.'

Sundy said that they keep on pushing it onto the players and saying that we have to sort ourselves out, and our attitude isn't right. 'What about yours, Don? Are you finally going to move down from Wolverhampton? Are you signing with England? Are you staying with Arsenal? We don't know. Does that mean your attitude isn't one hundred per cent?' That sounds silly, but if it were a player who was negotiating a new contract, Don would say, 'Your attitude isn't right, because you are worried about what is going to happen next year.' But Don wouldn't accept that.

Graham Roberts is dangerous. He sees the ball and he'll take off about ten feet away. There was one ball down on the right-hand side corner flag. I chased it, but it was a little bit too long for me. I might have got it, it just bounced up nicely, but I saw him coming across out of the corner of my eye. He'd seen the ball and was going for it, and he took off, coming in very high. I could have tried to nick it round him, and he would have gone flying past me. Or I might have ended up in hospital. There's no doubt that if he'd caught me I'd have been on a stretcher because he is stocky, he is a weight, and he was flying in with a lot of power; I tried to lift it over his head as he came in, but at a distance, so he took the ball.

Tottenham have this reputation for good football, but they have their quota of hard men. We were playing against Roberts and Miller, and they were tripping us up off the ball, pushing us off the ball, and when the ball came really hammering into us, we'd lose one marker and then we'd be tripped up. I played a one-two with Paul Davis, and Roberts just came right across me and blocked me continental style. And I didn't get a foul. With Miller I went up a couple of times and knocked balls on, and as I came down he had his arms around my neck and I couldn't move; I was looking at the ref but he never saw anything, although Miller was holding me back. And you try and move out in front of him to get a ball while he's pushing you back and got his arms across you. You expect all that, especially in a local derby against Spurs. It's fair enough from their point of view, because all they were concerned about was stopping us scoring and they did their job. But what made me and Sundy mad was that we were getting all this, and then you look when the ball is being played up to their front men and they've been given a yard. Our back four should be giving a bit out to their front men, not pussy footing around standing a yard off them.

Stewart Robson will hand it out, but he goes a bit brainless sometimes. He kicks people when he shouldn't. The lads keep telling him, 'Don't stop tackling', but I think they should try and tell him when not to tackle as well. He's tackling on the edge of our box and giving away free-kicks. And he was sent off against them on Boxing Day. Hopefully he'll learn, but I wonder. I said something to him about it, and so did Brian Talbot, and he said, 'I can't help it. I just hate Tottenham, I'll always do it against them.' And you think, 'A first division footballer saying that? What kind of a league is this?'

But we could do with a bit more hardness. We miss Peter Nicholas. I think every team has to have someone like that in midfield and defence. I'm not saying you should go over the top, but you need someone to get stuck in, to put his foot in. At Forest we had Larry Lloyd and Kenny Burns. Archie Gemmill could be nasty when he wanted to. You need people in a team like that. People with some sort of presence which says, 'You've got to be careful here', with the sort of reputation that at any fifty-fifty ball you've got to watch it as you go in, because he's likely to catch you. Peter Storey and Nobby Stiles had it, Remi Moses has it at the moment. He seems to have picked it up this season. He never had it at West Bromwich, but it seems that this season when he got his chance in the team he was determined to keep it and he has done well for himself. Souness definitely has it. He caught me very high in a cup game at Forest. Everyone knows what he's like. But I'm not saying anything against him – I think he's a great player, and I think it's a good thing to have in your team. You can talk about being dirty, but I think every successful side has a bit of it.

And we *haven't* got it, though Peter Nicholas has a bit. Brian Talbot is a willing tackler, but he doesn't have the presence that the real hard men have.

5 APRIL

We went in to sort it out. We had a meeting, and Don put it all down to attitude, saying we do it some weeks, and then other weeks we don't. He said to me what he'd already said on TV, that he can tell the difference in my attitude when I'm with England. He said, 'You want to do it then, you want to be the best player, but you don't show it all the time at Arsenal, and you certainly don't let me see it in training. But it's a change when you go to England. It's a big game and it just sparks you a little bit.' And I said that I was physically tired against Southampton, but that it can't all be down to me. Why does it always seem to be my fault? They keep on to me about being inconsistent. I think I've been very consistent – I've been bad all year, in my general play that is; I'm not happy with it at all. I've been knocking in the odd goal, but that's all. I've said to them that my form is down to me, and I accept that. But I've never been in such a spell before when I haven't been happy with my form for a whole season. I've got to the stage where I don't think it can *all* be put on my shoulders, it must also be the way the team is playing.

'Is it my fault I'm not getting the ball, my fault I'm not playing well, my fault the midfield are giving the ball away because I'm not making the right kind of runs?'

'Yes.'

So I said, 'Do you think my attitude was right against Luton when I got three goals?'

And again he said, 'Yes.'

I answered that I had exactly the same attitude on Saturday, but that against Luton I got the chances and put them away. I really believe that. Okay I didn't play too well on Saturday, maybe I could have done a bit more. And against Luton I had wanted to prove Don wrong for saying I wasn't brave enough, but it just happened that three chances came along and I stuck them in. Don can just never accept that he may be wrong sometimes. Well, perhaps he can accept it, but you can't tell him and he won't admit it.

We said their attitude might not be one hundred per cent either, because we've had two or three previous meetings and each time we've said that people who aren't doing it should be dropped. And each time they've agreed and nothing has been done. Now they've said that's what they will do. But having said all that we've probably been a bit slack, and they've been a bit slack, so we are all in it together.

Don going on about attitudes to training annoys me. We had it before the Luton game too. I'm a person who can't give my all in training; when it's playing football I'm not the best trainer in the world. It doesn't give me any buzz to do it. When we have a hard morning running I put it in – I'm always up the front, I've got the best times and all that. But when it comes to playing football I often can't whip up any enthusiasm, any sharpness to go out and do it. On the occasional day I might, but I find it hard. There's nothing to play for. I like to take it easy because that's the way I've been brought up, and I think I know what it takes to get me right on Saturday. I've had success by doing nothing under Brian Clough, so that's been instilled in me. But Don's had success by really training people hard, so that's in him.

I enjoy shooting, practising getting your technique right and putting the ball into the net. That's enjoyable and beneficial. You could say practice matches and five-a-sides are beneficial too, but I can't get into it, it just isn't in me. And obviously Don doesn't like that.

Now Graham Rix is different. Rixy trains really hard, he's enthusiastic about everything he does, although he moans all the time. But it gets me when he starts moaning and getting onto people on Thursdays and Fridays. I don't mind it on Saturdays when it matters.

Another big discussion at the moment is team spirit. Don keeps going back to the 'double' days, when if one player wasn't doing it another would get him by the scruff of the neck, 'You're not doing it. Get it done!' Well, that used to happen at Forest, but it didn't come about overnight. The more success you have the closer you get together and the more spirit you start to get. It comes through winning matches and having success – you can't just will it. You can tell that, because after two or three good results people start to come together. But our problem is that we get a couple of results and things start to slacken up a little. Part of the trouble is that there aren't as many 'characters' in the team as there should be, so we haven't been able to hold on to it when we've had it. Also, if anyone has a go at someone he won't accept it. So now we've tried to sort it out and if that happens we are all going to get onto a player.

That was one of the main things in our own meeting, which we had without Don and Terry. We were totally honest with one another, saying exactly what we thought and saying, 'Look, we've really got to get it together now.' We've only one game left before the semi-final. And we've agreed that if anyone isn't doing it we are all going to get onto him, and that people have got to accept it. One or two people said that if they had a go at some players they are likely to say, 'Bollocks', rather than accepting it, and that caused a bit of uneasiness. I said that if Rixy or Kenny shouted at me I was quite likely to say, 'Get on with your own job,' but they would see that they'd got through if I did chase the next ball.

At Highbury we are chopping and changing every week. Don and Terry's attitude is that we are good enough players to see how the opposition are playing and adapt our game. And some of the players said in the meeting that they thought we should be good enough to adapt, but I think the other way round. To me you start off with your own pattern, and then maybe if you can't get through you have to say, 'We can't get through here, we'd better try and change it.' At the

86

moment I don't know what is going on. Some weeks they tell us to come for it to be played to feet. Other times they say we come too short too quickly, and want too much played to our feet. So now I'm thinking, 'Shall I go and get it or shall I look for one over the top?' And if I'm indecisive, I don't know what the player on the ball is thinking. He might think, 'He's coming for it to feet but they are telling me to knock it over the top.' No one knows what anyone else is doing.

When Rixy gets the ball I don't know if he's looking for me straight away. And you should have quick thinking in a team. When you get the ball in certain positions it should be a quick glance up. Woody or Sundy there? Yes. Right, 'Here you are, here's the ball.' It should be the first thing that comes into a player's mind.

I said in the meeting that I thought the main thing was to get some sort of pattern in our play, which we all know. And if it is not working you can try and adapt. But I think the first thing is to decide how you want to play, and let the opposition worry about us, rather than us adjusting to what they do the whole time. We shouldn't start off by looking at the other team and say, 'How are we going to stop them?' and 'How are we going to play in response?' If we've got a big man in there we should try and hit him as early as possible; if we've got a real flier we should work on getting him in the clear as quickly as we can. But at the moment we just don't do that. If you look at Liverpool or Manchester United you see a certain move and you can say that's a typical Liverpool or United move. That's how they play, that's what they are aiming for. But at Arsenal we don't know what we are aiming for, we haven't got anything you can say is typically Arsenal – except passing back to the keeper, according to my friends.

At Forest you could definitely say, 'That's how Forest play.' You knew John Robertson was going to bring it down, and either try and get past his man or knock it up the line to someone's feet. And you knew he was going to turn and get a cross in sharply, so you went to get on the end of it. Although the opposition knew too they couldn't stop it. I've heard Don talk about what Arsenal tried to do when they played Forest. And I can imagine him setting all these things up and saying, 'You go here, and you do this, and you do that', but we used to beat Arsenal every time – well, quite often.

But with Cloughie, and Michels and Weisweiler to some extent, when they had a team finely tuned and playing well, they didn't like to change things even when you were under the cosh. They believe in what they are doing. Weisweiler would change things slightly to take account of other teams' styles. But for Cloughie, when we were doing well, it didn't matter if we were getting a hammering: he'd still play the same way. If their right-winger was giving our left-back a roasting he'd just say, 'He's got to get on with it and cope with it and we'll get our own game together sooner or later', he wouldn't change our formation or style. And we would battle against it until we could force our own game into it. If Robbo wasn't getting the ball he might tell him to move into midfield a bit to pick it up, but that was as far as it went.

There was only one occasion when Cloughie changed our pattern, and that was for the European Cup first leg match against Liverpool, which I've already mentioned. He said in the team meeting, 'Tony Woodcock. You play a bit deeper and go down the right. They are expecting you and Robbo to be over on the left, and I'm sure they will try and clog that area up, so you play on the right.' I had quite a lot of the ball, playing a bit deeper and going on runs all over the place. As I said earlier, I gave Garry Birtles the ball for the first goal and headed it back to Colin Barrett for the second, both from the inside-right/centre-forward position. But that was the only time we were asked to do anything different.

We had a big discussion with each player. We said to David O'Leary that with all his ability he should be scoring goals as well as defending – he's got so much ability. I've had a running joke with him and Kenny Sansom for months now that I'll buy them a bottle of champagne if either of them score before the end of the season. David should be coming up and playing one-twos and getting into their box. But he was worried about Don saying he should be defending if he did come forward, and all the lads said, 'You should be big enough to overcome that, you are your own man, do your own thing out there.' David also said he was worried about Chris Whyte, that he felt he had to cover for him, so he said, 'Look Chris, you've been in the team long enough now to take responsibility for yourself, and I'm not really going to be thinking about looking after you.'

Making sure your own job is right is what we've all got to do at the moment, which is what Dave was saying; because we've given away a lot of goals this season, and it's been difficult to pin down who is responsible. I think in the next few weeks it will become clear, because we said that people had to take responsibility for their own area. Too often in the past it's been, 'Why weren't you at the back post, Dave?' and he'll say, 'I was over there covering Chrissie', and that sounds right, but obviously there's not enough talking going on at the back. So now it's all been set down.

Of course the defence still has to work as a unit. You mustn't go too far on individual responsibility, because you can end up with what happened sometimes in Cologne. You lose 6–0 and a defender will come off with the attitude, 'My player didn't score so it's not down to me.' That's no good. But what we've decided will make each person's job a bit more specific. The whole game is about understanding, and I don't think we've got it, and not just in defence. If Graham Rix gets the ball I don't really know what he's going to do with it. With John Robertson he would get a ball and I could see from the way he was shaping up what was in his mind, and I would know whether I should stay out of the way to let him take his man on, or whether I should go out there for him to knock it up the line. Whereas Rixy will sometimes open up and I'll go wide and then the ball goes inside again. Or the continual complaint about people getting to the bye-line, and you go for the near post and then they check back onto the other foot. So next time you don't go and it's whacked in first time. It's been like that all season. Don says, 'You should gamble. Get to the near post.' But you've gambled twice and both times they've checked out, and that never gets mentioned. But this understanding will only come with winning matches. You've got to start winning matches first and progress from there.

But I think the meeting was very good. Saturday is a fresh start for us, and not just for this season. We might get to Wembley. We obviously aren't going to win the League this season, but we really believe we can qualify for Europe.

But really we are thinking about next season: thinking let's get these remaining nine or ten games under our belts, and do them properly, and see if we can sort things out ourselves as a preparation for next season. Hopefully we *have* got things sorted out a bit more, and starting on Saturday we'll show a bit more togetherness. I think it will be a new beginning. Whatever happens to the result – and it is better trying to start afresh against Coventry than against Liverpool – I think all the players will go out and give it everything they've got. I think we will really be geared up to run and fight and put one hundred per cent work in and help each other. And I think that has been lacking on some occasions – people have a tendency to say, 'Well, I'm all right, it's not my problem', but you get that if a team is not doing well. When you've got this team spirit and a good team going for the championship people help each other all the time.

I've had this groin strain for some weeks now. With so many games on top of one another I've carried on playing, although it has been niggling a bit. But after yesterday it is a little bit sore now. It's no real problem – it just needs two or three days' rest.

6 APRIL

We are not getting a day off this week, although we didn't do anything today. This evening there was a programme about the Falklands, about a lad who had got very badly burned, and when you see that, you think, 'What am I worrying about a bad result for? What does an international match matter, we'll win the next one.' Of course you still worry but it does put it into perspective. I saw Ian Botham on TV talking about the disastrous winter tour in Australia as well, and he just wants to make the critics eat their words, and that's as good a motivation as any. We'll just have to try and do that against Coventry on Saturday.

You can go so far in saying the service was bad, but you have to be careful you don't let that take your thinking over. You've got to think positive and think, 'I'll make it happen', and get your own game right if at all possible. But it is going to be a lot easier if the team is in tune with you. I've thought a bit over the last year or so how nice it would be to be in a sport like tennis, where you are there by yourself, everything depends on you whatever goes right or wrong. In football you have ten other people to depend on to get the best out of you. It must be nice to think you are in control of your own fate and when things go wrong there's only one person to blame.

When Kevin Keegan first came back to England he was dogged with injury and I'm sure that was a reaction to coming back, to playing so many games and not recovering from them. There's a bit of bad luck involved too, but I'm sure the difficulties of settling in have something to do with it. People were writing him off after that first year, but then he went from strength to strength again. I'm sure it was just a reaction to coming back and having to fit into a different team and a very different style of football, which as I have said, is also a real problem for me.

Even in this country if you look at players who have moved clubs you can see how hard it is for them. Garry Birtles to Manchester United was a classic example; and even Frank Stapleton has not fitted in one hundred per cent, although he's fitting in better all the time. But in his first season there was definitely a question mark against him.

And I've got nineteen goals this season. It could have been twenty-nine if I'd been a bit more clever here or taken a couple of chances there. I could have been up there with Rush and Blissett in my first season. As it is I'm going to finish with over twenty in my first season back; I don't think that's bad because I don't just classify myself as an out-and-out goalscorer. That's especially true if you compare it with Frank's position in Manchester United, who after all are a much more attacking team than Arsenal. We've only scored more than two goals twice this year, so you can't say we are the most attacking team in the first division!

7 APRIL

Chris Whyte was taken off at half-time on Monday: Terry didn't think he was doing it. Yet in the cup match against Aston Villa he was outstanding. He seems a bit inconsistent at the moment – one week he'll have a really good game, then he'll let it slip the next week. We've tried to get some sort of consistency into his game, tried to get him to talk a little more at the back, and to be a little more demanding, telling players what to do. He should be getting that into his game now, because he has been playing in the first team for two seasons now. And when he is on his game he can do it. In training this morning he was doing it, getting his tackles in and winning balls, and getting up there over people and banging into the back of them.

I was able to do a little bit, my groin was easing. But I said to Paul Davis as we walked out of London Colney, 'These games keep coming. We've got another one in two days. I've still got knocks from the Greece game a week ago, and we've played Tottenham and Southampton since then. I find it difficult to put any enthusiasm into coming training.' He said the same thing, and there are so many games coming up it's unbelievable. I think that's the most difficult thing about re-adjusting from Germany. We seem to be playing football all the time. But then in Germany I used to say we seemed to be training all the time.

It's a question of what you are used to. I played a hell of a lot of games at Forest, because we were always involved in lots of things, so I thought when I went to Germany, 'I can handle training. No problem.' And then I went to Cologne – and the *training*! The first six months I was so tired – I was really exhausted. I used to go home at lunchtime and have a sleep between the morning and afternoon sessions. But when Weisweiler saw that it was getting on top of me, he used to send me in sometimes half an hour before the Germans, and he saw me holding out of things sometimes and he would accept it because I was doing my stuff on a Saturday. He might say, 'All right, that's enough for you, you can go in now.' And gradually I built up to it, although I still found it difficult. Then in my final year Michels came and even the German players found his regime tough. We did a hell of a lot of running, and I was still having to go to bed at lunchtime.

Coming back to England, although we don't train so hard, we have a different type of fitness. You don't get kicked in training like you do in games, and playing three in six days as we've just done really takes it out of you. When you are playing a lot of games you need to spend a lot of time recovering, not on the training pitch, whereas with just a game every Saturday you can spend more time training.

8 APRIL

We lost Alan Sunderland today. We were in the gym and he went to play a ball and just went down with this pain in his groin. It was really bad and he said he thinks he could be out for the rest of the season – just what we don't need.

'I'm really wary about training in the gym at the moment because I seem to get more stiffness after a session there. What I need is a rest to allow it to recover, but with all these games there just is no opportunity.

9 APRIL

Arsenal 2 Coventry City 1

We went out and we started well enough. We went two up and then it was the same old story – we lost it again. We slackened off in the second half when we could really have steam-rollered them. I think everyone did put in one hundred per cent, which was what we were really after. You can allow for mistakes, allow for bad play as long as everyone gives all they've got, and we did. It's just the way we are playing at the moment. We got the result but we would have expected that anyway. It comes down to the fact that we are not a particularly good team at the moment.

Even though I haven't been playing well overall, I'm getting a fair number of goals: I got my twentieth today. That's partly a reflection of the different way I'm playing. At Forest I was back on the half-way line, then getting into the box or going wide to put crosses in for other people. But at Arsenal I've probably been in the box eighty per cent of the time; if you are in the box a lot, and you have got a bit up top and realize what is likely to happen, you are going to pick up the pieces. In my last year in Cologne I got quite a few by getting parries off the keeper. And I got today's only because I timed my run right. We had a free-kick on the edge of the box.

In Germany we used to have this one worked out with Klaus Allofs taking it. He would run up and I would run square and at a certain time dart in so I wouldn't be offside. It is amazing. You don't get picked up and the number of goals I got as a result I couldn't guess.

The one against Coventry was a classic of its kind. It is just a matter of timing it right as the person taking it strikes it. It was amazing – I arrived there to stick it in and there was no one around me; I was completely by myself. That happened a few times in Cologne. The first time I thought, 'Crikey, where is everybody?' Of course you still have the goalkeeper to contend with because he has parried the ball and is coming after it, but there is no one else near you.

That was also the occasion of one of my most embarrassing misses. We were playing Bochum. You have to know who is taking the free-kick and whether he is likely to lash one. This time Bonhof was, and he often has a go from twenty-five yards, and you can tell whether they are building up for a shot. So Bonhof hit it and the keeper parried it. I darted in. The keeper was lying on the floor and the ball was bouncing back towards the penalty spot, and I was on my own in the box because the defenders had rushed out. All I had to do was sidefoot it home, but I had been having a bad spell and I really wanted to see the net billow, so I smashed it, and it bent and just clipped the outside of the post. I couldn't believe it. I just wanted to dig a hole and crawl into it right there on the penalty spot.

13 APRIL

We started thinking about the semi-final today, working on free kicks and corner kicks, working on not just tossing them in because of McQueen. Sundy made a half-hearted attempt to train today, but I think he knows he has got no chance. So Graham Rix will probably play at the front, as he did against Coventry. He's played up there before so it won't be anything new to him, but we will obviously miss Sundy, and it would be nice to have Graham in midfield. And it looks as if Vlad will play. He came on against Spurs and played against Coventry, and although he had a quiet game there's always the chance he will do something. We don't know about Pat, who hasn't played since Luton. His injury is taking a long time to heal.

There seems very little excitement about the game outside though. It's completely different from Nottingham before a big game, and Brian Talbot said the same about Ipswich. At Forest if we got to a semi-final or final there would be an atmosphere in the city, and especially at the stadium, for weeks before. It builds up from the moment you qualify for the semi-final. The evening paper mentions it every day with reports on training, injury scares and all that sort of thing, and there are groups of people coming and going at the ground to buy tickets or just hanging around. But in London it just doesn't seem to be mentioned.

14 APRIL

We had a practice game today. Pat played, and will wait until tomorrow to see if there is any reaction.

This morning's *Mail* confirmed that Steve Coppell is definitely out – which had been in yesterday's paper – and said Muhren is out as well, which is even better for us. But Steve Coppell is a major player for Manchester United. When Frank Stapleton has been playing well, Steve Coppell has been doing well, and I think they are going to miss him more than anyone.

15 APRIL

The atmosphere is building up a bit at last. We came up to Birmingham quite early, and before going to our hotel in the centre we went to have a look at Villa Park, which is really in good condition – especially after Highbury, which has been a mess for months.

Pat is not going to play, which is a blow, although George Wood is a useful replacement. I think Pat was keen to play, but he's a pro, and he's had this bad foot for ages, which means he can't take goal-kicks. And he probably thought to himself, 'What if I make a mistake through the injury – it could cost the lads a trip to Wembley.' You need people who are completely fit, especially in semis, because they are a real battle. But having said that, *I've* been hobbling around for the last couple of months.

16 APRIL
Manchester United 2 Arsenal 1 FA Cup Semi-Final

Our cup run ended with their first goal. That was the end for us really, because I don't think there was any belief throughout the team. We never know where a second goal is going to come from. From that point it was only a matter of time before they scored. And to give away a goal like that at a time like that. . . . We really thought at half-time that we could hold out. The lads were buzzing: there was an excitement there. We'd had the perfect boost with our goal. When it went in I thought, 'Crikey, we've got a goal out of nothing. Let's see if we can hang on to it,' because I could never see us scoring again unless it was going to be another fluke. I think it was a shock for us when we scored, because it was the only shot we'd had. But when you go into a game thinking, 'If things go right we can beat them,' suddenly you think, 'Hey, we're on our way. We're one up.' And you can imagine what they must have been thinking, because they'd been attacking us for half an hour, and all of a sudden they are one down. And especially as it was a mucky goal from our point of view, let alone theirs. Stewart Robson did really well though. Rixy played a very good ball into him in the first place and he, the goalkeeper and a defender all went for it together; Robbo crunched someone – it might have been the keeper – and it bounced out to Vlad who tried to knock it in to me. Bailey parried it down, Robbo picked it up and scooped it across and I was able to knock it over the line.

From there until half-time we battled well, never gave them an inch, particularly Stewart Robson. We were biting everyone and winning the ball and he was just unfortunate that he made one of his lunges and injured himself. We expected that as soon as they kicked off for the second half they'd really come hammering at us, and they'd be knocking the ball about. I know it was only five minutes, but they didn't start off with any fire, they weren't putting any passing together and I thought, 'They are going to be a bit shaky here.' The passes they tried to put together were going astray and Frank mis-controlled one; Bryan Robson had a real go at him and I thought, 'This could be the beginning of their downfall.' It looked like we'd dampened them already, and I thought, 'If we can keep this up for ten or fifteen minutes we've got to have a great chance,' and then we gave this stupid, stupid goal away.

All week we had been discussing not playing it around at the back. All week Don stressed that if one square ball is knocked, 'Let's get the next one forward to put them under pressure.' Even if it's going to come back don't let's knock too many square balls because we've been losing out that way. Sooner or later you make a bad pass and lose goals because of it. So, 'Let's get it up there.' And especially in the first ten minutes of the second half, when if you can hold out for ten or fifteen minutes. . . .

So what happens? Chris Whyte plays a square ball to Kenny. Kenny plays it back and Chris tries to play a square ball to Johnny Hollins. It was on, but he just hit this terrible ball. It gets cut out, and the next moment it's in the back of our net. To make matters worse Brian Talbot slipped, and perhaps if he hadn't Robson wouldn't have got inside him. Even then Robson knocked it wide and I thought, 'Well, he's not going to score from that angle, he's knocked it too far,' but there it was. Back of the net, and it all went back to that pass. And that was it. Perhaps you could also ask questions about the way Whiteside got free for their winner, but from the moment that first goal went in it was only ever going to end one way.

Virtually from the moment we kicked off I couldn't run, I was so stiff around the groin. I said to Fred Street at half time, 'My groin is really painful at the moment,' and he said, 'We'll have a look at it next week.' But as soon as the second half started I felt this really sharp pain. It always seems to be worse then. When I sit down at half-time it seems to stiffen up. And when I come out for the second half I'm not as mobile as I'd like to be. It's been that way for two or three months now. I haven't had any zip or sharpness; I've had some discomfort all the time, I can't run without problems, and it just preys on your mind.

The dressing room afterwards was very quiet. There were a few moans about the first goal, because it has happened so many times. No one wanted to blame Chrissie, it is hard to say, 'It was your fault,' but he did make the pass.

We went out to a pub afterwards as a team and had a few drinks and tried to forget about the game. Inevitably we did chat about it though.

17 APRIL

A depressing day. I spent most of the day sitting around, and helping with the packing. We are at last going to have our own house. We've been living in a club house since November after five months in

Peter Shilton driving himself hard in training as always.

Peter Withe bashing his way through a brick wall — Butcher and Osman in this case.

Dieter is thinking: 'If it's a two-
yard tap-in, I bet I beat you to
it.'

Some people will sell you
dummies. Littbarski's whole
body weight goes one way then
the other — perfect balance.

hotels, which with a small baby is not ideal. The club house is an improvement on the hotels, but we've been living with boxes of stuff not unpacked, and it will be nice to move in and get settled.

You can't help thinking about the game though. I don't think we really went out thinking we were going to win. We thought we could win, we thought, 'Well, you never know what's going to happen, we may have a chance,' and 'If everything goes well, we're on our game and they are a bit off.' But it wasn't the sort of confidence we had at Forest, where we really thought, 'We are going to win,' not 'If we do our stuff we can beat them.'

At Forest we thought we could win anywhere, beat anyone. We thought we could get a result home or away. Before we beat Liverpool in the European Cup everyone expected us to lose, but we thought we could beat them. And as far as we were concerned to take a two-goal lead at Anfield was fantastic. We never dreamed of losing two goals, not even of being forced into a penalty decider. Even in the Cologne game, when we had been held 3–3 at home and everyone had written us off, we thought we were going to win.

And I don't think United are as good as everyone says they are. They are very strong in midfield, they play it around, but they are definitely not that good at the back. I like Duxbury and I like the left-back, but I think they are there to be taken. We didn't put that much pressure on, but the little bit we managed when we chased them made them look very shaky – half-hearted clearances which were going to no one, going into the stand or bobbling away. They are certainly not in Liverpool's class. When we went there in the League before Christmas we outplayed them. It was 0–0, but we should have won 3–0.

In the papers it said Terry had made a statement after the game pointing out the success Arsenal have had under his management. He's under some pressure because of all the rumours. And the trouble is two semi-finals isn't success at Arsenal. We are meant to compete with the Uniteds and Liverpools, and we just aren't good enough at the moment. We need new players to be able to do that.

18 APRIL

Some of the lads did a bit of training. I just went in and had treatment – heat treatment to make the blood circulate quicker. I've been having it for a few weeks, but they said it was just a bit of stiffness and as soon as I got warmed up it would go. And for the last couple of weeks that had been the case – towards the end of a training session I've been feeling all right. But during the semi it was more painful than it had been, so I must have done something else.

Understandably everyone was a bit down. Rixy was fighting back though. He's pointed out a few times he's been an ever-present this season, and he said, 'I'm really going to carry on working. I'm going to put me lot in and make sure I don't miss a game all season.'

19 APRIL
More treatment, and then they sent me home because I was sick.

The England squad for the match with Hungary was in the paper. I had a look to make sure I was in. Mr Robson has left two places vacant, and is going to watch Peter Withe play against West Brom tonight. Surely he knows what Peter can do? Rixy has been left out. The *Evening Standard* headline was 'Rix Axed', which wasn't very nice for him to see. Yet in the practices before the Greece game he was brilliant. I felt very disappointed for him, because he's played well for Arsenal. He's a battler and really tries hard. And Kenny and I haven't had the best of seasons, yet we are still in.

20 APRIL
Norwich City 3 Arsenal 1
What a day. It started off well enough. Carole, Jack and I had our first morning in our new house, which was a relief. And when we get settled in in a few weeks it will be smashing.

Then it was announced that Graham Rix had been brought into the England squad. Why Mr Robson waited to do that I don't know. He must have known when he announced the twenty whom he was bringing in; it just meant Graham had twenty-four hours of feeling miserable. Then he goes and tears a muscle in the game, and it looks as if he might be out for the rest of the season. Ironic, after his comments on Monday.

Peter Withe was brought in too, so he must have done well last night, although a journalist I saw at Norwich said that he and John Wile, the West Brom centre-half, had just had their normal kicking match. We travelled down and then they said, 'Are you all right?' And I said, 'No. I can feel it now when I walk,' so I didn't play.

Nor did Vlad. The team we put out! and here's an international player who can't get into it. He is in and out in and out. It must be destroying him. I am rooming with him now, and he is despondent. He loves Arsenal. He wasn't really involved in the semi-final. Vlad needs to be playing in a good team really for us to see the best of him. He is a very good footballer, but he's never going to adapt unless he plays regularly and is given a fair chance. Now they could say, 'You are in for six games, let's see what you can do.' That's what he needs.

Vlad can't understand what they are trying to do. They are trying to bring other things into his game, which he has got to learn somehow. But they aren't saying, 'This is his game, and this is what we have got to learn to bring into our game.' It's a little bit the same with me. He is a good passer of the ball, and instead of concentrating on getting him to defend, to get in front of opponents and that sort of thing, why not concentrate on getting people to give him the ball a bit more. Maybe if they brought him into the centre of midfield or played him just behind the front two so he could set things up from there.

I thought earlier that they'd decided about him, when they left him out after the Birmingham match. But then they keep bringing him back, so perhaps there was a little doubt in their minds. But that is never going to be resolved unless they give him a run.

We tried to play a bit differently, with Colin Hill coming in to mark Channon and Chris Whyte marking Bertschin, David O'Leary sweeping and Kenny and John Kay pushed virtually into midfield. We got the goal and although they had a couple of half chances which they should have done better with, we didn't seem in any danger. And then it all fell apart.

It was the first game I've watched for ages. Watching from the stand I felt that we just don't seem to play with that much confidence. There were loads of occasions when players could demand the ball and they didn't, they let the other player get on with it. Someone could say, 'Give it to me and I'll have a look and see if anything is on,' especially with free-kicks around the half-way line, but they don't. They say, 'Toss it into the box.'

There was virtually no width at all. Everything was coming right down the middle. Not once did anyone get to the bye-line that I can remember; certainly not once did anyone get there and hit the near post or far post with any conviction. Oh yes, David O'Leary did. He has started to go forward on occasion. Against United a couple of times he went to the edge of their box in the first half, and he did too against Norwich. In the first half he started in his own half, went past somebody, played a one-two and got to the bye-line, and we got a corner. If he can do that more regularly it will be a definite plus, because so much opens up when he strides into their half. Defenders don't know whether to leave their man and go to him or not. If they don't, who is going to take him? And if they do he can just slip it to someone.

We've been on to him all season to do it, and although he isn't doing it that much at the moment, at least he's beginning to come out a little. And if he can keep doing it it's going to be a tremendous help for the team, and for himself, because he looks in a different class when he does stride forward, more confident, and maybe he is going to get a bit of permanent extra confidence by doing it.

A defender's job now is not just defending, he has got to bring a little bit to the attack. In West Germany the sweepers, or libero, defend, when they have to. But in some games they don't have to defend at all, and it is a great position to be noticed in. They might make two or three surging runs, and that catches the eye, and all of a sudden they are 'man of the match'. If Dave only realized that. He's got a good reputation now, but he could really go.

Part of his problem, even defensively, is that he lacks aggression. When he has his mind on it, when he gets a bit wound up, then I think he's good. Maybe he's like a boxer, if he gets a good thump in the face early on, it makes him a bit aggressive, and then he's strong. But you've got to clip him first. And at the other end he hasn't scored this year, and I can't remember him even coming close. He's got so much going for him, yet he hasn't scored a single goal this season. I keep saying to him, jokingly but meaning it as well, 'Dave, get a goal. I haven't seen you score. How can I go through a whole season without seeing you score?' There are people with much less ability – just big bruising centre-halves – who are getting five or six and looking dangerous at set-pieces.

He's not that powerful at attacking the ball in the box, but you see that with a few defenders. They can be commanding in their own penalty area, but when they get up the other end something just seems to happen. It used to happen with Larry Lloyd. In his own box balls would come in and he'd thump them away – sometimes nearly to the half-way line. But when he went up for a corner, the ball would come in and although he'd win it, he'd be glancing it instead of thumping it. Cloughie was always getting onto him about it.

21 APRIL

There's been a lot of talk in the papers about Peter Withe being our secret weapon against Hungary. There was one story which said Hungary were banking on Trevor and I playing, and they are going to play the same as Greece did to stifle us. But it wasn't the two of us they stifled, the way we played did that. If we are going to play that way again, he might as well put Terry Butcher up there with Peter and Paul Mariner, and just keep tossing it in. If Trevor and I are going to play then we've got to think generally about the play we do before we get to the penalty box. And if we do play together it looks as if we are going to be under severe pressure to produce the goods; even though it is not our problem alone, it's the kind of football we are playing. But if it's a 0–0 draw they automatically look at the front two players.

I think, though, he will play Withe and Francis from what's being said in the paper. I read in a paper when he brought Peter into the squad that he said, 'Without Paul Mariner, the best centre-forward England have got,' and yet Paul has had such a hammering in the press over the last few England games he's played in. Then Bobby Robson says, 'Without Cyrille Regis available,' yet he left Cyrille out after the game against West Germany. I can't understand what he is getting at – I'd be better off not reading the papers because it mixes me up.

If I am left out I shall be very disappointed. I can only say I got into the side, and I got one against West Germany, two against Greece over there and one against Luxembourg; so I've got four goals in four games, yet it appears I'm definitely struggling to get a place. If I'd had three or four chances against Greece at Wembley and missed them all, I'd accept it, I'd say well you've got to be looking at someone else. I didn't get much of a kick in the Greece match, but I didn't get one chance, and I couldn't say now, 'I was bad against Greece and it was my fault.' I would really resent being dropped.

I don't know who else is scoring goals, but over the last few months I've been the most consistent goalscorer. If I'm given the chance I'll put it away, and I can't say more than that.

I'm sure Luther was upset at being left out after scoring a hat-trick, but I think he has got to look at his own performance a bit, because he could have had nine goals. And when Bobby Robson said afterwards that against top class opposition you only get one chance and you have to put it away I'm sure that's right.

But Luther does make things happen. He bustles. His first touch isn't that good, it might bounce a yard off him, but he'll put his foot in again for a second go and that'll bounce off somewhere else and he'll go and get that. And he did get a hat-trick, although when he played against Wales up front with Paul Mariner he didn't score.

We are coming back to the same old story again. Half-way through the European Championship qualifiers and no one knows what the team is. It should be virtually the same squad every time, like it is in Germany. I mean, Mr Robson knows how all the players who are in contention can perform, and ought to decide which ones he wants. Perhaps he might say if someone is really in form at the time, hitting hat-tricks every week, that kind of thing, that that guy is a likely candidate if the people in possession aren't doing it. But apart from that make your mind up on the squad and leave well alone is the best motto. It's a bit complicated at the moment though, and I think there's no doubt the press influence selection and the way we play.

22 APRIL

They asked me if I was fit enough to play. I said I could still feel the injury. It's settling down now. Before it was a general stiffness, but now there are two definite sore points in the right groin, which I probably got in the semi.

But as I said, they tended to think it was just a little bit of stiffness, and that once I started running around I might forget about it or it would ease off, although it would be stiff and painful after the game. With Lee Chapman breaking his nose at Norwich and Graham Rix, Robbo and Sundy also out they were obviously desperate for me to play. So I said, 'As long as you realize that if it's still there after twenty minutes I might have to come off. If you want to take that risk, I'll give it a try.'

23 APRIL

Arsenal 3 Manchester City 0

I knew after five minutes that it was hopeless and I would not finish the game. I went through to half-time to see if it would ease, and also because we were on top and you always think a chance may come along and you'll put it in. I said to the lads, 'I'll be all right if I just stand in the penalty box; you give me the ball and I'll put it in.' Unfortunately it doesn't work like that. You have to chase around and I just couldn't do it, so I came off at half-time.

But we got the win we needed – if we'd lost we would be drifting down towards the bottom again. City are in a dreadful state: they could get relegated. They've got some good players, and they knock the ball around well enough, but they are terrible. I think it's confidence as much as anything – they just haven't got any.

24 APRIL

Obviously I shouldn't have played yesterday. But at least, looking on the bright side, it made my mind up for me about whether I was fit to join the England party. It was better to have found out against City that I've got a problem than to go out against Hungary and have to come off after twenty minutes.

But I've decided that's it. Even if it means I don't play again this season I'm not going to play until this is cleared up. I've said in the past that I'm never going to play again when I'm not fully fit, but this time I mean it. It's gone on too long – virtually since Christmas, when we played four games in nine days in heavy conditions. When it goes on that long you really start worrying that it might mean you are finished, and I'll do anything as long as it doesn't mean that.

27 APRIL

England 2 Hungary 0

All I've been doing is going in and having treatment, morning and afternoon, this week from Roy Johnson because Fred Street is with the England squad. The lads moan about the treatment sometimes, but that's true at every football club. There's not much they can do except give me some heat treatment to help it along. Tomorrow I'm going for X-rays, not for the injury I did in the semi-final, but for the discomfort I've had for the last few months in the lower pelvic region. They are worried that it might be the thing Trevor Brooking has had with a bit of movement from the pelvic bone in the middle – which is pretty serious.

I went to the international. Hungary played very well for the first fifteen or twenty minutes – I thought they gave us a bit of a lesson in changing play and in three or four-man passing movements – and I thought, 'Here we go again.' They had one really good chance which Shilts smothered, and two half-chances which the fellow failed to control at the last moment. They cut through us a few times really.

But once we scored they just threw the towel in. They went to pieces. In the second half they made a feeble attempt to look as if they were going to have a go and attack us, but as they went forward we just took the ball off them and broke. For us in the second half it was virtually like an away performance, because they were coming at us without showing any conviction. And they kept losing the ball, so we were just breaking away and getting scoring chances. We had so many! It was like shooting practice by the end.

I'd like to have played, because there were a few chances flying around. It was a different game to the one against Greece – at least Hungary tried to come forward a bit. In the second half especially it was pretty easy for our forwards – the defenders were standing a yard off them, and they weren't even getting clattered. Trevor Francis got kicked on the calf early on in the game, but apart from that I can't remember a bad tackle. In fact in the second half they weren't getting tackled at all. England had a field day, because whenever they got the ball the defender was a couple of yards off. Peter Withe was getting the ball played up to him and laying it off, and Trevor was all over the place. The only one who didn't do so well was Luther, who was playing behind the front two, ironically the position I wanted to play in, but which is the wrong position for him.

28 APRIL

I went for the X-rays, the second lot I've had. The first ones didn't show anything. They said it was just wear and tear. This time they X-rayed me from all different angles, standing on one leg, the lot.

Looking back on it now, playing that forty-five minutes against City has put me back weeks. I shouldn't have played. But if I'd not played then and played yesterday, I might have done myself more harm than good. If I'd gone to the England call-up and given a bad account of myself because of the injury it would have been unfortunate.

The Arsenal tour is at the same time as the England tour of Australia, so I won't be going on that. I think it is fair enough that Arsenal have first call, particularly as other clubs are touring. It might not help my international hopes, but who can say. I could go to Australia and have three good games but I don't know that it would mean that much with players from United, Spurs and Liverpool not being there. My biggest concern at the moment is to be one hundred per cent fit for next season, and start the season well, so that I'm in for the European Championship games.

29 APRIL

I had a chat with Kenny about the England game, and about the one thing which had really disappointed me – the way the back players hadn't pushed forward. Alvin Martin has got the ability to do it. But he and Terry Butcher would get the ball on the D on the half-way line, and there would be twenty yards for them to go into, but they'd play the ball from there instead. In that situation the back player should push forward. They might go ten yards, they might go twenty. If they go ten something might start to open up, if they get twenty yards in who knows what is going to happen. And if you go ten and there's nothing opened up for you you haven't lost by it, because the worst thing that can happen is that you have to kick it forward from there instead of ten yards further back: but they just didn't do it.

Kenny said that he thought they were on edge, and were frightened to push forward as a result. He thought a few of the lads were nervous because there had been so much emphasis on this being *the* important game. Bobby Robson had been saying all week, 'This is the big game, it's important to the public.' And it is true that even in the build-up to the Greece game he was looking beyond that to Hungary; he was saying, 'This is not the big one, the big one is next month,' which is wrong anyway.

At our new house we have contract gardeners who come twice a week. They all jump off the lorry, rush into the garden, rush about looking busy and then rush out. The first time they came the boss came to see me and said:

'Mr Branch (the previous owner) liked to mow his own lawn. It took him about two hours. Do you want to do that?'

'Not really,' I said. 'No.'

'Well,' he said, 'I'll have to charge you an extra six pounds a week.' So I wondered if we could work out a deal; I said, 'I'll tell you what. How would you like two tickets for every home game at Highbury for a year?' We get eight complimentaries at every home game, and I very rarely use them if it isn't a big game. I usually end up sticking my head out of the dressing room window and look for some kids coming by or people who look like real Arsenal supporters and throw my spares to them. The standing joke with some of the lads is that they expect them to come flying back through the window the way we've been playing. So I thought I'd give him two tickets and get my lawns cut for nothing.

He said, 'I can't make it myself, but that sounds interesting. My son-in-law goes down there sometimes, perhaps he'd like them. I'll come back to you about it.'

He did today. He said, 'I've thought about the tickets. I'll take them, but I'll still have to charge you four pounds.'

What I should have done was threatened him: 'If you don't cut my lawn I'll give you four tickets.'

30 APRIL
Watford 2 Arsenal 1

I thought we played quite well. There was only one team in it for the first half hour – we knocked it around and Watford chased after it. We had a few really good chances which we missed; then Watford had two sitters which how they missed I'll never know. But everything was going great, we had been really confident. Then we scored just after the interval – and it was the same old story. As soon as the ball went into the net we seemed to drop. And Watford started attacking us, missing a few more chances. Then Kenny and Paul Davis got free with only the goalkeeper to beat, and they both missed, or the chap saved it.

It was like that: end to end stuff. But having been 1–0 up we shouldn't have thrown it away.

Colin Hill has come into the side and done really well. He's come into a struggling team, one that has been giving a lot of goals away, and played well; not just his tackling and enthusiasm, but his actual laying the ball forward too. He's knocked quite a few thirty-yard balls which haven't just been tanked forward – he's looked and played them, inside and outside of the foot. Not bad for a centre-half.

We again played with the two full-backs pushed into midfield and had a man-to-man marking system at the back. I think it is a good way to play. It gives our defenders set responsibility, where earlier in the season they were leaving it for one another. No one was being decisive and saying, 'That's my ball.' Now you can see if someone is not picking a man up, or is making mistakes.

I said to Kenny afterwards, 'David O'Leary will score before you do, and then you'll really be in trouble.'

Watford have one thing in common with the approach we had at Forest, although the styles are very different. They don't care if they lose the ball. They have two wingers with pace, who can do a bit on the ball, who can beat a man and get a good cross in. And they and the others are obviously told, 'Come on, get at them, and if you lose the ball okay, but if you get by them everything opens up.' At Forest it was, 'Get in the box, get in the box, take people on – if you get through once it's been worth it.'

Then I moved to Cologne and they wanted the opposite. If I went running at defenders and got past one there would be nobody coming with me, and if I lost it they'd say, 'No. Don't do that. We've got to take our time.' That was especially true under Rinus Michels. He wanted us to hold the ball, hold the ball, wait for an opening to appear, but we thought we had good enough players to spot things quickly and get in there straight away.

You really need a happy medium. To keep running and banging your head against a brick wall is daft, because there are times when you *can* slow it down. Last season at Cologne when we played well we got a balance. We knew when to take risks, and that's what you've got to find. I like that kind of game, when you slow down and wait and then do something quick. The best teams can do both: you always go back to Liverpool.

With Watford everyone knows what they are going to do – they just kick it forward. I'd score a lot of goals playing for them and being in the box, because there are a hell of a lot of chances with the ball bouncing around in there. But I wouldn't enjoy the build up, with everything hammered towards the corner flag and 'go chase'. It's a hard game for their forwards, because they are running all the time. But they do all run after it, they all chase; if one misses it, another gets it. If someone knocks a cross in and it is headed out, it goes straight back in again. And with all those people putting it back in there's got to be one that's going to bounce free somewhere in the box. I can understand why they score a lot of goals. And the forwards at least know what to expect: as soon as they see it bouncing in midfield it's a question of setting off and hoping it comes. A couple of times their midfield players got the ball with time to turn and play it, but the feller kicked it half on the turn. I suppose he knew where it was going – he must have done. I think Graham Taylor is a good manager, and I'm sure if he had a player like Glenn Hoddle in midfield he'd play somewhat differently, although he'd still want to get the ball forward quickly. And anyway, their style certainly suits the players they've got. The forwards also know that the ball is going to come straight back. They got their second goal that way. We headed the ball clear, and some of the lads came out, some stayed back. It was hooked back in and Blissett was unmarked on the edge of the penalty area because David O'Leary was trying to play offside while half the defence had stayed back.

Vlad came on as substitute today, and I think he really wanted to do something. He went out wide. There were players running towards him with the ball and he'd say, 'Give it me', but they'd turn away from him and give it somewhere else. When young John Kay first came in I'd said to him, 'When you get the ball, give it to Petrovic. I'm not trying to take anything away from you, but if there's nothing on, if you can't see anything straight away, just give it to him. You can always get it back from him.'

And I think Don and Terry should be telling players that, telling players to get him into the game, to really make a conscious effort to give it to him – because no one is doing it at the moment. They aren't good enough, that's why; so Vlad's inevitably going to go now. He'll probably end up as European Footballer of the Year somewhere else.

2 MAY
Arsenal 3 Manchester United 0
David O'Leary scored! So the pressure is really on Kenny now. But after the way he missed that chance at Watford, when he was right through, tried to place it and the goalkeeper got a hand to it, I don't fancy his chances. He got forward more though. He's always on about this. He says it's the way he used to play at Crystal Palace and when he first came to Arsenal – if he was out of position someone would fill in for him. He thinks it's the way he should play. But this season it has either been taken out of him or he has lost it. He hasn't got to the by-line for months. I think he's trying to get it back on his own, he's thinking about his own game where in the past I think he was worried that if he went forward there wouldn't be anyone behind him.

Ron Atkinson evidently said to the pressmen afterwards that an Arsenal player had told him at Wembley that we had a combined plan to get Moses! I confess all. I went up to him at Wembley and said, 'You had better watch out for Moses. We're going to get him.

108

Our hard midfield, all our hard back four are going to kick him all over the place. And we're going to get him sent off.'

What a farce. The lads don't like Moses. Not many people do, because he's a bit nasty. In the League Cup semi at Highbury he caught Nicho very late and very high. Well, you could account for that perhaps because of the conditions. But then it's happened in other games. In the return at Old Trafford he butted Brian Talbot. And he's been going over the top. He caught me in the semi-final at Villa Park. We're not the hardest of teams. You get some teams – it used to be true at Forest, and I think at Arsenal a few years ago, and it is at Liverpool now – that if anyone got kicked retribution followed. If a defender kicked me, Archie Gemmill would do him, if he went into Larry Lloyd's area it would be, 'Bang!' then Kenny Burns would go, 'Wham'. There was that sort of spirit. I think that's there in all good teams, they are so tightly knit together that if someone's been kicked, no matter who, one of the others will get the offender.

Whiteside is going to have to be careful he doesn't let his aggression take over his whole game. He is a good player, I've seen him play some great games, but he's pushing and elbowing all the time. I've nothing against that when it's on, but as he's doing it all the time, and leaving his foot in, it makes him look a bad player. It's as if he's got nothing going for him but his aggression. He also wants to watch it because one day he is going to run into an old pro who will time it right when he's left his foot in and do him, and he'll end up with a broken leg. One or two people have commented about that. But Moses had to go. I was watching him, and just before he was sent off there was a tackle with Nicho; the ball sprang away and Nicho was on the ground. I thought Moses kicked out at him, went for his head, but fortunately he missed. Nicho didn't know what was happening. I asked him afterwards, 'Do you know what he did?' and Nicho said, 'No.' Then there was the next tackle. Nicho got up and said, 'You've got to watch yourself, you'll be sent off here,' and all of a sudden Moses butted him. I saw him. All the people sitting around me in the stand saw him. He had to be sent off for it.

He has to be stupid to do it at the end of a fairly meaningless game when you are nearing Wembley. It's the same with Steve Foster getting that booking on Saturday. How you can get booked for dissent when you are going to be playing in a Cup Final if you stay out of trouble I will never know. I just can't understand it. I'm not saying don't tackle, you've got to do that. But butting or going over the top! You can still play football while avoiding the heavy stuff, particularly when the Final is coming up, because you may never get there again, especially if you play for Brighton! It was all so unnecessary, and it was especially strange because United just hadn't seemed all that bothered previously. They looked terrible in the first half. Then it blew up in the last ten minutes. And our back four said that when we were substituting John Hawley, McQueen raced over to their bench and shouted, 'Get Remi off, he's going to be sent off' – that was five minutes before he went.

Wilkins's tackle on O'Leary looked bad too. He went jumping up into him and caught him on the chest. It was getting a bit out of hand by then, but I think he just went for the play. Butch is one of those who couldn't kick anyone if he wanted to.

One disappointment out of it is that we won't see Moses and Case confronting one another at Wembley. Some friends were having a discussion about which is the harder the other day. I don't think there's any contest: Case would just steam-roller him.

Charlie Nicholas was at the ground today for talks. He's been linked with Liverpool and Manchester United, with United as favourites according to the papers; but I have an informed source – who has never been wrong yet – and he says Charlie will come to Highbury. We'll see.

I've only seen him on TV. He looks a good player. But he is playing with Celtic, who along with a couple of other teams, dominate Scottish football, and they score a lot of goals; so you would have to judge him by his performance in another team. The proof will be when he joins a top English club. Obviously the ability is there, the technique is there and he can finish. But whether he'll do as well as Dalglish is another thing. It happens to a lot of players that they come through at twenty-one or twenty-two, they start playing well and getting a lot of goals – but it's what happens in the years after that which tells.

Look at McGarvey, who is playing with Charlie at Celtic. He's getting a lot of goals there too. He was the coming man when he came down to Liverpool, yet he couldn't get a game there. He didn't even get in as sub, and they said he was 'brainless' and all sorts of things like that. Yet when he first came down they said, 'He's very similar to Tony Woodcock.' Thanks, lads! But I don't think another expensive forward is our priority. A system of play, and the strengthening of midfield seem more important to me.

Brian McDermott's done quite well since he has been in the side.

I would have played him a few months ago as a winger or right-sided player, because he goes past people and whips the ball in. He's a good crosser of the ball. He does things too quickly at times though. He had a great chance today, but he rushed at it. I spoke to him about it afterwards, because he could have taken his time and pushed it on a yard. And playing him in the middle is a waste of time, because he's never there. He's a bit like Trevor Francis in that respect, he goes out wide all the time and crosses to no one. Okay, when we were really on top Noddy got on the end of a couple, but generally there was nobody there because that was where Brian was meant to be.

He's not the most intelligent of players, when he's got time he doesn't really know what to do with the ball. He's one of those players who will get the ball and twist and turn, go round in a circle, prod the ball out and go after it and whip a cross in without knowing where it's going. But if they gave him a free role to go down the wings his strengths at getting past people and hammering in crosses could be used.

It all comes back to having a pattern we feel comfortable with. But having a good midfield would help. If you look at our midfield, we've got a young lad Paul Davis, who is making his way. You've got Noddy, who has scored a lot of goals in the last few weeks with his two today. You get the best from him when you can let him run all over the place and let him come into the penalty box late, but not when you ask him to be anchorman. Peter Nicholas is the anchorman at the moment. He'd be a good person in the right set-up to be holding there and crunching people in midfield. I'd like to see Graham Rix playing on the left-hand side and getting forward down the left-wing position, and just restrict him to that area. But you've got to have someone to give him the ball, because he won't stay there unless he is getting a regular supply. And we haven't got anyone to do that. When you compare our midfield with Liverpool's and Manchester United's, which are the teams Arsenal should be compared with, we haven't got a Souness or a Wilkins and a Muhren. I'd like to see someone like Glenn Hoddle or Liam Brady in the team – and I'm being self-interested in this – because it would help my game to have someone who can see things early and play it. Petrovic might have done. He knocked a couple when he was playing, even in his first game against Swansea. At the risk of sounding like a record with the needle stuck, they should have given him a run.

But who was going to give him the ball on the right? We don't go down the right.

3 MAY

There were petitions around the ground yesterday, got up by supporters demanding that Terry and Don be sacked. And those friends of mine who are Arsenal fans think that is the only solution. I don't say anything. But there is talk about them getting new three-year contracts. If they sign them and buy anybody, and then it still doesn't happen next season there will be hell to pay: because there have probably been only a couple of times this season when it has been worth going to Highbury.

Terry made that statement on semi-final day about his record. And when you look at it, it is a fair record, but you shouldn't say, 'Compared to the rest he has done well.' Arsenal should be striving with the best, should be compared with Liverpool. United have done it by spending all that money. They haven't won anything yet, but they are a lot closer to it than we are, because we seem content just to be getting by with a nice bank balance, not owing anyone any money.

My first season in Germany I remember watching Arsenal play at Forest, and the performance was on a par with Liverpool except they missed four open goals. But I've never seen anything better than the way they played. They pushed it around and ran for each other, ran off the ball well – the passing was good. They got it, looked, played it back. But at the moment they aren't confident enough to do that kind of thing, although I think we've got the players to do it if we get some kind of settled system.

The last few years have been a story of getting by, getting to the semis, qualifying for Europe. But hopefully they have now realized that that is not good enough for Arsenal. Arsenal should be one of the leading clubs in Europe, never mind England. So they've got to go out and try to get that back. It's not about getting by and bringing young players in. They should be going for international players. A lot of players in Europe would love to play for Arsenal. So what if the club have to pay over the odds to get them – you aren't taking a big chance in buying good international players.

But maybe not qualifying for Europe this year was the best thing that could have happened to us, because it may finally have sunk in that we are not good enough, and it will speed things up. Something has got to happen. They will have to buy someone if only to get the interest back among the supporters. They've got to spend a million pounds this summer and get two or three players. There is no way they can start off next season with just the same bunch. And they have also got to get their buys right. They bought three this season, and I'm the only one who has ended up playing regularly.

But I still think with a couple of additions to the squad we could do something. We have the nucleus of a good side. A couple more players and a system which we can all play and which will help develop understanding between players, and we will be all right.

The X-rays showed that there was no movement in the bones, but I've got a couple of strains to the attachments onto the bones. They said all I can do is rest, and they are hoping it will clear up in the close season. It's not surprising really. In the last three years I've played thirty–thirty-four matches a season, playing one a week. This year I've played nearly double, playing twice a week at least. We've played eighteen cup games this season, and that's where your troubles start. When you haven't had a proper summer break either because of the World Cup, something has got to give somewhere along the line. It's not suprising you suffer from wear and tear. And I've played at least seven where I shouldn't have done. That farce with the broom handle! But I was daft enough to let them do it and say, 'Yes, I'll go out and play,' when I just should have said, 'No.' But you always think well, one chance will come along and I'll put it away and it'll be worth it. But they never seem to when you are injured. Or you get one and miss it and you think, 'Oh, I shouldn't be playing today. That would have gone in if I'd been fit.'

But I haven't really done anything for two weeks now, and I can feel it getting better, so I'm just hoping that four weeks off in the summer will see it right. Without being one hundred per cent fit I can't perform at my best, and that has been the case for three or four months now, although it has only just hit home. Even though I've been getting the odd goal or two I haven't been able to do as much as I'd want to in terms of running and closing people down. I've had to wait for the right moment to give my lot in two or three sprints because I've known I couldn't do it all the time. So even if I miss some games now and don't play on tour it doesn't matter as long as I'm right for next season. But it is the most games I've ever missed.

4 MAY

I'm not going to play again this season, although we've got three matches left: a disppappointing end to a disappointing first season back in English football.

I can't say I've been over impressed with the English game since I returned; coming to it from Germany gives you a different perspective, and makes you question things you accepted as normal before. There are too many games. There is too much football, and it is a bit kick and rush at times. Everyone talks about us needing more skilful players, but you can't have skilful players if the ball is flying around you all the time. I think we should try and slow it down. I'm not advocating losing the good qualities we've got, like being direct, but we do need a bit more subtlety and control in our game.

It can be done. Liverpool don't play kick and rush; Ipswich, during their good couple of seasons, would play it around and be direct with it. But at the moment there are a lot of players in the English game who are making a living because they work hard and are good, honest players; defenders especially – they get stuck in, kick it out for a throw-in, keep getting it away from goal. When you compare them with German defenders you've got to say that the Germans have a little bit more to their game than just defending and clearing the ball.

I was watching on Saturday and seeing some of the passes being made made me think, 'What can he expect him to do with that?' Because the ball was being played at knee height, and there's no way that's how a pass should be played. But a lot of defenders don't think. They give you the ball to get rid of it. I see a lot of defenders get it, push it forward and go, 'Whoof!' If I've got a player on my left side I want the ball played to my right. Maybe I think they are better than they are, but I think they should be able to do that; it sometimes seems that if they hit you at all they are quite pleased, without thinking about what side you want it on.

At the moment I'm undecided about whether it's because the game is so fast. I've complained about it a few times and they always say, 'Well, you don't get the time in England that you get in Germany or Italy or somewhere like that.' And I think yes, it is that, they are under pressure all the time, they are being closed down a lot. Yet then I look back to the way Juventus played against Aston Villa. Villa were trying to put them under pressure, but Juventus took their time and had the confidence to play it about. And players weren't frightened to give it to somebody who was marked – but they didn't hammer it at him, they appreciated the kind of ball which was needed.

Thinking back, teams tried to do it to us a few times in Cologne. And we were pressured into mistakes a few times and gave the ball away, but it didn't stop us trying to play it out. And German defenders didn't just tonk the ball away unless they were under severe pressure.

That problem is looming large at Arsenal because we've had a bad season and people just haven't got the confidence. It's affecting everything. Very early on in the season we played Huddersfield, and I missed a couple of chances which I'd normally bury, but I was not happy with the general lack of understanding, so I went to see Don afterwards. And he said, 'If you had stuck those two in you would have been all right.' And I said, 'I wouldn't, I would probably have been happier, but I think you should be telling players when they get around the box to get it in to Sundy and myself.' And he said, 'We've got no Liam Brady there now, and you've been used to playing with good players at Cologne,' and making all these excuses. And I said, 'Surely you don't need good players to get the ball under control and pass it ten yards?' He agreed with me, but nothing's been said since.

When I first came I thought the reason it wasn't happening was that last season they only played with one forward, and all the thinking was, 'There's no one up there to hit, so play it square,' and I thought it was just going to be a matter of time for them to realize that they've got Sundy and myself now, that we're always there for them to play it in to feet. But now I'm not so sure. After watching these two games there's just a general lack of confidence. When we get past the half-way line there's not much movement, and there aren't enough people wanting the ball. Players should want it even when they shouldn't be given it. But if Kenny gets the ball there's no one dropping off for him to get it to, so there's nothing on for him. The rest are saying, 'Go on Kenny, knock it up there and we'll compete for it up there.' We've got to have more people wanting the ball. I've tried going back to get the ball, to make myself available, but when I do that no one goes forward in my place, no one for me to hit to. I want to get more involved in build-ups, to go at players and play one-twos, but there's no one for me to play one-twos with when I drop deep.

Our midfield tend to drop back a long way anyway, perhaps because we worry about their midfield too much. You have to do that to some extent when you are defending, but we tend to have our defence and midfield very close, then a gap between midfield and whoever is playing up front.

Of course Don has a reputation for being defensive as a coach, and he doesn't like giving goals away: no one does. Cloughie didn't. Michels didn't. Weisweiler didn't, although he was more adventurous, and was happy to win 5–4 as long as we won. But all top coaches base everything on not giving a goal away. We never gave goals away at Forest, but the difference was we used to score a lot.

Most teams can defend if they set about it like the Greeks. If you are well organized you are going to be hard to break down. But to actually go and score goals is difficult. You need to be good to create and score goals, and we are probably not good enough to go and get them. And that's not really down to Don.

Where I would question Don is that he is a bit overpowering for the young players, which I hadn't expected from how he is with England. Perhaps that's because he isn't with England on a day-to-day basis and because he has got better players. But at the club he is so caught up in the game that he wants to play it for you, and I think that affects the young players. I don't know what I'm doing now, and if he can get me a little bit muddled, I think it must be worse for the less experienced lads.

He is right in a lot of the things he says. If I'm wide around the box with a defender on me, after being in Germany for three years, I tend to go and get it to feet. He tells me to check off for a ball over the top, which is good advice, except I don't think we've the players with the craft to see it and play the ball quickly enough. If he'd got Glenn Hoddle there, it would be a different matter, but if we had got that type of player in the team I think I would realize that anyway and would go looking for it.

Effectively that was the end of Tony's season. He carried on having treatment for his groin strain, but he was unable to play in either of Arsenal's two remaining games, nor join the England squad. Instead he went as a passenger on the Arsenal tour of Burma and Malaysia as part of an extended holiday – his first summer break for two years, with swimming and tennis his main sporting activities. His most demanding task in that period was to act as studio expert during the Northern Ireland v England match on 28 May. That diary entry is also used to make some further comments on the position of English football.

116

28 MAY

Northern Ireland 0 England 0

It is difficult, being a member of the squad, to sit on TV and criticize individual players. You really can't, so I had to concentrate on the performance. It was a terrible game. I don't know whether the players were tired at the end of a long season, but there was just no sparkle – and so many mistakes.

Perhaps England were working to instructions to get the ball forward early, but you've got such good players in there you don't want it hammered forward for them to chase. They want it to feet, and we never did that. Against teams like Ireland you want to play it around and get them chasing the ball for a bit to take some of the fire out of them. And the most alarming thing is that we didn't create many chances over ninety minutes.

The formation seemed misguided to me anyway. If Bobby Robson is going to play with one player tucked in behind the front two, which I think is quite a good formation, he shouldn't use Luther in there. Luther is the one player who doesn't want it to feet; he wants to chase balls knocked forward. I'd like to play there myself – I think I could do it quite well – but with the players last night it would have made much more sense to play Luther up front and slot Trevor Francis in behind. Trevor drifts back there half the time anyway, so you end up with two:one instead of one:two, which defeats the whole object. You can rotate it, but that wasn't really happening.

It was difficult to see what we were aiming for. I spoke to Trevor on the phone and he said Butch Wilkins was brilliant in training, but he wasn't even on the bench. Instead Robson said it was Glenn's chance. I wonder if it was. Glenn was by-passed a lot last night, he wasn't really in the game. You could play him in behind the front two. But if you play him there you have got to give him a lot of the ball, so there won't be a lot of high balls going into the box for your strikers. You want him there to play balls in to feet, and play defence-splitting passes. So you would really then want Trevor and myself as the front pair for him.

In the end though, you have to wonder where we are going. Bobby Robson has had eight games in charge now, and if he had everyone available to him I wonder who he would pick. It is difficult in England; because we have so many games there is little chance of keeping an unchanged team over a period. But if Paul Mariner and I had been fit, I wonder who he would have picked. He has got to pick his team, say, 'I think he is a good player, he is my player,' and leave it at that. We all have individual preferences, but I can't see anything easier than just saying, 'I'm the England manager, and I think that is my best team – that is the one I'm playing and sticking to.' But at the moment, apart probably from Bryan Robson and Peter Shilton, no one is sure of playing. Kenny Sansom was desperate to go to Australia because he is afraid Statham will come in and do well and take his place.

Even more fundamentally, Robson has got to decide how he wants to play the game, and I am not sure that he knows at the moment.

25 JULY

Our first day back. And we went straight into things. We got the photo-call out of the way in the morning. In the afternoon we went to the training ground and had a fitness test. We did exercises and press-ups against the clock just to check how fit we are. It was really hard, everyone pushed themselves to the limit.

We did this small exercise – a twenty-five-yard shuttle. That sounds nothing, but is really quite demanding. From the start line you run out to a five-yard marker and back, then to a ten-yard one, and so on up to twenty-five yards, so the longest run is the last one. You had to do it in thirty-five seconds, then you got seventy seconds rest, then you went again. And if you finished it in under thirty-five seconds you did it again. So if you only did five, you did five, and that was that. But most people were doing ten and really pushing themselves. The object of the whole thing was just to check our starting fitness. We are going to keep doing this range of exercises throughout the season to keep a check on our fitness and how it is improving.

Charlie Nicholas was there. I think because of all the publicity we had wondered what to expect, but he seems a perfectly ordinary footballer, not a bit like the flashy image. He fitted in straight away. Players do. There's rarely any awkwardness coming into a new club. When I joined last year I felt accepted on day one, and I'm sure Charlie felt the same this year.

George Wood wasn't there. He got fed up waiting to get Pat's place, and has joined Crystal Palace. In his place they've signed John Lukic from Leeds. He's played for England Under 21s, so he is regarded as a promising keeper, but our only experience of him was in the Cup last year, and he looked a bit dodgy. I also think it's a bit hard on Rhys Wilmot, because I'm very impressed with him.

Fred Street wasn't there. It seems impossible to think that we won't be seeing him every day. He was part of Arsenal, like Ken Friar or Herbert Chapman or Dennis Hill-Wood, but he has retired and is going to work at a clinic, although he is carrying on with England. Roy Johnson has taken over. He used to work with the reserves. They advertised the post, but have given it to him, which I think most of the lads wanted. I don't think he has got the formal qualifications, but he knows his stuff.

There was this incredible story when Fred retired. I was in Highbury having treatment and he came up to me and said, 'What do you think of this?' It was a bit of paper with an Arsenal F.C. Ltd heading and it said Fred owed Arsenal thirteen pounds as an expenses advance from 1957. Alan Bevan, who did the accounts – he actually retired at the same time as Fred – had given it to him. Evidently when young players came down to King's Cross or Euston, Fred used to meet them off the train and transport them around. And on the day he was leaving, Alan Bevan had given him this slip of paper saying he owed thirteen pounds from fifteen years ago. I thought it was a joke, but no. Fred had put his hand in his pocket and paid the thirteen pounds. He is going to have it framed and put it on his wall. Instead of a gold watch he got a bill.

27 JULY
The shuttles have become harder. We are now having to do twenty, and the time has been cut to thirty-three seconds.

31 JULY
Today we began a trip to Germany with a game against Mappen, an amateur side. It was nice to win, but meaningless. It will be harder later. After the game we went out to Heneff, where we are going to train and be based for a couple of matches against German first division teams, Werder Bremen and Bochum. I knew Heneff quite well, because it is only half an hour from Cologne. It's a sports school out in the woods – the type of place continental clubs often take their players out to; it doesn't happen much in England.

1 AUGUST (Heneff)

This place is unbelievable. There's this hill we have to run up, which we've nick-named Cardiac Hill. It's something like one in three. You go up through trees and it's got steppings like railway sleepers; because it bends, you get some steps which are narrow and some that are wide. You have to check your stride the whole time. And you have to shoot up there. The average time is probably about twenty seconds. I do it in about seventeen, as do one or two of the others, like Kenny. And we have to do that six times.

Coming down you can't walk properly because it is so steep – your legs wobble. You hold on to a tree then stagger to the next, and you feel so knackered. I couldn't believe it until I did it. When you were watching people do it before your turn you knew it was going to be hard, but when you actually did it! But the lads are really giving everything. Everyone was joking and having a laugh about it, but really getting their teeth into it. Running up, the lads coming down would encourage you, yelling, 'Go on Tony, get the best time,' that kind of thing. Nearly everyone was competing against one another, and there was really good fun involved as well. I think everyone is feeling a bit guilty after last year, and determined to put everything in as a result.

2 AUGUST

We have a new captain. Rixy has been asked to do it and has agreed. I think he is a very good choice, not just because we are good friends. He is very outgoing and speaks his mind, and he always says what he thinks in team meetings. David is a quieter type; Rixy has a little more edge to him, so he'll be a better leader on the field. He will take the job very seriously too. When we were on holiday he said he thought it was up to us to set a good example in training. He said we were international players and we had to set an example, that we shouldn't complain if there was hard work to do because that wouldn't help young players like Paul Davis and Chris Whyte. I agreed with him, and the fact he was saying that even before he became captain showed he was thinking along the right lines.

I don't think David will be too disappointed. I think it will do him good, because it means he can just think about playing football, whereas I imagine the extra responsibility will improve Rixy's game.

And at least David didn't have the embarrassment of having his team mates vote for it to be given to someone else. That happened

120

in Cologne when I was there. The players used to get two votes each for who they wanted to be captain every year, a first choice and second choice. Everyone had a vote, right down to the youngest professional of eighteen, who would never actually play with the captain.

Cullmann was the captain when I got there. Then Bonhof was voted in. I think Bonhof was the right man for the job, not just on the field but off it as well, but having been captain for five years it must have concerned Cullmann a little that he was sitting in a room with all his team mates knowing more of them have voted for someone else to do the job. It's much less embarrassing if the trainer comes in and says this is who it's going to be.

The other problem was that people voted for their mates. Toni Schumacher canvassed all his friends to vote for him.

When Michels came he had every player in for a chat with him before the first game. He asked where you liked to play, that sort of thing, and the last question was who do you want as captain. I said I thought he should choose, and he said he normally did. But as he didn't know the players very well, who did I think? And the voting system carried on for a couple of years after that.

3 AUGUST

Cardiac Hill gained its first real victim today. As we have the game tomorrow we had this afternoon off, but we made up for it this morning. First we played football – man-to-man marking, a hard, physical game. Then we had to do six hills. Kenny flew up five times; he got the best times, but at the end of the fifth he collapsed at the top. Roy Johnson went up there and Kenny was just lying there, flat out. He couldn't move his arms or anything. We had to leave him there for what seemed about twenty minutes. We were a little bit worried at first, but he was all right, although he couldn't complete the sixth run.

Sundy has got some sort of problem with his new boots. They are a new style, very high at the back. He has been having a lot of pain; it looks as if they've damaged his achilles tendons, put too much pressure on them and bruised them or something. He is going to miss the game at Bochum.

4 AUGUST

Last night we went into Cologne to watch them play Grasshoppers. I sorted out the tickets, and before the game I went in to see the players. There are big problems there. The relationship between Michels and Schumacher is even worse than when I was there. Schumacher is saying, 'Michels must go; the President must go; the players must go.' He is extraordinary. There is a lot of unrest in the camp and it showed on the field. They won 2–0, but there was no confidence, and they weren't working for one another – although that was usual anyway.

The game was boring, and it gave Don a lot of ammunition which he used this morning. 'Who would have wanted to pay to watch that? Square football is out. You've got to entertain the crowd, play the ball forward.'

Toni Schumacher is a showman. He is too much sometimes. Everything happened for him very quickly. He went from being Cologne's number two keeper to the national team goalkeeper in a short time. All the fans loved him because he was a bit of a showman, and it went to his head. When I first went there I used to say that Peter Shilton and Clem were the two best goalkeepers in the world, and throughout the three years he would say, 'Shilton and Clem? Schumacher is number one!'

He was captain for a while, and he was a bit full of himself. He is a bit of a flier, a bit of a loud mouth. And when he was captain and we had a bad game he would say things to the papers about his colleagues. When we played Ipswich and lost in the UEFA Cup we didn't do well. I was marking Mick Mills! They told me to mark Mick Mills, so as you can imagine I was really buzzing before the game. 'You stop Mick Mills getting forward!' That was really inspiring that was. After the game Schumacher said to the papers that they should sell me because I didn't fit in with Cologne, they could get three million Deutschmarks. And he slagged everyone. 'Dieter Müller? You can forget him, he should be out of the team. Play Schumacher centre-forward!' 'Bonhof? Too old,' and so on and so on and you had to go training with him the next day.

I had a few arguments with him while I was there. My first one was quite satisfying, because I knew then I could speak German. It was after a game when we had been under pressure; and most goalkeepers in that situation when they get the ball will hold it for a moment and say, 'Let's calm down.' But Toni got it and just tossed

122

it straight out, and they would knock it back in, so we were still under pressure. And he tossed one up front and because I had about three defenders on me, they robbed me and put it straight back in. So he came into the dressing room and said to me, 'Fight for the ball.' I went mad. 'You must be stupid. When you've got it you've got to hold on to it, give us some breathing time. What do you want me to do against three defenders? You are the only goalkeeper in the world who does that.' And he sat there for about five minutes listening as I went for him. The rest of the lads couldn't believe it. Berndt Cullman pulled me off him and said, 'Calm down.' So when we got onto the coach to go back to the training ground after the match I said to Cullman, 'Did you understand all that, then?' He said, 'Oh, yes. It was great!'

That really chuffed me, because I had let fly with this great storm of German and I thought, 'Tell you what, my German is really coming on now.' Another time we had a row in the tunnel at half-time. We were playing Duisburg, and I had made 1,000 positions in the first half, I was everywhere, but they wouldn't give me the ball. And going off at half-time Schumacher said I had not been chasing and said, 'Get running around.' So I said something back to him and he pushed me. I wasn't happy, but I thought I'd better not argue with him there. But he didn't speak to me after that for two days. He was such a big name, or personality, that a lot of players in the club wouldn't say anything to him if he did anything wrong. They would say, 'Oh, he's wrong', but they wouldn't say anything to his face because he would shout them down.

After a couple of days I thought, 'Flip, I'm not having this', so when he came in in the morning I said, 'We've got to talk about Saturday. We can't go on like this,' and we sorted it out. But if I hadn't taken the initiative it could have gone on much longer. It was like that in Cologne. When players had a grudge against someone it took them a long time to come round. Schumacher did do some stupid things. When Karl-Heinz Heddergott was trainer there was a lot of unrest. The crowd used to shout, 'Heddergott Out', that sort of thing. At the time there was talk about Cologne selling both me and Schuster, and there was a big banner in the crowd saying, 'Heddergott must go then Woodcock and Schuster will stay', because they thought we had something against Heddergott. Schuster had, but I hadn't.

At this one game there wasn't a big crowd, and the fans from Cologne's equivalent of the North Bank or the Stretford End moved round to behind the trainer's bench, all shouting, 'Heddergott Out! Heddergott Out!' Then for a bit of variety they shouted, 'Toni, give us a wave', and he waved to them – which, as they were there abusing the trainer, was not very thoughtful of him to say the least.

The incident during the World Cup just about summed him up. When he flattened Battistan even the Germans turned against him. I've been told – although I can't vouch for it – that he was on TV last season, and they asked him about the foul. And he said, 'I'm a professional, blah, blah, blah', so they said, 'Well, you know you knocked his teeth out don't you?' and he pulled this wad of D-marks out and said, 'Well, I'll buy him a new set of teeth. I'll pay for him to go to the dentist.'

He may have quietened down a bit since then, but before that he was a bit strong. He was a big name in Germany, on TV every other week doing long interviews. Because of his personality everyone wanted to know him, and he really did think he was number one and acted accordingly.

We always had a lot of people watching training in Cologne and he would usually put on a show for them. He was very agile, and trained very hard. And he was very competitive in training, he would come sliding into you. But having gone there and thinking originally, 'He can't play', by the time I left I had changed my mind.

There is an English prejudice. You see the ball fly into the net and because it is a German goalkeeper you think, 'I couldn't see Shilton or Jennings letting that in.' But then you see him make a great save, and you think, 'What a great save that is.' And if you see the highlights of English football on TV, you see the English goalkeepers always making mistakes, because they show the goals like we do in our short clips. So the Germans could not understand how I could say Shilton and Clemence were the best when every time they saw them on TV in Germany they'd be dropping a ricket – like in the League Cup Final where Andy Gray got that goal against Shilts, or the Bonhof free kick against Clem. And that was all they remembered, those little slip-ups, although I think after the World Cup they rated Shilton pretty highly.

The goalkeeping requirements there are slightly different. I remember someone saying in Germany that they thought Jimmy Rimmer would do well for Villa in the European Cup because he was a tremendous shot stopper. In Germany there aren't many high balls coming into the box, so the goalie doesn't have to come out and collect them. Instead there are more people coming at you with one-twos and shots. So you don't have to be good at catching the ball, you have to be good at stopping shots, and they think that continental goalkeepers have the edge in that regard.

Schumacher, though, was a great one for charging out of his area and trying to dribble round whoever was coming in if he got there first. He tried that a couple of times. Once he lost it and we were fortunate not to have a goal scored against us by being a bit too flash. And he also liked to fly around and tip the ball all over the place.

Coming from playing with Peter Shilton at Forest I was prejudiced about that initially because Shilts was so correct in everything, even in training, while Schumacher was really unorthodox, and so I thought, 'He is not as good.' But at the end of the day what it boils down to is whether he stops it going into the net, and if he does that it doesn't matter how he stops it. If he gets his body in the way, that's fine. And he was an excellent shot stopper. He was as brave as anything. He'd get his body in, he'd dive in feet first or head first, and as long as he kept it out of the net that was good enough for me, it didn't matter whether he did it with style or not. And he had some fine games for us. I wouldn't want to have to choose between him, Pat and Shilts.

5 AUGUST
Bochum 1 Arsenal 1
We played really well, it was very encouraging. It was our first real test, while they'd had about a dozen games, so we ran out of steam a bit in the second half. That's why they got a draw. But in the first half we put them under a lot of pressure and their goalkeeper did well for them.

Our new approach worked well for us I thought. We were really together as a group, and we just wouldn't allow them to settle. If they played a ball to one of their team mates a red shirt would be there, bang! And if it got played again there would be another one there immediately. We were winning the ball in their half and creating chances.

The crowd appreciated it too. We were applauded off the field at the end.

The only worrying thing so far is the injuries. David O'Leary went off at half-time with a foot injury. He thinks it might be because of his new boots, the same as Sundy. More seriously Peter Nicholas was taken to hospital. He got this knock on the leg the other day, and didn't think anything of it, but next day it was swollen. He got caught again this evening and was rushed to hospital. They think it might be a cracked bone.

7 AUGUST

After the game at Bochum Terry got onto the coach and said, 'Right, you are off until Sunday lunchtime.' The sports centre was virtually closing down over the weekend. So we had all day Saturday and this morning free. We went into Cologne in the afternoon for a bit of shopping, then we had a really good night out. Six or seven of us went to a friend of mine's restaurant, then on to a nightclub. I think it was good judgement on his part. He knew we would have a few beers, but he also knew how hard we had been working, and obviously thought we had earned it. And because we had been putting it in, I think if he had said, 'Right you can go out to a club for a couple of hours, but there's a curfew,' it wouldn't have gone down too well.

They said Nicho hasn't got a fracture which is good news, but he is in some pain.

9 AUGUST
Werder Bremen 2 Arsenal 0
In spite of the result we were really quite pleased. They came second in the Bundesliga on goal average last year, so they are a good team, and we should have been three up at half-time. I missed one, Brian Talbot had virtually an open goal, and Charlie missed one. Then in the second half we ran out of steam again – they've played a lot of games already – and they took over. John Lukic came on for Pat in the second half and he did quite well.

Don had a go at Charlie for hanging on to the ball too long – there were a couple of occasions when he could have slipped me in. But I think it will come. He's obviously a good player.

10 AUGUST
Don has changed our approach this year. He admits it himself. He says he has had a long think about it, and that probably over the

last couple of years we've been playing too much football – too many square passes and too much possession. He wants to do that sometimes when we need a breather, but the whole emphasis is to be on going forward. Virtually from our first day back he's been stressing that whenever it's on, the ball must be played forward quickly.

The other thing – or complementary to that – is that when it has been a bad pass to a forward, say into the corner of the penalty box, we have to get after it and the whole team has to press up, not just forwards. We've got to press them in and win the ball back in the last third of the field. We have been watching a lot of films of Liverpool, and when they are playing at their best that is what they do. And the amount of goals that are scored that way is incredible. Don has been throwing a lot of statistics at us to prove that theory, and a lot of film supporting it; things from the World Cup, which showed that most goals are scored from three or four passes, not eight or nine.

It's the Watford method, but Don wants us to be a bit more sophisticated than that, to do it a bit more like Liverpool, because he thinks they have got good players. He says they don't just toss it forward like Watford, but *play* it forward.

As soon as we landed Terry and Don shot straight into London. So we think there must be a signing on the way. When Fred Street was the physio you could always tell. He'd turn up at Highbury in a suit, so you immediately guessed he was going to the hospital for a medical. You hear things on the grapevine.

13 AUGUST
Aberdeen 0 Arsenal 1

Now that really was satisfying, to beat the European Cup Winners Cup holders on their own ground, especially as they've played eight games already and this was only our third. A good return to Scotland for Charlie – the crowd were giving him some stick, but he had the last laugh.

It was quite an open end-to-end game, but we really played well. The application was excellent, and the defence is looking much tighter even without David O'Leary.

It's too early to tell too much about how we will do as a pair at the front, because we haven't played any home games yet, and so we are always battling and chasing and closing people down and hitting them on the break. It's when we play teams at home and can put them under sustained pressure that it will start to happen; when you have got teams penned in, partnerships work on the edge of the box. But I can't see there being any problem.

We are playing with three up front at the moment, and are creating a lot of chances, getting a lot of shots in, which is always a good sign. Last year we never knew where the next goal was coming from. It was always a scramble or a cross which someone would put in out of the blue. This year when people get in certain areas we know what they are going to do. It's going to be whipped in hard, crossed at the earliest opportunity.

The crowd were shouting 'Chocolate Charlie' at Charlie. We asked him what it meant afterwards and he said he didn't know. I can only think it's short-hand for that stock Jock phrase for being conceited – 'If he was chocolate he'd eat himself.' But that's unfair. Whatever the press makes you think Charlie just isn't like that. He's really fitting in and working very hard for the team like everybody else.

15 AUGUST

I hear on the grapevine that we are trying to sign Butch Wilkins. What an asset he would be.

16 AUGUST

My groin is reacting a bit to playing and training on these hard grounds. I feel a bit stiff the next day. It is not the problem I had last year, I don't think, but I haven't been able to train for a couple of days because it really stiffened up after going to Aberdeen.

London Colney is bone hard at the moment, so I've been playing in rubber studs on the pitches, and running in flats on concrete. I suppose you've got to expect some reaction after not doing anything for three months, and I feel as if the old trouble has cleared up. As far as running and training go I've been really pleased. And when the weather eases up and we get some rain it will be all right. The start of the season won't be a problem anyway because the grounds will be watered.

Sundy has started full training. He's missed all the pre-season games so far, and he obviously won't be playing at Portsmouth on Saturday.

They signed another forward yesterday: Ian Allinson from Colchester. They've got him on a free transfer because of a technicality over contracts, so if he comes off he comes off, and if he doesn't they haven't lost anything.

People keep on saying that Lee Chapman will go, but he is a one hundred per cent better player this year. You can see it in training. He is a much better player now than when they signed him. His touch is much better, he can control the ball. He lays it off well, whereas last year he couldn't control it. We tell him that. Lee says it's because last year he didn't have a good pre-season. He was in dispute with Stoke, so he never really got going until the season was here. And if you don't put it in then it is difficult to make up for it. But I'm sure every player at Highbury would say he has improved, and he has been scoring goals.

And with the strikers we've got at Highbury, we haven't got one who will win a high ball if it's tossed in. So if we are having a bad time he would be another option. You could always bring Lee on and say, 'We'll change it, start tossing the ball up for him to win it', and we will pick the ball up off him.

Sundy's injury has given Brian McDermott a chance. In training he is very confident, he looks a very good player. In the first team he is just lacking something, and maybe it is confidence. But if he is given a chance when the serious stuff begins he could hold on to it, because he is a good crosser of the ball, he can get a cross in out of nothing. And he'll stick to the wings. If Sundy comes back in we'll have to take it in turns to go out there. The idea is that Kenny and Rixy will take the left; I'll play up front in the middle with Charlie; and Sundy will be pushed wide on the right. But he is not keen on that.

Several of the lads have remarked that Don has really got his enthusiasm back. Last year with the World Cup Finals it had been twelve months football, and I think it affected both him and us. Before pre-season last year he asked the lads who had been at the

World Cup, 'How do you feel? Do you think we ought to slacken off a bit?' and on some training sessions he sent us in before the rest. That was fine at the time, but thinking back perhaps we should have done everything. It might have been better to have had a few days off, but when we were training we should have done everything they did.

This year we have had a long break, and we've come back refreshed. It was the longest break I've had for six or seven years, and I can't wait to play. It's been really hard this summer, but everybody has responded really well, whereas last year, although we didn't realize it at the time, we'd say, 'Oh, God, we've got to go running up this hill', or 'This is going to be hard, we don't fancy this.' Everyone has buckled down now and really put it in. And when some players have finished they'll stay and encourage the others to push through.

We've worked hard every morning, then, when the work is over, played football. This week we've been in morning and afternoon every day – in fact apart from the weekend in Germany we haven't had a break. But Don has kept everything running along smoothly, we haven't been getting bored because he has been changing things – it's been a really good pre-season. People like Rixy and Sundy who were around then have said that the training is back to what it was when they had that run of Cup Final appearances.

The whole atmosphere in the club is buzzing. It is different from last year. We had three major signings then so that kept things bubbling along, but this year it is as if the players feel we are all in this together. I think we are very disappointed with last year and determined to put it right. Last season was probably the best thing that could have happened to us, because everyone is determined not to let it happen again. Our attitude has definitely changed. We were a bit out of order last season, we just thought we could go out there and turn it on when we wanted, we didn't really bother that much. We realize now we can't do that.

We do think we can beat everyone though, hold our own with the best, provided we get the consistency and application which wasn't always there last year. I include myself in that. Looking back I didn't always apply myself properly, didn't always give everything I'd got because of the way things were going. This year I think it will be there every time.

You can see the results of the new attitude in the games we've played so far. We are much closer together, working for each other much more now. I think last year there was a bit of a tendency to go out and look after ourselves, where this year we are more compact, more of a unit. I'm convinced of it.

Our whole attitude to playing has changed. It keeps being drilled into us that we have a responsibility to entertain the public and bring them back into the grounds. And even in friendly matches where people have come to pay money to watch we have got to go out there and give one hundred per cent.

This year we are beginning to have the makings of a squad. They talk about getting a right-back and a centre-half, and if they do that and get Butch Wilkins too, we will really be in business. It would be nice if we were all internationals, but at least the competition is going to be there. In the forward spots already no one can be guaranteed a place. Last year when Sundy and I were both injured we were struggling to put out a forward line, but this year Charlie, Sundy, Ally, Lee, Brian McDermott and Raphael Meade and I are all competing for the striking positions. Just being a big money signing is not going to be enough, you will still have to go out and do it, because there will be people in the reserves who are challenging, which is the way it should be. Last year that was never the case. I probably knew that if I played badly I would still be in the team every week.

That competition has carried over into training too. If Don sees you aren't giving everything he has a go at you. He's had a go at me, at Charlie, at Graham Rix, which is right, because if the younger players see him have a go at us they know they have to put it in.

Don has been on John Lukic's back, really training him hard, putting him under pressure, moaning at him. John's never known training like it: the cross-countries when we first started, the running up Cardiac Hill. He never imagined it could be so hard. But he knows it's for his own good. He has been a bit shaky in training sometimes, but in the games in Germany when he came on he did well.

18 AUGUST

Nothing is being left to chance. We went over to Brentford to a sports clinic for a series of fitness and health tests. They took tests on our heart and lungs. We also had a questionnaire with about 200 questions on it – a kind of personality test, and they divided us into different physical types. Say I was an explosive player and should do sharp stuff to reach peak fitness. If I do a forty-yard sprint I can reproduce it twenty seconds later at the same pace, but I can't run up and down the pitch four times on the trot, while other players who have greater endurance do that.

One of the most interesting things was that different people needed different activities after games, depending on the amount of lactic acid they build up during a game. Some just need to relax to build up for the next game; and the way to get rid of it is by just doing light work, jogging or just a warm-up, rather than keeping it in your body for the next training session. Funnily enough, while we were in Germany I saw that Hamburg are doing that, and I know the West German squad did it before the World Cup.

We've started doing very long warm-ups after games, jogging round the pitch and walking for about fifteen or twenty minutes, and I've felt better doing that than the normal Monday morning warm-up. Don went to see the first leg of the Brazilian Cup Final, and the next day the team did a cross-country run. They weren't under any pressure, it was just a three- or five-mile run to get all the acid out of them; it's supposed to get rid of the stiffness.

19 AUGUST

Carole and Gill Rix are planning a party for all the wives and girlfriends for the first day of the season to try and build a bit more togetherness. They used to do it at Cologne – the President's wife would invite all the players' wives, and they would go and meet the wife of the first President, Herr Kremer, who really built the club.

I think Carole was initially a bit worried about how it would be received, but Don came up to me today and said he thought it was a brilliant idea, and that they should have thought of it years ago.

20 AUGUST
Portsmouth 2 Arsenal 1

That was a bit of a set-back. We had enough chances to have won, but we weren't quite sharp enough. I've never done well in pre-season as far as goalscoring goes. And I've only got one this time – although I've had a lot of bad luck. But it doesn't worry me. I know

I'm virtually guaranteed to score next Saturday, because I'm really looking forward to it.

The defence was a bit less convincing yesterday. It was the first time anyone had really got at us, because we have been so compact as a team. We were so tigerish in the tackle in midfield and even up front that we just weren't letting teams settle. But Chrissy Whyte got the blame for both goals yesterday.

Afterwards Don kept to his main tack. He had a go at midfield, said they weren't getting the ball forward quickly enough. And they were picking the ball up and running with it and the space was getting tighter and tighter all the time. They'd finish trying to poke a five-yard ball in, which was not very good. Don said, 'As soon as you get it, the first thought is "Can I hit the forwards?" ' But I wonder after last year whether we've gone to the other extreme in a way, and sometimes we are trying to force it, trying to pick players out when we shouldn't do. We won the ball back in their half on quite a few occasions. But because we did want to get it forward quickly, players were rushed. Rixy was so anxious to put it in someone's path he rushed it a couple of times. Pre-season that's not a bad sign, because it means everyone is thinking of going forward, and that can only be good for Charlie and myself, but once we settle down and start playing I'm hoping we can say, 'That's not on, so now we've got to play it square', rather than trying to force things.

I had a drink with Pat this evening. He's retiring this season. He says that after games and the next morning he has aches and pains, and they just aren't clearing up now. He's had an achilles injury for some while, and he still feels the groin injury he got against Tottenham two years ago. He just can't get rid of it; he said it was really sore. He's playing in Bill Nicholson's testimonial tomorrow and he said he wouldn't be able to kick the ball, he'd have to throw it out. Obviously he knows better than anyone how he feels, but he still looks good.

21 AUGUST

A couple of papers have gone really over the top this morning about yesterday. We didn't do as well as we can, but calling us flops and saying we will finish about half-way up the table is just ridiculous. We are so confident, and so eager to prove people wrong after last year that we've been talking about putting a bet on ourselves to win the League. *That's* how confident we are. We are so much together as a squad – which we weren't last year – that we are thinking of putting in five pounds each and backing ourselves. I won't say we will walk away with it, but we have a fair chance if we keep putting it in as we are at the moment.

Everyone thinks they are going to see the same old team, but I think they are going to see such a difference. Last year I thought we were going to do well, but I was completely wrong, yet I'm sure everyone will see a change this year. I think we were unfairly criticized last season at times. Some games we played some extremely good football, some really good attacking football at that, and the ball just didn't go in the net three times, so they said we were boring – and that's a load of rubbish. But that is the way it is with Arsenal. If we don't win 4–0 and turn it on, people say we've given a bad performance. Even after the Aberdeen game, which was a great result for us, we didn't get the credit we deserved. Mike Langley in the *People* admitted we'd deserved our win, but then said, 'Aberdeen looked short of match practice', and they'd played eight games and it was our third. I think we deserved more credit than that. I really believe we will do well.

There certainly can't be anyone fitter than us in the first division, so we hope we'll be able to steam-roller people: we'll wear them down if we can't do anything else.

It said in the paper this morning that we are looking at the Blackpool right-back. We do need a right-back, but Butch Wilkins is the player we really need. I think he would fit into our style of play, because he can pass the ball. We want to get forward quickly but we are rushing it, and we need someone who can make the controlled forward pass, someone who can switch the play. Rixy is playing on the left now, which I think is his best position, and if we can get someone who can supply him, and switch the ball from right to left it will really help.

I hope we get Wilkins. My source tells me it is just a question of haggling over money at the moment as United have said he can go. If it's that, I think we should pay the extra £100,000 before United change their minds. Everyone says he had a great game in the Charity Shield; and the sooner we get him fitted into the team the better.

23 AUGUST

At Arsenal they don't think I pass now. I said to Rixy today, 'If they don't think I passed last season, wait until they see me this year. I'm hitting everything.' This year the slightest half chance I get of a strike on goal I'm going to hit it. I was influenced a little by watching the last few games of the season. I was amazed, watching them, because from twenty to twenty-five yards out people weren't having a go. I was probably guilty myself on a few occasions too; I was laying them off or teeing them up for other people, but watching from the stand I thought, 'That's worth a shot', particularly with those Tango balls which fly in.

People say we don't have the finishers that Germany and Italy produce. We do. You see them in snippets on TV, and it is, 'Cor, what a fantastic goal', but you probably don't see the ones which are missed. And if you do, sometimes you'll see them try a shot from thirty-five to forty yards, and if it rolls to the keeper or flies over the bar the commentator doesn't say a word. But if it was an English player trying it they'd say something like, 'That's a bit ambitious', with the tone of voice telling you that they really mean, 'What an idiot for trying that.'

When I was in Germany I was encouraged to shoot from anywhere, from any angle, because it didn't matter who was in goal, there was a chance it might go in. And this season I'm turning on everything and hitting it as soon as I get it. A lot of it comes down to confidence and how the game is going, but I'm going to be a bit more selfish, because I can do it. In training I can connect well with both feet whatever the height or bounce. Even getting a bad bounce I can score from thirty-five yards in training. And in a match it only takes one to go in. So I'm going to shoot. I've told Charlie I'm going to let him do all the running around and getting up there and nodding them down for me when the crosses come flying in.

Charlie is already expected to score twenty goals this year, just because he got fifty in Scotland last: that's ridiculous. If he gets twenty he will have done brilliantly. It is a lot of pressure. When I joined, they didn't know what was going to happen or how many I was going to get, because no one knew how many I had scored in Germany.

Trevor Francis said when he came back for the Greece game, 'We don't take goals seriously enough in this country. We don't realize what a good thing it is when the ball goes in the net. In Italy it is

135

great if someone scores a goal. Here it's, "Okay, that's what he is there for".' I think he is right. In Germany they appreciated it, but managers and coaches here just take scoring for granted.

24 AUGUST

Our pre-season has been really excellent. We've worked hard, really hard, but it has been done to put power in, not training to make you sick. Some people say the training isn't hard enough if you aren't throwing up. But Don has done all this research, and come up with the news that if you can get 4,000 odd yards covered in forty or forty-five minutes that is best for your body, and that's really what we've done.

Every morning we have played football, which finds you out quicker than anything when you are not fit. It really tires you out. Passing the ball, stops and starts and turns, all the little things which happen in games are tiring. Then in the afternoon we have had the physical stuff. But it hasn't been 'run up here, run up there', it's been thirty to forty-five minutes' maximum effort. Because you knew that in half an hour you were going to be relaxing in the bath, you would push yourself to the limit. After that you would be tired, but your recovery rate was quick. Fifteen minutes later you were fully recovered and felt you could do it all again. It was really hard but good.

25 AUGUST

We have decided to cut down on our night-clubbing. We had a get-together today and decided we were a little bit out of order last year. We used to go out a lot as a bunch. If we went to a function we'd always end up at a nightclub, generally Stringfellows.

So we said, 'Look, we'll have a night out now and again, but not like last year.' I think we all realized it. We didn't get blind drunk, but we were out a lot and we thought it wasn't right, so we will cut it down a lot this year.

At Forest, because we were winning things, the social life among the team was very good. Eight or ten of us would have lunch together at least once a week, either after training, or on a Thursday, particularly when we had played Wednesday night. Then we'd have a couple of drinks after the game and say, 'Okay, we'll meet for

136

lunch tomorrow.' We'd go to a wine bar and have a couple of bottles of wine.

Everybody was really together. And if there was a special night, if anybody was doing a charity show or anything like that, all the lads would be there in force to give him support. It was lovely. But success breeds that togetherness. When I went to Cologne it wasn't there. There was a tradition that at the beginning of a season if there were new players you all went out to a restaurant and the new players – or any who had been there under two years – footed the bill. So we all went to this restaurant and had a smashing meal. There were about ten of us sharing the bill, so it didn't work out too expensive. But we finished the meal about 10.30, and I assumed we would all be going on to a disco or nightclub. But it was, 'Okay. Thanks very much, see you tomorrow. Cheers.' And that was it. I got home about 11 o'clock. Carole couldn't believe it. 'What's happened here? Are you all right?' 'Oh,' I said, 'they've all gone home.'

The social life was very different. We didn't go to the theatre or cinema like we do in London. We used to meet players and their wives occasionally. We used to go out with Rainer Bonhof and his girlfriend and René Botteron and his girl on Saturday nights, because René had been in Switzerland and Rainer in Spain and they were used to it. René found the fact that there was little social contact very strange, so that was why the six of us went out together. We tried to expand it, but after a while even that seemed to tail off. And there wasn't any, 'Let's go for a coffee', or nipping down to the pub after training. I missed all that.

26 AUGUST

All the publicity Charlie is getting could be counter-productive. I can't believe some of the things I read about him. I know the press are trying to build him up, because with the way football is played at the moment, there aren't many personalities about, and they are trying to make him one. Charlie is a good player, but all the stuff they are writing is incredible. And if he has a bad season, they are going to blame all his activities outside football and all the publicity for it. I think the message has got through to him too, because he said today that he thinks he has been involved in some silly stunts, and that he is not going to be any more.

The anticipation and excitement have been building up all week.

I am determined to make a good start, to claim a place in the England team, to do so well that Robson can't leave me out. I want to be England's number one striker from now until the European Championships. I think I've done enough to be given that chance in the next game, but quite honestly I don't think he thinks so at the moment. It looks like he has chosen Trevor Francis. Even when we played well without Trevor he was saying, 'Well, I've got Trevor coming back.' So it looks like there is one place up for grabs. I think I should have it. Just on past record I think I should be given the chance to hold on to it. I've played four games under him, and got four goals, yet these seem to be taken for granted.

That makes me a little angry, because they discovered in Australia how difficult it is to score goals even against bad teams. I'm sure if I had gone I'd have scored goals. But when anyone's looked back to that tour it's been, 'We didn't have Robson or Hoddle or Withe or Mariner', but no one's said, 'We didn't have Woodcock.' There was a piece in one of the papers a couple of weeks ago about the failures of English forwards to score goals in the international team. It went through Francis, Withe, Mariner, etc. – how many games they had played and how many goals they had got. Although my goals to games ratio is good I never got a mention. I've got twenty-eight caps, and six or eight were for coming on as sub, yet I've got eleven goals, and that's with never having a real run in the team. I got twenty-one goals for Arsenal last year, and that was when I was not having a particularly good time, still re-adjusting to English football, and at a new club which wasn't doing particularly well. People talk about Frank Stapleton, say what a good player he is, what a good centre-forward. And he is, I'm only using him as an example, because he is the player everyone holds up as the best, and because he used to be at Arsenal. But he didn't score that many goals for Manchester United, who are in the top three, play more attacking football and score more goals than Arsenal do.

Things like that really get to me. I know I can live with the best. I was playing for one of the top few teams in Germany when they won the European Championship and reached the World Cup Final – so I was playing with the cream. I came back to England, never get a mention and I'm struggling to get in the team.

It's difficult when you are away – for some of us anyway. When I went abroad Kevin Keegan was playing regularly and Trevor was in and out, so I was coming back and getting the odd game and doing well but then dropping out again. Whereas Kevin, when he was abroad, came back and went straight into the team. He was 'Captain of England' so he knew he didn't have to fight for his place. He played well too, and everyone said, 'What a good player he is now he's in Germany.' The same thing is happening now with Trevor. He's coming back from Italy, he's had a couple of good games for England and they are saying, 'Francis is a much better player now he is in Italy', yet with his injuries he played only half a season over there. While I came back, got the odd showing now and again, and was left out again.

A lot of people say we've got to learn from the Europeans. Well, I think my game has changed from playing in Europe. As I've mentioned, Weisweiler always said to me, 'You are not an English player, you are a continental footballer.'

Obviously I think I am the best man for the job: everyone should think that. But since coming back and getting two or three games under my belt and getting goals as well as doing reasonably well, I think I should be given an extended run. Even if I'm not involved or having a poor game I'm still confident that if a chance comes along I'll put it away. In that Greece game the tactics were completely wrong and it was a bad team performance, but I still thought Bobby Robson should have left me on on the grounds that if a chance did come along I was the most likely to put it away. But he obviously didn't see it like that. I don't know what his thinking is. We are at the stage anyway where he has got to make his mind up, and say, 'These are my two strikers.' Obviously I think I should be one, although I'd happily play behind the front two as Luther did at the end of the season, if that was the only way to get in. But Robson has to decide now whether it is 'Francis and Woodcock' or 'Francis and Mariner' or 'Woodcock and Mariner'. He's also got to decide what tactics he wants to use. If he plays me and Trevor there is no point in tossing in high balls from the back – although I don't think you could win a major competition playing that way anyway.

This season I'm going to train hard, I'm really going out to make the position my own. If my game is on, there's no way they can leave me out. I just wish they would show a little confidence in me. He could have mentioned my name a few times. He could have said I was in possession of the shirt. Against Greece it shouldn't have mattered if I'd had a terrible game, I should have stayed on because of the three previous performances. Trevor has a bad game and he stays on – like he did against Greece.

Klaus Fischer had this spell when he wasn't scoring any goals in the league. He was having a terrible time. But he was the German centre-forward. And because Germany were a good team and were playing well he was putting the ball in the back of the net, because the manager had said, 'He is my centre-forward.' In Germany you rarely got all the demands for changes you get here. It was never, 'He had a bad game, get someone else in.' You knew what the team was, it rarely changed. If Fischer had a bad game and was substituted, he was still back in the team for the next game. Whereas here, apart from Trevor, it doesn't seem to work like that. No one can have any confidence that he is going to be playing. And this whole thing about England going to Australia looking for new forwards – we don't need to be looking for new forwards. Mariner, Francis, Peter Withe and I are all good enough to play international football. But the press are always trying to find someone else, and I sometimes think that influences the manager.

I told Kenny I was certain to score tomorrow. I've never done well in pre-season, not because I don't want to, but because there isn't that extra excitement there. Those games are just to get your fitness. Kenny said he's going to get five goals this season. We've had a bet on it. I've told him he has got no chance. But if he and David O'Leary could get a dozen or so between them – and with their ability they should – it would make so much difference to us.

27 AUGUST
Arsenal 2 Luton 1

I said I'd score. We are definitely on our way. We played really well, and even after we gave them an equalizer with a silly own goal, we came back and got on top again. The last ten minutes we could easily have got a couple more we were so on top. So we have got the start we wanted. And Luton aren't a bad team. I got the first goal. Charlie stumbled through a couple of tackles. It looked like he should have had a foul, but Paul Davis picked it up and did really well. He got into the box, faked to cross, then beat his man and took it on and crossed. It was a great ball but a difficult one because it was bending all the time. I was quite surprised when it just dropped down and I nipped in front of one of the defenders.

Then we played some really good football until we gave that own goal away – a terrible own goal when you think about it. It had been worked across our box through our bad marking initially. Walsh drew back his foot to shoot from a difficult angle, but before he could kick it Stewart Robson rushed in and hammered it past Pat. Pat was lined up for the shot and all of a sudden it was flying over his head. Why Stewart hit it so hard I'll never know, but that's the sort of player he is, he sometimes has a rush of blood. So that put them back in it just before half-time. But we got another goal when I turned a defender in the box and got brought down. The ref was just about to give a penalty, but it ran to Brian McDermott, and he put it in.

The wives' and girlfriends' party evidently went very well. It carried on after the game when some of us went into the players' room for a drink and joined it.

Football Focus had a profile on Charlie. It was quite funny, because they showed all these pictures of Charlie posing in different clothes. He just put his head in his hands, and all the lads were diving in taking the mickey. He'd be standing there with a leather suit on and some girl hanging around his leg, then they'd flash onto another picture. Everyone cheered every time another picture came up – he was so embarrassed. Ever since we played Aberdeen, if anyone sees a picture of him they say, 'Oh, look. Here's Chocolate Charlie.'

29 AUGUST
Wolves 1 Arsenal 2
We were bursting with confidence and strolled it really. The only surprise was that it took us so long to get our second goal. We lost a goal in the first few minutes – another bad one. But we knew we were going to win. We took the game to them, and we were never in any danger. Wolves were nothing. They must be relegation candidates already, and how they got a point against Liverpool on Saturday I'll never know.

Charlie got both goals. The second was a penalty. After he had scored that he really played well, he was beating people, jinking about.

There was a full page colour picture of Charlie in swimming trunks in this morning's *Daily Star* – ironic coming so soon after his statement about cutting out that sort of thing, although it was obviously taken before then. Sundy came with us and he had it on the coach and asked Charlie to autograph it. On the other side there was a 'Star Bird' so Charlie got some terrible stick all round. Sundy is so sharp as soon as you give him the slightest opening, say anything slightly wrong, he is straight in. Kenny, Rixy and Peter Nicholas dive in too. They are all pretty sharp, but Sundy is undoubtedly the squad leader.

30 AUGUST

I went home to Nottingham after last night's game, with Jon Holmes. I'd one or two things to sort out. I went to see Notts County play Birmingham this evening. Birmingham looked even worse than Wolves. And Notts County aren't as good as us!

31 AUGUST

The club is really buzzing at the moment. We honestly do believe we can do something. On Saturday we go to Southampton, and we are confident we can win there after our first two games. Then next week we've got United and Liverpool at Old Trafford. That will tell us how good we are. If we beat them we'll not only be top but we'll have a lead on them too, and even at this stage of the season to be ahead of them means they've got to make the points up. And Spurs have got off to a bad start – they're already five points behind us.

3 SEPTEMBER
Southampton 1 Arsenal 0
We really went expecting to win. We are so full of confidence at the moment, and at the start we penned them in. We didn't create any chances, but we kept them on the run. Then we slackened off – that old fault appearing again – and we gave away another bad goal: that's three now. This time Rixy lost it in midfield and they went down and scored.

We didn't deserve to lose. We should have had at least a point. It was just one of those things really, one of those results that happen from time to time. But our commitment and people working for each other was there. Charlie didn't have a good game. Don had a go at him afterwards because he didn't think Charlie was putting the effort in.

6 SEPTEMBER
Arsenal 2 Manchester United 3

We got the ideal start against United, an early lead, which should have been just what we needed. Then five minutes later we throw it away: five minutes, when you should be at your strongest. All of a sudden it's a bouncing ball. Someone heads it down, someone is unmarked, and it is in the back of the net. And that has happened countless times in the last twelve months.

United played well, but we want to look at ourselves as well. We've played them a couple of times at Highbury now and they've created quite a few chances. Once they've got a couple of goals they dominate midfield, so you can't really ask any more of them, but you have got to look at the opposition they are playing against. Although we worked hard, we lacked the craft to trouble them. And we also lacked someone to say, 'Come on, let's sort it out,' and get us together to snuff them out that way.

Don said afterwards that we needed someone to get hold of the game, to realize what was happening and push and pull people about. We were working hard, trying to get our foot in, but we weren't doing it very cleverly – we were diving in a bit. So although they played well, it is not the most difficult thing to do when people are diving in. Of course you are desperate to get the ball off Wilkins and Muhren, but if you dive in at them they just play it past you, so you need to be a bit clever.

The service we get is bad. That's a constant forward's complaint, and I've been making it for twelve months now, but it's true. Forwards get enough complaints from midfield players and defenders if they forsake their defensive duties. If you don't chase a full-back straight away when he's got the ball, they are soon complaining. It's, 'Come on, get across, block him out, help us out.' But they sometimes seem to think it doesn't matter what kind of ball they play up to you; they seem to say, 'Get it up there and let them sort it out for themselves.' I had a go at Stewart Robson in the first half and then told him at half-time. He'd get the ball and he'd knock it, but he'd knock it onto your chest when there was a space. Or there would be a defender on your left-hand side, so you'd want the ball on your right, and he'd just knock it anywhere between you – and that's just lack of thought.

The service to us was awful. But having said that, Charlie was a bit subdued. It's no good standing there hoping. You've got to go out and get it and try and make things happen.

I'm sure the partnership will be all right. We've only played two home games together, and until we've played a few home games the partnership won't take off. It's difficult to develop it in away games. A couple of times so far perhaps he should have layed it off to put me into the area, and a couple of times I maybe should have given him the ball, but that will come.

Provided they are good players I don't really mind who I play with. It doesn't have to be a big player. I've played with all different types and it has worked well, and I'm sure Charlie and I will get it together. He is a good player, has got good skills, but I think he has got to be a bit more forceful, put his weight about a bit more than he does at the moment. He's trying to turn players without using his body, trying to go past people just with his skill on the floor alone, and he's being knocked away from the ball.

I still fancy my chances against them at the back if you can take the ball up to them. I got that early goal when Rixy knocked it in behind them and I got free, and I thought that I gave them some problems. In the second half they had Moran stick close to me, they tied him down to one job. But they are vulnerable through the middle if you can get in amongst them, especially if you are sharp and have good control. I think that's the case everywhere. If you get good enough service and the control is there defenders can't do that much to stop you – legally at any rate.

Arthur Graham, signed by United from Leeds, must be the bargain of the season. He looks really good. £40,000! Arsenal have been looking for a right-sided player for ages, he comes along and what happens? . . . he goes to United.

After the match a lot of people said he had given Kenny a chasing, that Kenny had given him too much space and got a run around. I find it difficult to tell how players in other positions are doing unless they are really having an outstanding game, so I wasn't aware of that. And Kenny never looks as if he is having a bad game, because he doesn't get skinned, he never gets left for dead. So even when his opponent starts really producing things like Graham did, Kenny still looks as if he is doing all right. It's only afterwards that you see Graham has made one goal, hit the bar, and generally done well that you think, 'Well, Kenny wasn't quite on his game tonight.' But even then you tend to say, 'Arthur played well', rather than, 'Kenny played badly.'

Frank played well too. Frank had a couple of chances I thought he should have done better with, which was uncharacteristic. I'd like to play alongside him. But then, looking at United as a whole, I'm sure if I was playing there I'd get an awful lot of goals. But Whiteside isn't. Last season at Highbury I said that his main attribute in that last game had been his aggression, but even that seems to have left him now. It might just be confidence. Because when you are confident, on your game, you are excited, bubbling and you will put your foot in because you feel strong. But he has had a lot of criticism, and it might be getting on top of him, especially as he has had a few chances which he missed – so he has probably started to worry about it a little. Whereas before everything was going for him and he was putting his foot in, and his elbow; it just seems to have drained out of him now.

Don had a go about individual mistakes which had cost goals. But basically he said, 'You've all tried hard and that's all I can ask for really. The other things are just mistakes which we have got to tighten up on and not do again.' And we did try hard. Even when we were 3–1 down we didn't give in, we kept going.

7 SEPTEMBER

Last night I said to Butch Wilkins before the game, 'I expected you to be wearing the red, not the white.' He just smiled.

It's easy to be wise after the event, but Terry and Don should have grabbed him when he was available. Until Moses got injured he wasn't going to be in United's team at the start of the season. But I think they thought, 'Well, if he's not in the team when the season starts the price will come down', so instead of paying the asking price there and then they waited. If they had paid it we could have had him. Now we've no chance of getting him.

He has done very well. He has had a funny couple of years with the England and United captaincies being taken from him, and getting injured and coming back. And when he played in the reserves he stayed really cool under pressure, didn't start complaining and slagging people off, stayed the nice person he is, and waited for his chance. Now he has grabbed it with both hands: all credit to him. They say he is a quiet lad, not outspoken, but there's obviously real character there to do what he has done. There are a lot of players who would have buckled under the sort of pressure he has been coping with, especially at a big club like United. I've got nothing but admiration for him.

He's been criticized in the past for being negative, but I think it all boils down to what sort of team you are playing in. Perhaps he has changed a little, and begun to put more emphasis on looking forward and putting the ball in there; but the way the team plays dominates your style to some extent. When he was criticized in Manchester they weren't doing well as a team. Now you are going to go forward at United because the whole team is going forward. They've got a good midfield and the amount of chances they create for their forwards is considerable. Balls are knocked in to Frank, he knocks it back – a simple ball – and there's Wilkins getting on it with two moving for him. So he is encouraged to play it forward. Whereas in the England team when he got a lot of stick for playing square balls he didn't have those options all too often. But when you look at the England side for the game against Denmark and say, 'Who do you want, Wilkins or Hoddle?' there is only one answer on form, especially with Bryan Robson there, because they've got a good understanding.

I'm sure if I was playing in front of United's midfield I'd have a field day. This season I'm feeling sharp, strong and fit, where last year I wasn't. And I know that even if I have a bad game whoever is marking me will be on his knees by the end of the match from following me because I want the ball so much. And I think I'm losing my man so often that if I was playing in front of United's midfield – or someone like Glenn Hoddle, who can spot things, I'd be in constantly.

I might be wrong, but with some of the moves I'm doing I think, 'I'm in here if they can get the ball to me', but it very rarely comes. Maybe I am expecting too much, I don't know. But I think basically we are not good enough. I sometimes wonder if I should have been more aware of that when I chose to sign for Arsenal instead of someone else. But I wanted to join Arsenal and I thought they were a big enough club to get that sorted out. I like living in London. Football is on Saturday; the rest of the week I wanted to live in London. And when Liam Brady comes back next season it will be different!

People have linked Liam with United, but you couldn't imagine him being content to just sit out there on the left like Arnold Muhren does. Brady likes a lot more room, he likes to be the kingpin of the midfield and say, 'Right, revolve around me.' I'm sure he could sit out in that ten or twenty-yard patch on the left and do it very well, but I don't think he'd settle for that – he would want to be much more involved.

United have got a nice pattern at the moment. They all know what they are doing. Muhren's a good player but he is not in it that much. He subordinates himself to Butch in a way. Butch hits a lot of straight balls. He goes first time: bang; or he floats one from right to left. He is a straight passer. Everything he does is very precise. But Muhren is different. You find a lot of left-footed players bend the ball round or into people's path. Of course right-footed players can do it too, but it seems left-footed players do it more.

I'd love playing in front of the three of them, but Arnie might suit me. It's a discussion I keep having with Rixy. When he has the ball on the left I might make a run into the left channel, and Muhren plays them there. He used to hit Alan Brazil with those at Ipswich the whole time. John Robertson used to do it a lot too. But Rixy wants to play the diagonal cross ball, looking for Noddy Talbot coming through in the inside-right position; and I keep saying, 'Don't do that. If I get goal-side of the defender knock it down the left-hand side and I'm in the box.' I keep on at him saying, 'Just get it to me, just give it to me in the box', but he keeps coming and looking and then going 'bang' to someone coming in on the other side. And if that gets cut out we're stretched and exposed!

8 SEPTEMBER

Noddy came in this morning, while David O'Leary was on the treatment table. 'Dave,' said Noddy, 'I've been here six years and I haven't seen you complete a full week yet.' Dave's proneness to injury is a bit of a standing joke.

I get annoyed with David sometimes; because he has got so much ability, it's almost too easy for him. He's a nice placid lad, which is probably the problem, because he seems content to sit at the back sweeping up the bits and pieces when with his ability he could really take games by the scruff of the neck. I play against him sometimes in training. He's strong, and when he really wants to get the ball he'll go and get it. He comes in with his elbows and really thumps it. I think you have to get his back up. And we are still on at him to be more positive on the ball. He got one goal last season, which for someone of his ability is ridiculous. Willie Young got six or seven.

Kenny Sansom is definitely trying to win his bet. He's had two or three shots now. I said to him, 'Kenny, you are wasting your time. The keeper's watched you shoot, taken his cap off and stood waiting for it to arrive. When it does he threw his cap onto it and stopped it.'

Sundy scored in the reserves on Tuesday. I think coming up to Wolverhampton with us and not being part of things shook him up. I'm sure it suddenly sank in that he wants to be in the team. He likes living where he is in London, and he is really working hard in training and looks very sharp again. He looks like he wants to do it, and is really pushing for his place back.

Rixy asked him how he was feeling and he said, 'I want to play in the first team.'

Rixy said, 'It might mean playing down the right-hand side.'

'It doesn't matter. I just want to play in the first team.'

If that is the case it will be great for us, because he is a very good player. If you play three up front you've got to have one going wide, and out of the three of us he is the best equipped to do it. He must be pushing Brian McDermott very hard. In fact I will be surprised if he isn't playing on Saturday. And if he is in the team, when you look at our forward line you must say we are as good as anyone if we get it together, provided we can get the midfield to respond to us a bit. At the moment we are having too many long balls knocked at us. They are not mixing it up enough. You need the little short ones, then a long one. We haven't got enough craft in there right now.

We are lacking two or three quality players. We need a right-back. Stewart Robson is not a right-back. We need a centre-half. And we need a player like Wilkins in midfield. Everyone in the club knows it, including Don and Terry. It is just a question of getting the players.

It's difficult to decide which is the most important. We are giving away so many stupid goals rumour has it they are more concerned about a centre-half than a midfield player. And we got two goals the other night against United. If you keep a clean sheet you have always got a chance, you might produce something and win 1–0 or 2–0, which is what Arsenal used to do. Giving away silly goals like we are doing at the moment is so unlike Arsenal it's untrue.

I've got athlete's foot, and it's really painful. I've been putting cream on it but it hasn't cured it yet. If you get anything wrong with your toes, get them stamped on for instance, it is probably worse than anything else.

It is ironic, really, because I'm much fitter now than I was last year. Last season I got so many knocks and niggly injuries I couldn't train properly. And looking back I always seemed to puff and pant when I was playing. This year I can go for ninety minutes, no problem – I just don't get tired. The strength is there, the fitness is there, and I've suddenly realized that when you aren't completely fit you lose so much. If I'm ever a manager or trainer – which I think is highly unlikely – I would have a really hard pre-season, just as we did this season. I think everyone at Arsenal realizes the value of it. We've got it in the bank and we are going to benefit from it.

9 SEPTEMBER

Don has definitely got his appetite back this year. He was a bit like the rest of us last year, we were all rather down, and complaining about each other. I had my complaints about him, but this year he is really on the ball. He is a good coach. Training is ever so interesting – he never lets you get bored. You go in some mornings thinking, 'I don't really fancy it', but you soon snap out of it because he is so good.

He won't let it slip either. I don't think the defeats have knocked us back too much. We think United are a good team, and we got them on a good night. But although the papers said they gave us a trouncing, we didn't see it that way. We kept going, we didn't disgrace ourselves. And we think that if we beat Liverpool tomorrow we will keep plodding on and be there, or thereabouts, at the end. If we keep going with the same attitude, the same work-rate, we are going to finish higher than last year, at least in the top six. And if we get a couple of players to give us that bit extra then we could go even further.

10 SEPTEMBER
Arsenal 0 Liverpool 2
That was a knock-back. Losing at Southampton was one of those things, and losing to United could be explained away, too, but three on the trot is a bit of a blow, and does make us question our optimism a little. We might have got a point. Charlie hit the bar with a snapshot, a really good attempt from an angle, and we had them under pressure for a time in the second half. Grobbelaar made a couple of good saves, and there were a few scrambles in their goal-mouth which could have broken our way. Then they broke away and got their second near the end, when, if we had scored, we would have been right back in it.

But we didn't and we weren't . . . and once you go a goal down to Liverpool it is always an uphill struggle, especially when it is as warm as it was. They just took the pace out of the game completely once they'd got their first goal. It was more crushing than the United game for that reason. United play it a bit quicker, a bit more excitingly, and you always think you've got a chance to score against them. But Liverpool just took the sting out of the game. And you do have to look at things afterwards and say, 'Those are the teams we should be measuring ourselves against', and we've lost at home to the pair of them in the space of five days. So where does that leave us? And the answer is 'not quite there'.

11 SEPTEMBER
I flew over to Munich for the day. There is a big sports fair at Bayern and I go to a certain amount of functions each year for Pony, who supply my boots.

I met Rainer Bonhof. He had retired a few weeks earlier, which really shocked me. He had had an injury which he couldn't shake off, so he just packed it in – and he is only thirty-one. My first reaction was, 'Bring your boots to Arsenal and have a trial. Come and train with us. I'm sure you could do a good enough job.' But he refused.

If I looked back over my career at players who had been one hundred per cent professional, who give all they have got, who think about the game and how they prepare themselves, he stands out. There has always been one at every club. I imagine at West Ham Billy Bonds is like that. At Forest it was John McGovern. He was still playing at thirty-four or thirty-five, and looked only twenty-one. And whatever he did, even if he was having a bad time, he would still want to do the right thing: train hard and work hard, and never have a bad word to say about anyone.

John Hollins, from the little bit I saw of him, was the same at Arsenal. He was always smiling and happy, you could never knock him down and he always trained hard.

Maybe that is what we are lacking at Arsenal at the moment. I can't think of anyone. They were experienced players, and we haven't got any. I'd like to think that eventually I'll be like that, in games anyway, I don't mean in training. I'm not the world's best trainer.

16 SEPTEMBER

Rixy has really taken the captaincy to heart, and wants to do well. There are just a few little things which haven't been sorted out in the past, like the players' tea room. Too many people have been coming in there after matches, and he is trying to get that put right. And he is trying to organize a room for the players' kids to use if they have been brought to a match. He's generally trying to make things better for the players. I think he will do well.

He is a little disappointed with his own form though, and he is feeling inhibited about telling people what to do on the field as a result. He says he can't hit a straight pass at the moment, so he doesn't feel able to boss other people. I said he shouldn't worry about that, because I think everyone respects him, and they know he gives his all even when he is playing badly.

17 SEPTEMBER
Notts County 0 Arsenal 4

That's set me up perfectly for Denmark. We played well, and I felt really sharp. At the end of the game Don came running on the field to me, and said it was one of the best forward displays he had ever seen – which coming from someone you respect is very pleasing.

It was very funny too. In the papers this morning there was all this stuff from Kilcline saying how Charlie and I would know we'd been in a game by 4.40 p.m. We sat in our room – I room with him now – reading all this and kidding one another, saying, 'Oh, he won't get near us', because the implication was that he was going to kick us, to sort us out.

When we got to the ground I saw Larry Lloyd, who is now their manager, and said to him, 'I'm going to put on a big pair of pads today because I know what you are going to be telling Kilcline.' And he laughed. But I know what Larry is like, and he would definitely go in there before the game and say, 'Look, first chance you get, hammer him', and I accept that.

But then we went out and got a goal in twenty seconds, and then played really well. We were mobile, and one of us was pulling him out of position with the other going in behind him, and he never got near either of us.

Charlie, however, got an ankle injury and went off at half-time, so Sundy switched up front with me. And coming out for the second half Kilcline ran past me. Didn't say a word, although we know each other, just ran past looking really mean. It looked like someone had better watch out. In the first half they had been knocking balls into us hard, but I looked at his face and I turned to Kenny and nodded at Kilcline and said, 'Kenny, better watch out, he's looking mean.'

Kenny started to laugh, so I said, 'Anything you are laying up to us now, just roll it up so we can come off him. Otherwise he's going to come and do us.'

We were two up, and we had given him a bit of a roasting, so you could expect that in the opening five or ten minutes, the first time Sundy or I got it he was going to come in and clatter us. So Kenny said, 'Okay.' But there was nothing. We really took them to pieces, played some very good football. And he never touched me. I was amazed.

After the match we were having a drink and Larry came in. He had apparently given Kilcline a real going over in the dressing room. 'Well,' I said, 'I kept on expecting to be hit from behind or something.'

'I know,' he said. 'I told him that. I also told him you would know I was going to tell him that. You wait until I tell him about this conversation on Monday.'

So I answered, 'Just let me get out of Nottingham before you start to tell him.'

18 SEPTEMBER

I am so angry and disappointed. At the end of training this afternoon I pulled a muscle, and I should think there is only a twenty-five per cent chance that I'll be fit for Wednesday: I can't believe it.

To make it worse it makes me wonder if staying in Nottingham last night was a good idea. It seemed so at the time – see some friends and have a nice, relaxing evening instead of rushing back after the game. But I certainly didn't think we would do a heavy training session today. In the past we've sometimes done a little bit at Highbury on the Sunday, just to get the stiffness out of you, but not a major session. Being in a car for two hours to Wembley, and then getting the bus from there out to Bisham, was not good preparation for training. Yet I don't think that was the major factor. It was the decision to have a full session. They talk about abandoning League games on the Saturday before an international to guard against injuries, then we're asked to train when we are tired from playing the previous day. It didn't go down too well when we were told on the bus out to Bisham that we would be training this afternoon.

And it was a fair old stint. We left for the ground, which is about fifteen minutes away, at 3.15, and didn't get back until 7.15; and we watched a video of Denmark. I think expecting people who have played a League game on Saturday to spend most of Sunday on international football is just a bit too much. We'd all had enough of it, especially after four hours.

As far as I was concerned it was a bit of a useless session anyway. We were lucky really that we didn't get any more serious injuries, because we did this four against four in the box at corners and free-kicks, the forwards against the centre-halves. And when the ball came in from the right we were defending, and with people like Terry Butcher and Alvin Martin charging in at you you feel a bit exposed. I thought at the time, 'I don't fancy this, what is going to happen here?' because the keepers were coming out and punching it, and they were charging in on the ball, and the danger of cut eyes or broken noses seemed really high. But I got away with just a minor knock. Graham Roberts trod on my foot, so I hobbled around for five minutes. It was sore.

Then that finished and Bobby Robson said, 'Right, just to finish off we'll do three sprints.' I pushed off for the first and immediately felt a muscle go, which is very rare for me, because normally I can go out and play without even a warm-up. All I can put it down to is being tired from the previous day. Looking back I suppose I should just have gone through the motions. If I had done I probably wouldn't feel that training today was such a bad idea, but I did get the kind of injury I don't usually get, and so I would oppose doing it in future. The rest of the lads came through all right though.

19 SEPTEMBER

I had some treatment today, and I couldn't feel anything, so I thought I'd go out and try it. I didn't even get onto the training pitch. I was walking out there and this ball came flying over. I controlled it and felt my hamstring straight away. I knew then it was hopeless. I said to Fred Street, who is still with England even though he has given up Arsenal, that it would be better if I went home. Hanging around and being bored stiff and getting in the way would do me no good, and wouldn't do anyone else any good either. So tomorrow morning I'm going to go home and get out of the way and forget it.

Alvin Martin picked up an injury this morning, which I think was probably because he was still recovering from Saturday. I think training yesterday was so stupid. I've never pulled a muscle before; I've no history of it.

21 SEPTEMBER
England 0 Denmark 1

22 SEPTEMBER

We went to the match last night – Carole, me, Graham and his wife, Charlie and his girlfriend. Afterwards we went back to the hotel Charlie is staying in. It is such a nice friendly place, it is almost like being at home. It was closed, so Charlie took us in and we went into the bar and helped ourselves to drinks and just made a note of what we had. It was a fairly heavy night.

The match was really depressing. It's the same old story every time we play at Wembley – or at least every time a team comes here to play in their own half and to keep the ball, we just don't know how to break it down. We looked so predictable. The back four stayed at the back; the midfield stayed in midfield; and the front players tried to get on the end of fifty-fifty balls. Against teams like that you want a creative player in midfield, someone who can go past the other man and open it up. We just haven't got that type of player in the team, and over the last couple of years that is how we have let ourselves down. It's not a case of missed chances, because we don't create any chances. The only shot came from Blissett right at the end. And that came from a ball being tossed into the box, it bounced and there was a snapshot – the only one on target over the ninety minutes.

And I don't think they were a great team. Far from it in fact. They have some good players, and they created one chance in the first few minutes when they should have scored, but apart from that they offered nothing at all. I don't think the build-ups they got beforehand helped. It shouldn't affect you, and I don't think we were frightened of them as such. If I'd been playing I'd have thought, 'Come on, we can beat them 4–0.' As far as I'm concerned what the manager and press say wouldn't worry me. I expect to win every game we are playing in, but I think all that publicity about what a good team they were did not help.

The papers today were complaining about lack of commitment. I think there was something missing in that area. With twenty minutes to go, with us 1–0 down, when they got the ball at the back and were stroking it around across the back four, we were just letting them have it – which is ridiculous when you have got to win the game. You've got to press up. But it's no use the forwards going in there if the midfield don't support them; and no use the midfield going in if the back four don't push up behind them.

And I think that was because the midfield were frightened of taking chances. When you are against a defensive set-up like that you have to be prepared to lose the ball on some occasions to open things up. If you are going to take a man on you are not going to beat him every time, but if you do beat him it starts to open things up. We didn't do that.

Ray Wilkins came in for a lot of criticism afterwards. I think it goes back to what I was saying about being affected by what is happening around him. He is not the type of player to go past people, and we were very predictable last night. But when he plays for United he has got a lot of runners around him – they are all buzzing

– and he delivers. Robson goes steaming off ahead of him. Graham, Stapleton and Whiteside are all running all over the place, so he has got plenty of movement in front of him, to slot the ball into. Last night there was no movement in midfield and not much from the front lads.

Trevor was not very impressive. He was going back too deep, picking the ball up on the half-way line. I can understand him wanting to get into the game, you want the ball, but if he is coming back someone has got to go up there for him. From a team point of view he should be up there, you don't want him picking it up on the half-way line.

He was involved, unwittingly, in one of the less pleasant incidents. Phil Neal tried to chip a ball up the line over someone's leg and it went straight into touch. Of course the crowd gave him a lot of stick. But really it was Trevor's fault because he had held on to the ball too long instead of giving it to Phil straight away and when he did give it to him he played Phil into trouble.

Kenny was also complaining about Trevor after the game. He's just not the type of player who can read a situation. Those occasions against Greece when he ran into space I'd left for myself were just typical. Our midfield players and defenders knew I was taking their defenders one way so I could go back into the space – which you can do against sides which play with a sweeper – but Trevor couldn't read it. He'd just go running into it. And when I said, 'Trev, I set that up for myself you know, and now you've gone running in there', he just didn't see it. If two players were on the left-hand side and he thought he could get the ball he'd come over there as well, whereas he shouldn't. He should think, 'Someone's there, I'll just stay out of it this time.' I'm sure that playing in Italy will make him more aware. Because, apart from briefly at Forest, he hadn't been encouraged, or needed, to think about his game in a team pattern.

24 SEPTEMBER
Arsenal 3 Norwich City 0
They were terrible. Most of them can't play and some of them didn't want to. It could have been 6–0. Sitting watching in the stand the number of chances flying around was just unbelievable.

Charlie gave a good solid performance, which we have been looking for. You always see nice touches from him throughout a game, but you want more than that. He's been a bit troubled by his ankle injury. He didn't score though, and is still short of goals; maybe he is starting to try a little bit too hard at the moment.

He is taking a bit of a battering up front. Players are coming into him, hitting him, and he doesn't seem able to stand up to them. Whether it is a different game here from Scotland I don't know, but he goes down very easily. I think possibly we should try playing Sundy and me up front, with him just behind us. I think his strength really is when the ball has been layed up to someone and knocked back to him so he is coming at players, rather than facing the wrong way with a defender on his back.

I wondered beforehand how David O'Leary would play. He had been left out of the Ireland team on Wednesday – which must have shaken him, although he didn't say anything about it – and I wondered if it would spur him on to go out and say, 'I'll show them.' But he just played his normal game – and he could do more.

28 SEPTEMBER
I've been back in training for the last couple of days. Did some road work with Terry round London Colney; ran up and down the terraces at Highbury; and played a bit of tennis, and I had no reaction. So everything seemed fine. Then today I had an ache on the side of my foot. When I looked I had a bruise there. I've no idea where that has come from. But we went to train on the Astroturf – we play QPR on Saturday – and I couldn't run. I was hobbling, not because of the hamstring injury but because of this bruise. I can't put my foot down on the hard ground.

29 SEPTEMBER
My run earlier in the week with Terry has had its effect. He said today, 'I'm not going running with you again.' He says he is still knackered from that run.

It was quite a mix-up. When we set off from London Colney I thought we were going on the small circuit so I went off at a fair pace. Terry was keeping up with me so I followed his lead as far as directions went. After fifteen minutes he was starting to puff, and the next minute we were going up this big hill into Shenley Village. And I thought, 'Where are we going here?' Terry was puffing and panting, so I thought I'd better ease the pace. It was just as well I did, because we were out for an hour.

Don has been on the warpath after me for a few days. I've been keeping out of his way, but he caught up with me finally. I made this really silly mistake on the scales last week. I still think of my best weight as seventy-five kilos rather than thinking in stones. Seventy-five kilos is a little under twelve stone, but for some reason I got confused and thought it was the other way round. So I thought I'd better put down twelve stone three pounds or twelve stone four pounds so that they don't think there's any problem.

But of course when he looked at it for his records, which he keeps weekly, it looked as if I'd suddenly put a lot on. So he finally caught me and said, 'Come here, I want a word with you. What's this about your weight? You're putting a bit on aren't you?' So I explained about putting the wrong weight down. I'm not sure he was convinced. He said, 'Putting on three or four pounds, that's the difference between sharp and not sharp, you know! You can lose it by doing that.' So I tried to reassure him. 'Don't worry, Don. If I'm playing Saturday I'll be back down to twelve stone, or whatever my fighting weight is.'

'That's all right, then.'

He does chase people up. He looks at the weights every week.

30 SEPTEMBER

I had a try-out this morning, but I won't play tomorrow. If the game had been at Highbury I probably would have done, but on that hard ground it seemed too risky. So I said, 'If I don't play at QPR I will definitely be ready for Plymouth on Tuesday.' And they left it at that.

1 OCTOBER

QPR 2 Arsenal 0

I certainly wasn't sorry to miss that. It was a terrible game. If that is the standard of football you get on that pitch I wouldn't go every week. When Rangers went two up they started to play a bit, but apart from that the ball was bouncing all over the place. Maybe the players aren't good enough to control it, but I can't believe that people like Graham Rix, Charlie and Sundy haven't got enough skill to control the ball – yet it never seemed to be on the ground.

It was terrible to watch. You play on mistakes. The only way to play on that pitch is to get it forward, chase everything, rely on the bounce and wait for a mistake to happen. It's not my way of playing.

What made the pitch even worse was that if we had won it would have shot us up into a challenging position with two home games to come. So it was doubly disappointing. But all the top teams lost, so at least we didn't lose any ground. It's still wide open, and with Coventry and Forest to come to Highbury, six points could start us pushing up into the top four or five, which would be a great boost for us.

3 OCTOBER

I trained perfectly well this morning, ran hard, twisted, turned, sprinted and felt nothing. So it is all clear. I shall play at Plymouth tomorrow and be ready for Hungary next week. I expect to play in that one now – the one consolation from the dreadful performance against Denmark was that at least it meant I shall probably get back in.

Wilf Dixon's talk on Plymouth was a classic. We thought we were playing Real Madrid by the time he had finished. It was like here's Joe Bloggs at right-back, and he can do this, and he can do that, and he's a really good player, right through the team. And he said about the right-half, 'He's a very deceptive player. He does this and that. In the programme it says he is five feet eight inches tall, but I really believe he is five feet seven.' We fell about. Talking about an inch difference, as if it mattered!

Kenny has been unhappy for ages and is talking about asking for a transfer. He resents the fact that people like me and Charlie, and probably David O'Leary are earning more, when he is an England regular and he thinks he does well by the club. He probably looks around at where some of the lads are living and wonders why he hasn't got such a nice house. He feels the club owe him something.

I'm not that sympathetic. I spoke to him about it. I said, 'Well, you signed the contract. You aren't just responsible for football, you are responsible for what happens in the rest of your life as well.' I do believe that. When you are negotiating, then it is up to you to get the best terms you can, but if you sign a contract then you've committed yourself. He accepts that, but he thinks that if Arsenal know that they have got him, not cheaply but for less than they might have expected, then they should go to him and say, 'Here you are, Ken', and pull him in line with us. And there is something in that.

David Dein has been appointed as a director. He is an Arsenal

159

fanatic, and I think he will be good for the club when he has settled in. I'm sure he will go for the top players, and for whatever he thinks will be beneficial for Arsenal. He is a young man, and I wouldn't say he is impatient, but certainly when he wants something, he wants it as soon as possible.

I've known him nearly a year now. We met early last season at Nottingham, he was having a drink with Willie Young. We got talking and I said I was house-hunting. He asked where and I mentioned Totteridge among other places. He said he lived there and invited us round for dinner, and we became friends. Rixy and I go out with him quite often. It might make for a slightly funny situation with him on the board, but I don't see why it should make any difference. I think we've known him long enough for it not to interfere.

4 OCTOBER
Plymouth Argyle 1 Arsenal 1

5 OCTOBER
My muscle went again last night – it's the most disappointing thing that has happened to me since I began playing football. I've got no chance of playing for England next week now; and all because of the stupidity of having us train on that Sunday. To do that when this Saturday (by which time it is probably too late), there are no first division fixtures to protect the players for the Hungary game is unbelievable.

I played for forty minutes last night. It was all going fine, I was really springing well, and feeling no reaction. Then at half-pace I checked and turned inside and it just went. Maybe I was getting a bit tired. They said it looks like I'll be out for three weeks.

I went out and had a few drinks afterwards because I felt so down.

We went into the bar. I had this great strapping on my thigh, and it was slipping down all the time. So I took it off and put it into the ash-tray. I wasn't trying to be funny. I took it off, rolled it up into a big ball of tape and put it in the ash-tray, and didn't think any more about it.

Then we went out to a club and had a few drinks. Kenny and Sundy were arguing; there was a bit of friction between them. And

160

Man-for-man marking German style: Tenhagen in close attendance, the ball nowhere to be seen.

Classic shot of Klaus Allofs: ball under control at speed, mind one step ahead.

*Concentration, balance, skill —
Charlie Nicholas.*

*Even Charlie admits that some
of the pictures he poses for
look silly!*

when we got back to the hotel a fight broke out between them in the corridor – Rixy couldn't keep them apart.

There was a bit of a commotion, Terry opened his bedroom door, and Rixy said, 'Come on Terry, come and stop it;' Terry looked, then turned round and went back into his room and closed the door. Then Don came out in his underpants. He thought the hotel was on fire. But he said, 'Come on lads, break it up, break it up!' So they stopped for a second. And the hotel security guards were there too, so everyone cleared off back to their rooms.

But then Kenny went and knocked on Sundy's door and it all started again. So Roy Johnson, who is an ex-policeman, came out and pulled them apart. Sundy was still trying to get at Kenny, so Roy said, 'If you are going to hit Kenny, you are going to have to hit me first.' So Sundy did. But it all died down after that. It was nothing very serious, just the sort of thing which happens occasionally when you get a group of fellows together and a few drinks spark things off.

But coming back on the train this morning Terry came down the corridor and said he wanted to see six of us at Highbury – Sundy, Kenny, Charlie, Lee, Rixy and me. So we all trooped off to Highbury. He saw us each individually, so we had to sit around waiting for our turn. We thought it might have been about the fight, or about going out and getting in late at the hotel.

As it turned out it was all for different things. Charlie was told he had got to train harder as he hasn't been doing much because of his ankle; Lee because he was very down after being dropped yesterday to make room for me to come back in. He was very upset and had his head really down in the changing room, and Terry wanted to discuss that with him. With Sundy and Kenny it was about the skirmish. They had to write an apology to the hotel. Then it came to Rixy and myself. And it was about going out when we had injuries. Rixy went in first and when he came out of the door I asked, 'What's it all about?'

'He found your strapping in the ash-tray in the bar.' I found that quite amusing at the time, so I went in smiling to myself.

Terry said, 'Look, I don't mind you going out and having a beer, but you have got an injury and I think you ought to think about that.'

I said, 'They told me that I'm going to be out for three weeks. I'll have missed two important England games as a result. I'm not going to go straight to bed if I'm not going to play for that long. If they had said, "You've got a chance to play next week," then I would have done.'

He accepted that. 'Yes, I suppose you are right,' and that was the end of the interview. We had gone to Highbury thinking we were going to be ticked off, been there for an hour, and it was for nothing.

7 OCTOBER

Kenny has asked for a transfer. I just think he has gone about things all wrong. He went into see them to talk to them about getting a new house, and I don't think he got the answers he wanted, so he steamed ahead and demanded a transfer. He can't win that way. He has eighteen months left to go on his contract, so if they do put him on the list they are going to put a big fee on him, so I don't think he would be any better off.

He suggested a ten-year contract, which quite rightly they refused. But if he had suggested an extra two years with a rise, and gone and talked to the Chairman and Ken Friar about it, they might have agreed. I would imagine Arsenal would want to be fair with him, because they know that he has given them good service, and will continue to do so. I'm sure something could be sorted out which would be beneficial to both, but I don't think asking for a transfer will help anyway. I'm sure, knowing Kenny, that it won't affect his contribution, he is a good trainer and he will still give everything – but this is something we could have done without.

The trouble is, though, it is a bit of a waste of time talking to Terry about these things. When I joined Jon had dealt initially with Terry, but when it came down to the nitty-gritty he virtually had to start all over again with Ken Friar.

11 OCTOBER

According to this morning's papers Jock Stein said, 'Nicholas has still got to prove himself.' That's the last thing Charlie needs at the moment. There has not been as much bad publicity as he might have expected, because he isn't having the best of times at present. But he has stayed cheerful, and things seemed to have quietened down; what he needs at the moment is for everything to be nice and calm so that he is allowed to just get on with playing football. So he goes up to Scotland and the first thing that happens is that he is back in the headlines with that sort of thing, which isn't very nice for him.

Jock Stein probably didn't mean it to come out that way, but he said enough to make you wonder. He said, 'He's only played a good half-hour for Scotland', which is probably true, but I don't think he should say that to the papers and not expect it to be blown up. What Charlie needs was Jock saying nothing more than, 'Let him get on with his game', and I would have expected him to have enough experience to know that.

12 OCTOBER

I might be injured, but I'm making sure I don't suffer alone. I went running with Roy Johnson today, Terry having refused the invitation, and I got him instead. We went on Hampstead Heath, and we were running up one of the hills when he put his foot in a rabbit hole and tore all his ankle ligaments. Two down, two to go.

At the end of last week, between not training and having one or two nights out – medicinal, to help me get over my depression – I really did go up to twelve stone three pounds; but with the laps today I'm back down to eleven stone nine pounds. So it seems that with a few laps it just drops straight off. I keep telling them that the heavier I get the faster and stronger I get. They won't have it though.

13 OCTOBER

We have got the running joke of all time at the moment. It started a couple of weeks ago, and it puts Chrissie Whyte's bald patch completely into the shade. Paul Davis used to have this really rickety old Ford Estate, but a couple of months ago he finally sold it and bought a new XR3. It's always immaculately polished, the inside is spotless. The little car blanket is neatly folded, the *A–Z* in the right place. He's very careful where he parks it. He wouldn't leave it in the front row of a car park because someone might scratch it; and he never parks it near bus stops because there are a lot of people around them so someone might decide to vandalize it. And of course he drives it equally carefully. I usually pass him on the A1 when we are going to London Colney. He's got this nice, fast little motor, but he's driving along at a steady thirty m.p.h. I assumed he was still running it in. He's given me a lift a couple of times and I've said, 'Can I drive,' and he always says, '*No*. I'm the only one who drives this car.'

Well that's quirky, but not that exceptional – the proud new car-owner. But a couple of weeks ago Lee Chapman came in one morning bursting to tell us his news. He'd been out with Paul the previous night and Paul had told him that the man in the garage had said that he was only allowed to do thirty miles a day, anything over that was bad for the engine. So he gets up to thirty and then he takes the tube and things like that!

Well, of course we didn't believe it. So Lee said, 'I'm telling you. It happened last night. We went into Hampstead for a meal, and afterwards I said, "Shall we go into town now?" And Paul said, "I can't do that, I've already done thirty-two miles today," ' and that was how it came out. So of course as soon as Davo arrived we had a go at him about it. And he said, 'Yes, that's what they told me.' I cracked up. Then he said, 'No, I'm only winding you up, I'm joking.'

It was too late to say that though. And since then I've been checking the mileage on his car every day. He makes it easy because he winds the mileage back to nought every day. When he goes to London Colney there are nine on the clock, when it is Highbury it is fifteen, which means he has got exactly enough to get home in thirty miles.

So the other day at Highbury I asked him if I could borrow his car to nip down to the bank. All the lads were listening, and he knew exactly what I wanted it for, so he got this little grin on his face and said, 'Oh, yes if you want to.' He really didn't want me to, but he is taking so much ribbing about it at the moment that he keeps saying he was just having us on. But I think we got conclusive proof this week. Lee and he were out with Garth Crooks, and Lee tipped Garth off about the situation. So half-way through the evening Lee casually asked Garth how he was getting home. And Garth said, 'I'm going to have to get a tube or taxi, because I've done thirty miles in my car today already.' So Paul fell right into it. 'You've got a car like mine as well then, have you?'

Roy is hobbling around badly. He is going to have to have someone to run on for him on Saturday.

Liam Brady is over at the moment. He is going to the game on Saturday, and might be training with us tomorrow. There has been a lot of newspaper talk about him coming back at Christmas. Obviously I'd like him back. We all would. It's probably a question of getting him the right sort of contract. There's been talk about him going to United, but although you can never have too many good players, I don't know how he would fit in there. He likes to run the show, and Wilkins and Robson seem to have that sorted out at the moment, and as I said before I think he'd want to be more involved than Muhren is. He could be captain at Arsenal. In fact he could be the Chairman if he wanted: he could name his price. Graham would love him to come back. Graham is his big mate, and I don't think that Liam would come back if Graham was to leave.

Graham is in a funny situation at the moment. He wants to play abroad, but he knows that forward players get the best opportunities to go. In fact I think that deep down he doesn't think he has got much of a chance unless Arsenal are up there winning European trophies. He played in all the World Cup games when he was a free agent, and no one came for him. Then he sees Luther, who was under contract, so Milan paid a million pounds for him because they wanted him badly enough, and it makes him doubt himself. Yet he is captain of Arsenal, which he is very proud of. He and his wife are living in a flat, which they don't want. Graham would like to buy a house with a garden for his little girl, but I think he feels that if he makes that decision now he is accepting defeat, accepting that he is not going to move. I don't know why he feels that buying a house would tie him down. I told him a year ago he should buy one. Then if a move came up, sell it. And if the move didn't come up, he wouldn't have to start the rigmarole a year further on.

Roy Johnson was testing how far I could stretch this morning. There was a certain exercise I just couldn't do I was so stiff. 'I can't do that, Roy. It hurts me here and it hurts me here,' I said.

'Cor, you are terrible, you are,' he said. 'I don't know how you manage to play.'

But I told him that when Saturday comes round my range of stretches and movement are about fifty per cent better than during the week; not because I work harder, but because I'm keyed up for the game. On a Monday I can just touch my toes; and even if I don't do anything else during the week, if I try it on a Saturday, because it's the day of the game and I am keyed up, I can put my hands flat on the floor.

15 OCTOBER

I definitely won't be playing tomorrow, so Lee is back in. We've got a testimonial on Tuesday and a reserve match on Wednesday, so I might get a run-out in one of those.

The youth team and reserves are both top of their leagues at the moment, so the top dressing room is coming in for some mickey-taking from their trainers. Alf Field, who has been at Highbury for donkey's years, works with the youth team, which they say is the best they've had in five years. They've got some good prospects in it.

We have a game with them occasionally. I think it is a good idea to take a young player with you on away games, but that idea seems to have gone out of fashion. Some clubs used to do that years ago, and I know when I was sixteen or seventeen it was a boost. I think it is a good idea, it gives the youngster a feel of things, gives him a chance to talk to the first team, and see the things that happen.

They really rate Tony Adams, who is the England youth team captain. He is a big, tall lad, quick and good on the ball. I think depending on the situation they will give him a chance sometime this year – perhaps at the end of the season. He is very confident.

15 OCTOBER
Arsenal 0 Coventry City 1

We gave a terrible performance. Lee Chapman had a nightmare. It got to the stage where it was embarrassing, because he could not do a thing right. He was giving a hundred per cent but he could not do it. I've always defended him as a player, but I just couldn't after that showing. He's either lost it completely or he has just not got it.

And of course the crowd were getting at him, which just made it worse. Less excusably they also started booing Rixy. He gave a few bad passes and it started. That was terrible, it just proved that some of them don't have any idea about the game.

The main problem I've seen from the stand is that almost no one wants the ball. Rixy wants it, Sundy wants it. They will both accept responsibility, both say, 'Come on, give it me, I'll try and do something.' I think I do that too when I'm playing. But sitting there watching there are so many players who don't. Especially today. There were so many players saying, 'You've got it, see if you can do something.' And Rixy was always wanting it, always trying to do something. Okay, he kept giving it away, but his attitude was right, he kept on trying to do something with the ball.

If you look at the good teams, like Liverpool, they all want the ball and the player on the ball has two or three options where he can pass it. But watching us for the last couple of games we've got very few. The front lads aren't showing themselves too well, but then the service is crap as well. Everything has to work hand in hand, but if people aren't moving for one another and wanting the ball you have got no chance, and some players just did not want to know.

166

When I first went to Cologne I remember a midfield player making a point about how good it was to have someone always available for him. I'd made a fantastic start, so much so that I got some tremendous press coverage. And every week in the paper they would say who my marker was going to be in the build-up to the game. They call the marker a 'dog', and when we went to play 1860 Munich in the Olympic Stadium there was the news that 'Woodcock's dog this week will be Kapellman.' He used to play for Cologne. They called him 'The Doctor'. He was a Colin Todd type player, really sharp and strong.

And wherever I went he was there. I didn't score, but I thought I played well. I kept getting the ball and laying it off and making new positions. He was virtually inside my shirt the whole time, but I'd still say, 'Give it me again', and after the game Herbert Neumann, who couldn't speak very good English, said, 'I like the way you play, because if you are not doing much with the ball you still want it from me.' For another player to say that was very important to me.

Yet the papers all said I had had a bad game. I couldn't believe it. I thought it was a really good game and a really good contest because he was fair, he wasn't kicking, and I wanted the ball a lot, and I thought I'd played well. There was a funny postscript. I was standing combing my hair after changing and suddenly in the mirror there was Kapellman right behind me again. I said, 'You still here?' – I couldn't speak a word of German at that stage, but my face must have said a lot, so he laughed his head off.

16 OCTOBER

David O'Leary is having a golf day today as part of his testimonial year. Most of the players are going. I'm not because I can't play golf, and I don't want to spoil the game for whoever I played with – three people pay to play with one of the lads or a celebrity, and I can imagine that if I was there my foursome would wait for ever for me to get round. So I said I wouldn't play in this one, but I'll give it a go in the one later in the season. It makes you think though. Ten or fifteen years ago if a player was having a testimonial you would automatically assume he was either thirty-five or playing his last match. Yet here's David at twenty-five, with the best years of his career ahead of him; it can't be bad, getting a testimonial at twenty-five.

17 OCTOBER

According to John Sadler in the *Sun*, Charlie dropped a right clanger by joining Arsenal, because they are asking him to work too hard. That is ridiculous – talk about getting the wrong end of the stick. It's arguable that if he were in a better team he wouldn't have to work so hard because things would be going right. When the team is not doing so well you have to work extra hard. But look at the good teams – they all still work hard. United's front men, Frank Stapleton and Norman Whiteside work ever so hard. At Liverpool everybody works hard; it's just that because they are a better team things come easier. And when things are happening for you the work seems easier – if you are winning games you can play five games a week. If you are losing you are absolutely on your knees if you play two a week.

Charlie is in a bit of a trough of the moment, and he has got to battle his way out of it. He is not getting much help, because everyone is struggling. He shouldn't be asked to chase long balls, or challenge six feet tall defenders, because that isn't his game, although you have to do it a few times over ninety minutes.

Today we paid for David's golf day yesterday. We had this really strenuous morning. A lot of running as well as football. We did box to box. You go from the edge of one penalty area to the other and back, touch your partner and he goes. You do that six times. Then we went into a game, and after that we did more runs, this time from penalty box to half-way line, six times again, then back into the game. On top of that we did exercises and body work, and we finished with six short runs from the edge of the penalty box to the goal-line. And with the testimonial at Aldershot tomorrow we couldn't understand why we were working so hard. It all became clear. On one of the runs Don shouted, 'This'll get the white wine out of you!' So that was it. 'Here we go, it's from yesterday.' We've enjoyed ourselves, he's heard about it, and is going to run us into the ground. Typical of Don. I was a bit disappointed because I wasn't even there, I didn't have a drink all day. And Sundy shouted, 'That's not right, I never touched white wine. I was on red.' So he was complaining as well.

Kenny missed out on it. He went into hospital for two or three days for observation. He has got back pains. We told him they were growing pains. He gets terrible stick about his height. We've decided to send him a get-well card, 'Kenny Sansom, Private Cot. . .'.

Now he has got a beard we pull his leg about being one of the seven dwarfs, or a gnome. But he takes it well and joins in against himself. If he sees anyone really small in the street he'll say, 'I'll pick him up at corners.'

I went to St Giles' hospital for an injection. There's a slight spot where the tendon and muscle join, and on certain movements I can feel it. Everything has healed, and they wanted to disperse this bit of gristle. They said, 'It needs a helping hand, there won't be any lasting effects, and it won't do any harm', so off I went.

It means I won't be able to play in the game at Aldershot, but I don't think that bothers them. Probably a couple of weeks ago they would have said, 'Get a game under your belt', but I got the impression after Saturday's performance they want me out there whatever happens. If I'd got to go out on crutches they'd still want me to play.

There was a nice little incident in the training game this morning. Dave Madden, who joined us on a free transfer from Southampton at the beginning of the season – he had had a few problems with Lawrie McMenemy – and Sundy clashed. Madden crashed into Sundy and sent him flying. Sundy got up a bit riled. And the next tussle he saw Dave a bit off balance so he dived in to challenge hard and get a bit of his own back, but he just bounced off him. We were in the bathroom afterwards and Dave came walking through and everybody stepped back and said, 'Let him through, let him through!'

I've been very impressed with him. I think one or two of the lads are, but it often seems that players who impress their team mates don't get a chance. I think he should have been thrown in against Coventry. If I were the manager I would have no hesitation. He's the type of midfield player we need. His nickname at Southampton was 'Studs'. As Sundy said he's like a walking accident unit. But he's been scoring goals, he's good on the ball, he knocks lovely balls through. He goes past players, even though he is not the quickest player around, so he can play as well as getting stuck in. We need someone like that in the team.

It must be heart-breaking for our reserves at the moment. They are doing well, top of their League, and they must think they are never going to get a chance when they see a performance like the one against Coventry, because the team never changes. And I think that feeling has spilled over into the first team squad, because players keep getting chance after chance however badly they are playing. So they must think it doesn't matter; if they had a bad game, there's no one to replace them. And I think that is wrong, and that is coming from the management.

I know I've said this before, but it wouldn't have happened with Clough, or to an extent with Weisweiler. Clough would say it didn't matter who the player was, even if he was an international, if he wasn't doing it he'd put on an 'A' team player if necessary.

19 OCTOBER

In training today I ran with Tony Isaacs, one of the apprentices; Charlie and I were training with them; he was quick. We did six and a half laps to start with. I stayed with him for the first half lap, and I said, 'Do you want to run together? Slow it down a bit.' He said, 'Okay, fine,' but I think he got it wrong, because if anything he quickened up and we went on at his pace for the remaining six laps.

I beat him on the thrusts up the steep part of the stands though: I couldn't let him win everything.

I watched Tottenham play Ajax on TV. It must be nice to play with so many good attacking players. It's not just Charlie who would benefit from playing for a team like that, I should think every forward in the first division must think when they look at the midfield players Tottenham, Manchester United, or Liverpool have got that they would be a dream to play with. And conversely if you put Ian Rush, who I don't think is having the best of times at the moment anyway, into Arsenal's forward line, he would struggle.

In the morning someone asked Charlie and I if we were going to Tottenham. I said, 'No, it's too much of a hassle.' Charlie would like to have gone, but he got enough stick at Aldershot last night, so he could imagine what it would be like walking into the main stand at Tottenham. So we said we will go there when we are top of the League. Then we could walk in with a couple of big cigars and big hats on, just stroll in and take our seats. We could take it all then, but it will have to wait for now.

20 OCTOBER

I went in today looking to play football to start building up for Saturday. But we had half an hour's football then did doggies. I don't mind doing doggies, in fact when I'm losing myself in training

I quite enjoy it – I like trying to get the best times in short things like that. It's only a minute's work and a good blow out. You are supposed to give your all in the first run, pushing eighteen seconds. On the second if you are quick you might do it in nineteen or twenty seconds, and on the third it doesn't matter if you die on it and come down to twenty-three or twenty-four seconds, because to get the best out of it you are supposed to give everything you've got in the first, not save yourself for the third.

But today I didn't think that was what I needed, and I started to complain. I said to Roy Johnson, 'I've done enough running. I know I'm fit enough that way. I want to play football.'

So he went to Don, and Don came over and said, 'I know you've done a lot of running, a lot of hard work, but we've got to make sure you are okay. You shouldn't be worrying about whether you'll get your first touch in. A player of your quality and experience will have no problems whatsoever.'

But that wasn't what I was saying. My first touch is either there or it isn't. You can't do anything to improve it in games. Some days, most days (touch wood), the ball comes and it sticks. Other days you can't feel the ball. So it doesn't matter how hard I practise control, if it is not there on a certain day there's nothing I can do about it.

But what I meant was that I wanted to get into the swing of playing football, picking the ball up, running with it, doing different sorts of movements, the kind of movements I'd be doing in a game. But he just didn't see that.

I was running with Lee Chapman. Normally you just can't knock him down, he shrugs off a bad game and is remarkably resilient, but this time it is getting to him. He is really depressed – it's surprising really, it should have happened a long time ago, but he kept going until now. He missed some easy chances in the training game.

21 OCTOBER

I'm really looking forward to playing again, but I wish it had been last week against Coventry rather than starting back against Forest, not really because they are my old team. There is always an extra dimension when players play against their old clubs, but I haven't got much of that left now, because it seems so long since I was there. A couple of years ago I used to look for their result in the paper, but I don't make a point of it now.

I'd sooner have come back against Coventry though, because

Forest'll be more difficult. They have an impressive back four. I think Paul Hart must rank with Arthur Graham as the bargain of the season. How we didn't go in for both of them I'll never understand. We've been looking for a right-sided player and a centre-half, and those two came on the market for £40,000 and £60,000.

Then there's Viv Anderson, Colin Todd, who I still rate highly – in fact last season I thought I'd still play him in the England team – and Kenny Swain, who I thought was very unlucky not to be called up by England against Hungary. John Gregory did well enough, but if I were a manager I'd have wanted to have a proper right-back playing. And as well as being a good back four, they get lots of men behind the ball. The midfield players all drop back, so it is going to be difficult to get any sort of opening against them. I remember last year's game, and it was such a bore.

I can imagine what Clough will say in the changing room. He won't want me to score. When I was at Forest and we were playing against an ex-player, he'd always say, 'Get to grips with him. Let him have one early', or 'Let him know you're about', so it is going to be difficult, especially not having played for a month.

With Forest and then Plymouth in the League Cup on Tuesday, it is being built-up as a bit of a crisis week for Terry. There's a shareholders' meeting on Tuesday. The Chairman has been dismissing all the speculation, saying that the meeting is before the game, not afterwards, and that he is right behind Terry. At some clubs the Chairman saying that is the kiss of death, but I think at Arsenal it probably does mean something. And he said if they sacked Terry who would they get? He'd like Herbert Chapman, but it's a bit late for that.

But in spite of all that, these are two crucial games, because they are both at home and you are expected to win. The Forest match will be hard though. We should beat Plymouth, but you never know. If we lose that 1–0 we're out of the League Cup, and if we lost to Forest we'd be down in the relegation zone. And then I think something would have to give.

Kenny came out of hospital today. He has had a minor operation, but he's playing tomorrow.

22 OCTOBER
Arsenal 4 Nottingham Forest 1

Before the game Don said, 'Forwards have really got to want to score.' He said we'd only scored one headed goal in the box all season, and that was on the opening day against Luton – our first goal of the season in fact. So he said, 'Woody, and you, Charlie, you've got to want to get your eyes cut and your noses hit and get in there.' It's a favourite refrain of Don's. 'Get in there and get a few cuts.' It's quite a joke in the dressing room, the lads taking Don off. 'Do you want a cut eye? Do you want a bloody nose?'

But it's not quite right, not on today's evidence anyway, because I got our fourth clattering into the goalkeeper for a header without suffering any real damage, while Charlie came off with a thick lip and didn't score. In fact he hardly had a kick, and he ended up with a bruised thigh and a thick lip. Van Breukelen didn't get off so lightly, though, from our collision, I think he's quite badly injured. And they say I'm not aggressive! Don was delighted afterwards – not with Van Breukelen getting hurt – but with me clattering him. He never stopped talking about it.

I was a bit disappointed in the keeper. I thought he would have done me really. He knew I was going to get the ball first when it was hammered in, and normally when you head the ball you seem to go limp for a second, so I thought, 'Well, the keeper is going to clatter me.' And I had to concentrate on the ball coming in, so all I could do was try and stay solid and expect to be knocked. And we did really whack into one another; I think the ball then rebounded off him back onto me and then into the net. I got smashed in the face, and a thump on the thigh, but I came off best: I got the goal and he got the injury.

I found the other goal more satisfying. Rixy and I have been practising this move where I come short, and if the defender is trying to get in front of me I'll check and go for a long one. We seem to have got this down to a fine art at the moment. Rixy waits for me to check, then plants it over the top. This time he played a lovely ball. Anderson and Todd were coming in, and I just managed to nod it past them and then hit it past the keeper. David Dein said afterwards that it looked so simple, and I take that as a compliment. Footballers know when they've scored a good goal, and I thought that was one. It was a well-timed run, I held the challengers off and just knocked it past the goalkeeper, and made it look easy. I was quite pleased with that.

It was an eventful game altogether. We got the ideal start. Sundy scored a cracking goal. Then Colin Hill hit one in from thirty yards. He came to Highbury as a striker, and has a really strong shot. So we were 2–0 up after sixteen minutes, and it isn't often that Forest score three away from home.

I was really shattered. Just before half-time I thought, 'I'm not going to get through this', yet even though I wasn't playing particularly well the goals still came. And in the last ten minutes of the first half my legs felt so heavy I could hardly move. It just goes to show that no matter how hard you train, when you first play you are going to be shattered. While I was injured I did a hell of a lot of running and weights and things like that. I really worked hard. But you need a couple of games before you are going to stop blowing and start feeling sharp again. Getting tackled heavily and getting knocked down takes a little bit out of you when you've been running around as well, much more than just straight running does.

Paul Hart was sent off for a foul on Charlie. He shouldn't have been. Sundy and I both asked the ref to forget it, and so did a couple of the other lads. They weren't clattering us really – it wasn't a bad foul. Charlie goes over easily. I don't think he means to, he is just not resisting challenges at the moment. Balls are coming, he's waiting for them to come and defenders are making contact as soon as they arrive. Then he goes over when he should be resisting. It looks as if he's looking for a foul. In fact Colin Todd said he was a cheat doing things like that. But I said to him, 'It looks that way, it looks as if he is going down deliberately, but I think it's just he gets knocked down easily.'

Robbo and Ian Bowyer had a run-in. In the bath afterwards Stewart Robson said, 'That Bowyer went over the top to me.' He's got a graze down his shin. I said, 'Well, Robbo, you did clatter him two or three times in the first half.' He said, 'Well, I didn't mean to.' I told him, 'It doesn't matter whether you meant to or not, you did catch him. You hit him with your elbow once, and you went in late on a couple of occasions. And he's the type of player who will bide his time.' Which he did.

Then, when I went into the Forest dressing room, Bowyer said the same thing.

'Is he crackers?' he demanded. 'He's rushing around kicking people.'

174

'He's just said the same about you,' I replied.

I don't know whether it is over-enthusiasm with Robbo or what. He rushes in. When he wins it, all too often he gives it away again because he doesn't steady himself, which is what he has got to learn at the moment. He'll win a great tackle then he'll give the ball back to them. There was one occasion today when he ran the ball out and it looked as if he was going to go and tackle someone on the North Bank. He went charging after the ball, over the line and onto the track. I thought, 'Cor, what's happening here?'

I was pulling his leg yesterday. I said, 'Steady down, Robbo, I know it's getting near match day.' You can tell when it's Friday because he is already getting all excited, and on a Saturday morning he is bubbling over. On a Saturday before we go out he'll rush into the gym and start smashing balls around. You have to watch yourself in there sometimes because the balls really fly around. And it carries over onto the field. He needs to be careful, because he goes flying into these tackles, and sometimes you think, 'Watch it, Robbo, I don't want you to break your leg', because he goes diving in, sliding in, and he only needs to get someone nasty who he has crunched a couple of times and the next time he goes in we might see him getting done.

There was a bit of light relief too. Cloughie went and sat in the Arsenal dugout at one stage. I was standing with Viv Anderson and we couldn't believe our eyes. 'What's he up to now? Has he cracked up again?' We didn't know what was happening.

When I went into the Forest dressing room afterwards I realized there was only Viv Anderson and Ian Bowyer left from when I was there. Garry Birtles was injured, so he didn't play.

Cloughie was pleasant enough. 'Come in, sit down, how's the family? How are you doing? Do you know him over there? Do you know Frans, have you met the goalkeeper?'

There was one absolutely typical piece of Clough. Viv was staying down for the weekend. Cloughie said to him, 'If you fancy doing a bit on Monday . . . what do you think?'

Viv said, 'Yeah, I'll do a bit of training on Monday.'

So Cloughie said, 'Well, make it Monday afternoon. Come and do a bit Monday afternoon.'

And they'd just been beaten 4–1. If we had been beaten 4–1 we'd have been training Monday morning *and* afternoon. But that was typical of Cloughie. He's got his way of doing things and he sticks to what he believes. If you win 5–0 he'll say, 'Okay, see you Wednesday', and if you lose 4–0 he'll still say, 'Okay, see you Wednesday.'

Sometimes if we'd played badly he would have us down at the training ground. It was just a field with brambles and rough surrounding it. There were trees, and grass three feet high; and there was concrete and nettles in the grass, but he'd send you on a run through that. You'd be running in single file with your hands in front of your face to knock the brambles aside and the branches would all be swinging back onto the next person, and your legs would be getting whacks and nettle stings. And when you came out he'd say, 'Right, back you go in there again.' He'd do things like that.

When we trained at the Embankment he would either walk down with Peter Taylor and his dog, or come down in his car. And he would hide behind a tree or sit in the car and watch the training. If anyone was slacking he'd catch him later and say, 'I saw you today', and you would think, 'How did he see that?' You hadn't realized he was there because he'd been hiding behind a tree or walking the dog over the far side of the field.

But we never really trained much. He used to take us for walks or jogging. Sometimes he used to take us on the track running, and he'd suddenly say, 'Right, last man on someone's back', or 'Last man through someone's legs', or 'Last man up in the stand', so then you had to jump over the wall and run up to the back of the stand; or 'Last one out of sight', so you had to run out of sight. Just sharp things like that, and jumping over walls. Twenty minutes and we'd be finished.

We never used to do shooting, or tactics or corners. When we were winning we had things down to a minimum. Play on the Saturday. Do a bit of jogging on the Monday or Tuesday. Play Wednesday. Have Thursday off. Do twenty minutes on Friday. Play again on Saturday.

We did play a lot though, including a lot of testimonials, with Cloughie. As well as European Cup, FA Cup and Milk Cup games he would always fit the odd testimonial in. He'd never hesitate. We'd play at Southampton in the League on Saturday; go back to Nottingham; go down to play at Plymouth on the Monday; go back again, then down to Bristol Rovers on the Wednesday. It didn't worry him.

We played at Sheffield United one night. I can't remember who it was for. About five minutes before half time it was 0–0, and we were just stroking it around; suddenly we heard someone shouting from the directors' box. And we thought, 'God, he's here!' We hadn't thought he had come that night, because he hadn't travelled with us and he arrived late. So we went in at half-time and he gave everyone a pasting. I'd missed a chance, taken it half-heartedly. 'Call yourself an England player and you miss a chance like that?' At the end of the tirade he said, 'Right. I want five goals this half.' And we went out and won 5–0.

Things like that happened. It was almost uncanny sometimes the way things worked out exactly as he had discussed them. The time when we played Cologne in Cologne, which must have been one of our greatest results ever, and was certainly the most memorable match we played, it was almost unbelievable. Everyone had written us off after we'd drawn 3–3 at home. He said before the start, 'We'll hold them until half-time. Okay, if we score, we score, but hold them until half-time.' At half-time he said, 'Right, we'll keep it tight. If you get a goal with about twenty minutes to go that'll be ideal.' And we scored with about twenty minutes left.

When we played Southampton in the League Cup Final, we were losing 1–0 at half-time, and he was as calm as anything. We weren't playing well, but he said, 'Don't worry. All I'm asking you to do is pass it to a red shirt. That's all I want you to do, let's just get out there and pass it to a red shirt and we'll come back.' And we went out there and it was, 'Here, you have it. Now you' – pass, pass, pass, and we trounced them in the second half. He was brilliant before games. He used to get into the changing room at 2.45. He'd come in about 2.30 after his game of squash, go into the bathroom and have a bath and a cup of coffee, and come through about 2.45. He'd tell us about his game – if he'd won. If he'd lost he wouldn't mention it. He'd put his clean kit on, get his squash racquet in his hand and say, 'Right, here's what we've got to do today', and go through it in about five minutes. He didn't say a lot. 'Get the ball, put your foot on the ball and give it to a red shirt. Get into the penalty box. You won't score unless you get players into the penalty box', and that was about it. But it was enough. You were raring to go once he'd finished talking to you. He could really lift you, all you needed was a couple of minutes with him. I can't remember now what he said, but it must have been things like, 'You are a good player. They are terrified of you today, just keep getting into that box.'

Sometimes after a game he would say, 'You're a credit to the game.' And once he said that, that was everything. If he said that to me it kept me going right through the weekend.

We never really discussed the opposition. Peter Taylor used to watch them, but all he would say was, 'This bloke can't play. He's got no pace, can't do this, can't do that. You'll wipe the floor with him. All we've got to do is get our attitude right. The goalkeeper is rubbish . . .' and so it went on. I remember once when we played Derby he said, 'Take that Roy McFarland on. He'll be frightened to death of you. He can't run any longer. Take him on every time.' And that was it.

Peter had this classic before the first game against Cologne. 'I've watched Cologne,' he said. 'The keeper can't catch a thing. There's no height in the defence, they are very rusty on crosses. They've got no pace in the side.' We were two down after ten minutes and they were flying all over the place. Afterwards we said, 'Did you get the right report here, Pete? No pace in the side???'

24 OCTOBER

Don was very complimentary about me in the papers this morning. There have been a lot of questions about Charlie still not scoring, and Don said he was a young player who had a lot to learn, and that he should try and learn from me, a player who 'has won League championships and European Cups'. I hope he has changed his mind about me now. Last year when I came back I think he felt my attitude wasn't right, that when I play for England and when I really want to do it I go out and turn it on no matter what, but that for some games I wasn't in the mood. He may have been right to some extent, but last year I had so many niggling injuries and I just couldn't get it to work. And with playing football without a break for a year because of the World Cup I was jaded. But that long lay-off this summer has given me my appetite back, and I feel much stronger, fitter and more determined now.

But we have a better relationship this year. He obviously thinks I can play, and he is not trying to play for me in the way I thought he was last year. Last year Don said I wanted the ball played to my feet too much. I'd come off my marker, see that I was in front of him for the midfield to play the ball up to me. Don said I wanted them to play that pass too much, and that what I should do was come towards the player with the ball and then spin round and go the other way behind the defender for a ball played into space. He was constantly on to me about spinning away, spinning away. I disagreed with him at the time, but now I think he had a point, because I'm losing defenders. There have been a lot of runs when I've been pulling away because I've come towards the ball as if I wanted it to feet, and then checked out, and it is only because Don kept on and on at me to do it and sell defenders dummies. So he has undoubtedly added something to my game. The perfect example was Saturday's goal against Forest.

It is also because I'm re-adjusting to English football. Partly I have a slightly better understanding with the team. But I would love Petrovic still to be playing, because I think I'm losing my marker so many times that anyone with a bit of vision could hit me all the time. There are so many occasions when I think if I get the ball here I'll get a strike at goal. And the other players either can't see it or aren't good enough to get it to me. Whereas Petrovic. . . . On the few occasions I played with him I'd see something and think, 'I could go there, but no one will see me', and all of a sudden the ball would be there, because he'd got the ball, and he had seen it.

They gave up too easily on him. By those standards they should sell Charlie and Lee Chapman. Okay, Petrovic didn't tackle, he didn't do everything right. But Charlie hasn't done everything right, Lee Chapman hasn't done everything right. They should have given Petrovic a chance to settle in. I think we would really have seen the best of him this year.

Not all the papers made such good reading. The bloke in the *Express* said that petty jealousies against Charlie were invading the Arsenal changing room. That's ridiculous. Everyone wants him to do well, everyone wants to help him. But that is typical of the situation at the moment. The fact that Charlie hasn't made a huge impact, and especially the fact that he still hasn't got a goal at Highbury, is dominating all the coverage at the moment. It's difficult fitting into a new side, and as I said last season even really outstanding, experienced players like Stapleton, Fischer and Allofs found it so. But the papers and fans never seem to realise that – well the fans are really on Charlie's side – but the papers are carrying on as if they expected him to get a hat-trick every week. So the fact that he hasn't scored at Highbury is providing them with lots of material – Nicholas crisis', all that rubbish.

25 OCTOBER
Arsenal 1 Plymouth Argyle 0

26 OCTOBER
There was a dreadful incident. Whether it had anything to do with Monday's piece in the paper I don't know, but when Paul Davis had a shot instead of passing to Charlie the crowd started booing, which was outrageous. It said in the papers this morning that I should have passed to Charlie, because he was free, but there was no possible way I could have got it to him in time, so I played a simpler ball to Paul.

The ball came from the right-back position. They were attacking and we caught them half on the break. It came out high from our defence down the right. I took it on my chest, and as soon as it hit my chest I knew from the crowd's reaction that something was happening behind me. They were obviously shouting that Charlie was free. But I rarely hit things blind – if I know where players are I'll do it, but not on spec. I got the ball down and looked up, but by then everything was closing down. And I absolutely refuse to let the crowd dictate to me how I'm going to play, and play a ball which was probably going to be cut out in consequence. Trying to force things is ridiculous. So I played the ball to Paul.

He said afterwards he should have passed to Charlie, because Charlie was in a better position, but he chose to shoot. And the crowd started booing, which is terrible. I thought at the time the booing might have been for me. I just didn't know. But Paul said afterwards, 'No, it wasn't. It was me for shooting!' Booing a player for shooting!

All right, they desperately want Charlie to score. We want Charlie to score, but you can't give him the ball all the time, especially as he isn't losing his marker. He wants to beat his man with the ball at his feet all the time instead of making a yard so that the ball can be slipped to him.

I think crowds have changed. They don't seem to have the passion there used to be. You used to read about crowds lifting a team by getting behind them, but it seems to me more now that the team has to lift the crowd – they respond when you start playing well, rather than their encouragement pushing you on when things aren't going well.

Professionals often affect to despise the fans, but I think with the decline in support we've become more aware of them. We often talk about whether they come to watch good football, or just to see their

180

team win. And although everyone in the game pays lip-service to the belief that we have to provide good entertainment, we always end up by saying that the Arsenal fans – and others – want to see their side win rather than see a good game which they lose.

Charlie is very down at the moment. He had a poor game, and he said afterwards he doesn't know what he has got to do to get it right. But he doesn't seem to be talking enough on the pitch. Sometimes we are in each other's way. He never seems able to get away from his marker. And, crucially, he doesn't seem to get into the penalty box much. He had a good chance in the fifth minute. He didn't connect well, and the keeper saved it.

It is getting harder and harder for him at the moment. Celtic created so many chances, but we are not the most attacking English first division team at the moment, and chances are hard to come by; although I've had quite a few more this season. I put that down to myself, however, to wanting, as Don said, to be the best player on the field.

I thought it was a good game. Both chairmen came into the dressing rooms and said it had been a good game to watch. In this morning's papers, it seemed like a completely different game. We did miss a few chances. I missed one, but all credit to their goalkeeper, he tricked me.

I now know why Colin Hill was moved back to defence. I went down the right and cut into the box. He was running in slightly behind me so I laid it back to him, ten yards out with only the keeper to beat. He completely miskicked. So that's why they turned him into a defender!

Kenny Sansom is playing very well at the moment. He is looking much more confident on the ball, getting forward more than he has been doing, and looking more relaxed.

He still can't score though. Last night he sent this shot whizzing into the North Bank. He's a much bigger danger for the people there than he is to goalkeepers! He had a good chance on Saturday too. He's not the best in front of goal, but at least he is starting to get there and get his shots in.

Lee Chapman has obviously been bombed out now after his display against Coventry. He's got no chance. He wasn't even in the squad last night – possibly they don't want him to get cup-tied. Yet he is being measured for a new club blazer on Friday, along with the rest of the lads.

It would have been different under Cloughie. Lee would have gone by now, never mind losing £400,000. If Cloughie thinks someone can't play he doesn't want them around, doesn't want to be associated with them. He is not afraid to admit he made a mistake, even if it costs the club money.

I think one of Cloughie's great secrets was putting the right players in the right positions. Players who were happy and comfortable in certain positions were just asked to stay there. And that might be a problem at Arsenal at the moment. Colin Hill isn't really a right-back. Sundy, although he is playing well at the moment, is not really a right-winger. Rixy is playing on the left, which I think is his best position, but that leaves Paul Davis in the middle, and I don't think he's good enough to take that responsibility.

The other thing about Cloughie was that you all had a certain job, you were never asked to do two or three different things. You did your own job. He used to say to me, 'Get into the box, get penalties, create goals, score goals. Take people on, run at players.' With another player it would be something else. It was the same with the team. We had a pattern and stuck to it. But we really worked it all out among ourselves. When we attacked we *all* attacked, and when we defended we *all* defended. There was a classic against Leeds in the League Cup semi-final at Elland Road when we beat them 3–1. I shall remember for ever an incident from the TV recording of it. Leeds had this breakaway and they were really racing. Then all of a sudden there were these seven red shirts in the picture. It was one, then two, three . . . four . . . five . . . six . . . seven all straight back, and it snapped shut. We used to smother teams. And he never used to say, 'When we lose the ball, everyone get back.' It wasn't coached. We just did it, we just went out and played.

I've been feeling so fit, yet I keep getting these silly injuries. Last night I twisted my ankle. I've had more injuries in the last twelve months than in the rest of my career. This time I went past a fellow and he took me from behind. He caught me on the calf with his studs, and as I went down he was still on top of me and my ankle twisted under me.

I went out after the game with Graeme Fowler and Jon Holmes; Jon has just started handling Graeme. David Gower introduced him. I've never had much interest in cricket, in fact I didn't even know who Graeme Fowler was until the other week, but knowing David has made me watch out for him when it is on television, and I expect I'll do the same with Graeme now. He seems a nice lad.

I've suggested that Stewart Robson should join us. Jon is not one of those agents who gets as many players as he can together to take ten or twenty per cent from. It has to be something the player wants to do, and hope it attracts the kind of independent player we like to be associated with. He is also talking to John Barnes.

It's difficult for young players though. I remember Jon taking a couple of Midlands players out and saying to them, 'We'd like you to join us. We think you are good players and if your football comes right then it all follows.' But young players sometimes don't realize that football is the primary thing, and they were swayed by some fast-talking agent who promised them a sponsored car and a boot contract. So they signed a contract with him and they got that, but that was about all. He really couldn't care less how your career is going, whereas Jon sorts out everything, pension schemes, anything to do with your contract, and future planning. I've got over eighteen months of my contract to go, but we had a discussion last night and this morning about what we are going to do, what's going to happen. Jon thinks I should go and see Don and Terry at the end of the season and tell them I'm not happy with the way things are going if we have another mediocre season.

But that sums up the approach. Because I've only played at Arsenal for one year, and already we are talking about the next contract or the next move, whichever it is going to be. I might stay at Arsenal for ten years, but we are planning well ahead. That's why I cannot understand all the speculation you get in the summer when players don't know whether to re-sign, or if they are going abroad or not, like there was with Glenn Hoddle last summer. If it's on, you shouldn't leave it to the last minute; you can sign a contract six months beforehand if a club wants you.

27 OCTOBER

Ever since Paul Mariner asked for a transfer, there has been a lot of stuff in the papers about the money I'm on. It was supposed to be talking to me and some of the others when he was with England that made him discontented. When I see the figures quoted I keep wondering, 'Have I sold myself short?' I think Arsenal got quite a good investment, because when I look around and see how difficult it is to buy players they are going to have a difficult job trying to replace me.

Clubs and the public are funny about players' salaries. If Arsenal had met Frank Stapleton's demands I'm sure he would have been happy to stay; and they would have been better off financially and on the field, because they spent a lot more than they got for him between Charlie and Lee Chapman, and even when Charlie settles he will have to go some to be as good a player for Arsenal as Frank was.

I'm happy with my contract. I could have made a lot more by going to Italy, and I hope they realize that.

Paul did ask me something about his contract, and I referred him to Jon. I don't know what Paul earns, and I hope he doesn't know what I earn. I certainly didn't tell him. The only person I tell about my vast salary is my wife. And Carole doesn't know exactly, because you would have to tell her in pounds, shillings and pence per week, not spread over three years.

And Jon wouldn't tell anyone. He did Luther's contract with AC Milan in the summer, and although we work together and I would like to venture into that area when I stop playing, he wouldn't discuss the details with me. I don't mean I want to be an agent, although when you see the way some of the agents around at the moment rip players off it can seem like a good idea. But the kind of job I'd really like, if I stay in football, is to be a manager in the German sense, like Gunter Netzer at Hamburg. The man who does the buying and selling, negotiates the contracts and transfer fees. I really enjoy doing contract negotiations and I think doing that would be interesting.

28 OCTOBER

I haven't trained since the Plymouth match because of my ankle. I was having treatment today and Roy Johnson asked how I felt.

'Okay. I'll play, it's not absolutely right but I'll play.'

'We haven't got a big enough squad,' he said. 'You aren't a hundred per cent fit, you shouldn't be playing.'

So I said, 'Well, players do play with injuries the whole time. There are probably three or four at the moment who aren't one hundred per cent fit.'

That is true. It's just a fact of English football life, and with the amount of games we play I think it is inevitable.

We have a hell of a League Cup draw, Spurs away. It'll be great for the fans, it should really get them buzzing for the next couple of weeks.

Sundy broke a bone in his hand in the fracas at Plymouth. He has to have it strapped up before training and is getting a lot of mickey-taking. Someone told him today, 'Frank Warren's been on the phone for you. Who have you got on your next bill?', and there are all the comments about 'Getting taped up for the gloves, Al?'

29 OCTOBER
Aston Villa 2 Arsenal 6

Roy Johnson, our physio, had a really bad day today. On the coach up to Villa he said I shouldn't play; and he also said he fancied Luton to win at Anfield. I got five goals, and so did Ian Rush – Luton lost 6–0. Roy was given a very bad time afterwards, but he said it was the first time he had ever been really worried about letting a player go out. He didn't explain away the Luton tip quite so easily.

I think he had been genuinely worried. He said on the coach, 'You've got a badly twisted ankle. Really, you shouldn't play.' But I said I'd be all right. Then when we got to Villa Park, although I didn't know it at the time, Roy came out to have a look at how I went in the warm-up. But of course when the adrenalin starts flowing and you get a bit excited you tend to forget the knocks. And the pitch was absolutely fantastic.

In fact the main problem before the game was Terry. After the Forest game Rixy had said to one or two journalists that the change after the Coventry performance was because I'd spotted things in the stand about people not wanting the ball, and we had a meeting about it. Well, it wasn't quite like that. It was just that after a bad performance like that, if you've been sitting in the stand, you'll go into the changing room and they'll say, 'Well, you were watching, what did you think?' So I told them. But in the papers it came out as if it had been a special team meeting. Terry wasn't very pleased. He said, 'You know what you've said in the papers. Well, I've had so many letters asking why Don and I had to wait for you to spot it, or why hadn't we done anything about it, I've told them all to write to you.'

I don't know whether my talk sunk in, but against Forest we played some good football, and today we played some great stuff. When you got the ball there were always a couple of options open to you, and sometimes it even looked as if we had two extra men in the first half; that's because of people wanting the ball and also running off it.

It was one of those days. We started off very sharp, and even before we scored you could tell it was going well. We had a couple of half chances before the first goal, which came after about five minutes – it was probably the best goal of the five. I held on to the ball, went past someone and played a one-two. The ball came looping back, but it was behind me, and I managed to hit it in with my right foot.

The second had a good build-up down the right. I went into the near post for a header, which I glided past Spink.

For the third I played two one-twos with Charlie. I got the ball from Kenny's throw-in, turned, played a one-two with Charlie, got it back and put him in. He drew Spink and knocked it back and I walked it into the net – a classic goal even though the finish was only a tap-in.

With the fourth we hit the bar, and I just got in there first for the rebound. The fifth, which looked like a gift, was probably the most difficult one to actually put in. It shot across the box, hit the floor and bounced up and as it was going away from me I had to steer it back into the net. I did it as if it was nothing, but if it had been the first chance instead of coming along when I'd already scored four I might have been a bit worried about it.

You don't really think beyond the game while it is going on. It was only afterwards that people started talking about Ted Drake and his record of seven goals for Arsenal. But at the time when the first goal went in I thought, 'That's got us off to a good start.' Then the second and third came, and I thought, 'That's good, a hat-trick', but when you've got three you don't seriously think you'll get a fourth, even though it was still so early in the game. I couldn't believe it when I headed the fourth. And when the fifth arrived just after half-time it was becoming a joke. I thought, 'This can't go on', and it didn't. I didn't get another chance after that. But my only thought at the time was that the game had put me up to ten goals in the eight games I've played this season.

Looking back of course the record was on. I'm sure that if I had had another chance I would have put it in. When we scored the sixth I was in position to score at the near post, but Rixy put it over the back to Brian McDermott and he put it in. I'd certainly like the chance again to have five goals after fifty minutes.

30 OCTOBER

One or two of the papers said Charlie was very unselfish not to shoot himself for the third goal yesterday. I thought there was only one thing he could have done – any good player would have done it. It was to his credit, because he is under pressure and in his situation a lot of players would have hit it hopefully once they got into that position. But because he is a good player he did what you would expect of him.

31 OCTOBER

Noddy Talbot laughed his head off at me today. I was complaining, living up to Jon's statement that I've always moaned about not getting the ball enough wherever I've been. He said I moaned at Forest, I moaned at Cologne and now I'm moaning at Arsenal. Even when I'd got a few goals and played well I'd still say, 'So-and-so could have given me a better pass', or 'So-and-so should have given me the ball then.' I suppose this time really proved his point. I said, 'Charlie could have put me through at Villa twice. He hung onto the ball too long when I'd lost my marker and he could have slipped me in.' Noddy fell about. 'You scored five! What are you going on about that for?' But I think I'll always complain about that sort of thing. It's better this season though. Graham and Kenny have got to know me better now, they know how I like to get the ball, and there is greater understanding than last season. And I get a lot of supply from them because they are on the ball a lot.

I think I'm showing more determination too. If things aren't coming right I am making sure I get onto the balls and turn them into good passes. It's no use saying, 'Oh, that's a bad ball', and letting it go. But if it is a really bad ball, I will still say something about it. I get on to Stewart Robson a lot. He wins the ball so well and then wastes all the good work he has done because he loses concentration. He wants to get rid of it so quickly, and he does lose it. There was an instance against Villa in which he'd got the ball and I was in again. I was in the clear. He saw me go, which is well and good, but he tried to rush it, tried to hook it on to me, and put it out of play. If he had taken his time, taken it on his chest, I wouldn't have got the ball so early, but I would have received it in a much better position going in on goal. So if he had taken his time initially the whole movement would have been a lot quicker because he would have released a much better ball.

But I know I complain about the service a lot. I want the ball all the time. Obviously I can't have it all the time, but I think I ought to have it most of the time. I might be wrong, it might just be me, but the number of times I lose my marker and I think I'm in the clear if someone could get the ball to me is incredible – and I'm not talking about needing an impossible ball, only the ten- to twenty-yard balls. I might get the ball and play it and go straight away, and if someone's quick enough or clever enough to see me going, I'm in. But unfortunately we haven't got that style of player at the moment.

I didn't train today. My ankle is sore. Davo trained, but shouldn't have done. He felt an injury on Saturday, and training made it worse. He definitely won't play at Chelsea in the testimonial tomorrow night, and must be doubtful for Saturday.

He is still doing his thirty miles a day. I still check his car whenever I can, and although he denies it, I'm convinced. I asked him if he did sixty miles one day whether he had to give it a day off the next. I keep meaning to ask him what he thinks about his own body. Does he have to stop after he's run up and down the pitch a couple of times?

1 NOVEMBER
Chelsea 2 Arsenal 1 Mickey Droy Testimonial

2 NOVEMBER
According to the papers this morning, one of the chefs in the Chelsea restaurant came on in the second half. That summed up the game, because you wouldn't have known – he could have been any one of the twenty-two players on the pitch. It was a terrible night all round. There was some sickening crowd trouble. In a testimonial match! I just couldn't believe it. And to top it all my ankle went again.

Before the game Terry said, 'Just play the first half.' I said, 'No, I want to play the whole game.'

'I'm telling you. You play forty-five minutes and then come off. No arguing, that's all you are having.' So I said, 'Suit yourself.' But after about twenty-five minutes I went over on it in exactly the same spot as I did against Plymouth. It was as if I'd got a tennis ball stuffed down my sock. It was very painful. I went down on the far side of the ground away from the dressing rooms and when Roy Johnson came on he said, 'Right, off straight away', so I went to the touchline and sat down for a couple of minutes to allow the pain to ease.

By then the crowd trouble had started. There were a few Arsenal fans who had paid to come and support us, and obviously Mickey Droy was getting the benefit from their presence. They were behind the away-team goal. About five minutes before I went down these Chelsea fans had gone walking round the ground from the Shed to try and get at them. I just couldn't believe it. And even worse, the people in the main stand were shouting encouragement, telling them to do it, getting them all keyed up to go and bash the Arsenal fans up. It was horrible. There we were out on the pitch trying to have a nice, friendly game, and there was this fighting on the terraces. If it had been my testimonial I would have thought seriously about just walking off, saying, 'Thanks, lads, but it is not worth the bother', and taken the teams off. It would have been a shame for the people who were there to watch the game, but with that mob fighting, and half the main stand egging them on there weren't that many people there to watch the game.

When I got up from sitting on the touchline I wondered how to get there. Do I go past the Shed and risk all their abuse? Or do I go the other way where there is that horde trying to get at the Arsenal fans? It was a bit of a dilemma, but I decided to avoid the Shed and take my chances the other way. And that was all right, they didn't say much. But when I got in front of the main stand I got lots of abuse thrown at me. It was indescribable, really, really horrible.

Dave Madden played instead of Paul Davis. I've seen him play better, but I think he impressed a few people there.

Rixy was not very happy afterwards. He always likes everything to be spot on; he thinks the sort of sloppiness in yesterday's game is bad because it can carry over into the real thing. It's the same as his attitude to training: if you are sloppy during the week you get found out on Saturday.

We still have arguments about this. Of course if I know we've got to work hard I'll do it. I'll do the running and the doggies and give it everything. And if I do a finishing exercise, whether shooting or heading, I'll really concentrate and do it properly, because I know it is going to benefit me. But playing practice games and five-a-sides I can't. If we are playing football in training it depends how I feel on the day. Some days I can gee myself up to give everything, sometimes I can't take it that seriously. I can't work up the enthusiasm to do so. And so I'm still regularly getting the Friday vote as the worst player in the five-a-side.

At Arsenal I think they realize now that it doesn't affect my performance on Saturday. It is the same as that discussion with Roy Johnson (when I was out with my hamstring) about being able to do the exercise on Saturday, even if I couldn't during the week. And it was the same as not scoring in pre-season, but saying to Kenny Sansom that I knew I would score against Luton because I knew I'd be keyed up and sharp and wanting to do it. And at Arsenal they accept it. But Rixy doesn't; he still moans at me.

Yet there are lots of players who look world beaters in training, and you think, 'He's got to be given his chance.' But when he is you often find there is something lacking.

As usual after a testimonial, they had drinks laid on. I didn't stay long, but we had a chat about testimonials in general. Players' attitudes towards them are changing. There were 7,000 people there last night. Well, Mickey Droy didn't actually play that many games for Chelsea when you look at his record, but if you regard that as your reward for ten or twelve years' service, I wouldn't want to have to rely on it – particularly if it's a wet night; whereas in the old days players thought it was a great thing to have.

The other thing is that players think that although you've done that length of service, the clubs aren't giving you anything. Sometimes players even have to pay for the floodlighting. All the club do is let you have use of their ground, which doesn't cost them very much, so the public can come and give the player their money as a reward for a player's loyalty to their club. The clubs get off lightly; they think they are doing you a great favour by granting you a testimonial, but in fact they aren't really giving you anything much.

A friend of mine phoned me today to see how I was after he'd read that I'd been taken off last night. I said I hoped it would be all right for Saturday. So he said, 'It's next Wednesday you've got to be fit for.'

'Why, what's next Wednesday?' I'd completely forgotten about the Tottenham match. That could never have happened in Nottingham; you miss the build-up in London. It has its compensations though. In Nottingham virtually everywhere you went you would meet a friend or see someone you knew. In Cologne it got to ridiculous lengths; people would follow you around in the streets. They would walk up and stare at you, or follow you up and down. And they were roller-skating crazy in Cologne. If you went into the main shopping area you would have about twenty kids on roller skates circling around you. It was like the circus coming to town. I used to hate it. I didn't want to go out in the town with Carole; I'd walk with my head down and hope not to be recognized it was so embarrassing.

3 NOVEMBER
There's another Paul Davis story building up, it's a classic. After the Chelsea game he had some friends with him, and he wanted to go to the Valbonne nightclub. Usually, as footballers, you can get into these places, although in theory they require membership. Charlie is a member – he had a membership card sent to him through the post when he first came down. So Paul asked Charlie if he could borrow it.

Charlie said, 'You must be nuts, Davo. They'll know you aren't Charlie Nicholas.'

'Oh, I'll get in. It's just so if they ask questions I can say that you sent me down and here's the card to prove it.' So Charlie gave it to him. And of course, it being Davo, they took the card off him at the door. Lee Chapman saw him yesterday and was told the story, and he tipped Charlie off. So when Davo came in this morning he went up to Charlie and said, 'I've got a bit of bad news for you.'

'Don't tell me, Davo. They haven't taken the card off you, have they?'

'How did you know that?'

'Well, you said, "Bad news." That cost me £2,000. It's a life membership.'

'Really?'

'Yes.'

'Oh dear,' said Davo. 'What am I going to do about that? I'll go halves with you.'

'Halves?' shouted Charlie. 'Halves? I need the money, Davo, I've just bought a house. That's £2,000. Two grand!'

Paul looked really crestfallen, but he said, 'Oh, okay. I'll give you a cheque tomorrow.'

4 NOVEMBER
I haven't trained all week because of my ankle, but I shall play tomorrow. Paul won't play, but they haven't put Dave Madden in; they are putting Brian Talbot straight in and he hasn't played for weeks, nor even really trained fully. But it looks as if David O'Leary won't play, so Tony Adams is getting his chance even earlier than I

expected, so perhaps they are going for experience. I'd take a chance on Madden.

Charlie asked Paul if he'd got the cheque for him. Paul said, 'No, but I'll definitely bring it tomorrow.'

5 NOVEMBER
Arsenal 1 Sunderland 2
When we got to Highbury Paul had been having treatment. Then he came into the changing room with his cheque book. A few of us were in on the story. He was looking at Charlie, very downcast, and writing this cheque out when I walked past him.

'That's a bit of bad news that is, Davo.'

'Yeah,' he said. 'I didn't realize it was going to cost me this.'

So I said, 'Well, all the lads were shocked when you took the card. Because we knew if you had it taken off you it would cost this money.'

He said, 'I can't believe it.' He looked as if he was going to cry, but to do him credit he wrote out a cheque for £2,000 and handed it over, while everyone was suppressing giggles. And Charlie took it and ripped it up, and said, 'I can't accept it, Davo.'

Then everyone started laughing, and Davo couldn't understand what was happening. He said, 'Charlie, you really mean it, you really mean it?' He thought Charlie was doing him a favour. Eventually we told him. He was so happy, he could have gone out and played.

He might as well have done, too. It was the same old story: we have a couple of good wins, think we are on a run, then go and blow it at home against a side we are expected to beat. You can accept being beaten by United and Liverpool, but losing at home to Coventry and Sunderland! If we had taken the points from those two matches we would be second now. It is so disappointing.

There are two good teams: United and Liverpool, with maybe Tottenham, if they get it together, although I don't think they are as good as the other two. They've started to push up there now, but there's a long way to go. They will probably make it eventually, around the end of the season. But I was talking to someone the other day about the size of their squad. They've got twenty-two first-team players, and while it is good to have competition – we could certainly do with more – I think that is too many. He was saying, 'It's healthy

Paul Mariner in an Arsenal shirt — one of the most important factors in the club's turn round under Don Howe.

Photographers always try and come up with a new angle.

For a change, all eyes are not on Don Howe

Training under Weisweiler, hard work but very enjoyable.

Rinus Michels watching training — with him it was just hard work.

and good', but I think that's a couple too many. Players then think that they *have* to do well or someone will take their places; when that starts to happen players can play for themselves rather than the team. I think that has happened with England over the last few years, because players come in and their performance has to be right or they are out again.

Apart perhaps from those teams the rest are also-rans. We ought to beat all of them, and we only have United and Liverpool to play once more. The rest we know we can beat home and away, or should be able to anyway. If we could get a couple of quality players into the team we could hold our own with anybody – we should be able to push for the title.

It's just a question of consistency. The basis is there, I think, but we need someone badly at the moment, or we are just going to be in with the mob – although there are probably a few teams saying that at the moment.

Sunderland's two goals didn't help matters. They got one in the third minute, which really boosted their confidence. It was a good one for them, but a bad one for us. I was right in line with it when Tony Adams lost it out near the touchline, and I thought, 'If he curls this, he's going to put it in.' Pat was out of his goal at his near post and he was walking back in watching. It looked as if he was thinking, 'He's not going to shoot from there.' Then all of a sudden he curls it in and Pat thinks, 'Oh, he's shot!' and it was too late. I thought for once Pat was a bit slow, because you would never expect anyone to beat him from there.

The second just bobbled in. I don't know who headed it, but it bobbled in off two of our men. Someone kicked it, it hit someone else on the line, rolled in, Kenny slipped as he went to clear, and it was in the net. And that was that: another home defeat.

My goal had a good finish, but afterwards people kept on about the fact that they thought I'd have aimed for the other corner because of the angle I was at. Kenny chipped the ball in, and I was going for it when I saw Robbo going for it – so I checked off and shouted for him to back-head it. He did and I twisted and volleyed it into the corner at the nearer post. It went more or less where I wanted it to, but it was a little bit near the post for comfort, because I didn't quite catch it flush. I caught it reasonably well, but if I'd caught it exactly as I wanted it would have been a foot the other way instead of going inside the side netting. Leighton James, though, said to me on the field, 'You miss-hit that.' You'll sometimes say that as a joke when someone's really hit a blinder from thirty yards, but his tone of voice suggested he meant it, so I said, 'You've got to be joking. Are you serious?'

And he said, 'You caught that with your shin.' I couldn't believe it. I've heard people say his legs are going, but his tongue is still working. He never shut up the whole match; he got on my nerves. And when he said that. . . .

Then Pat said afterwards that he'd been in line, and 'You'd think it would have gone in the other corner.' I was quite heated. 'I meant it to go in that corner!' I was amazed that people kept on about expecting me to go for the other corner.

Noddy got injured again. It was probably the same as me against Plymouth. You go through forty minutes all right, and the injury has cleared up, but your muscles are getting tired and you don't realize it. That's when it is likely to go again, which is what happened to him in the second half. He had been doing quite well, and then he knocked this ball and it went. He had to stay on and hobble around for the last twenty minutes because they'd taken Sundy off a few minutes earlier. He probably wasn't having the best of games, but looking back it seemed a strange decision, given that Noddy was having his first game for weeks and had been plunged straight in to the first division and so was likely to get a bit tired.

6 NOVEMBER

In the *Sunday Times* today Brian Glanville said that Charlie and I looked like two inside-forwards in search of a centre-forward. He'd said something similar before the start of the season, that Charlie and I were similar sorts of players.

I don't see how he can say that. I've got eleven goals in nine games this season. Do I need a centre-forward to play with? I don't care who I play with. I would like to change things a bit. I'd put Sundy up there with me and say to Charlie, 'Tuck in behind us and see if it is any different', because he is obviously getting no joy at the moment.

He had a reasonable first half yesterday, but he is not getting in the box enough to score goals. If you don't get in the box and gamble you are never going to score goals. It's a question of getting in there, and getting in before defenders, not waiting. Then you get the ones that hit you and go in off your knee or your face. But Charlie wants to jink past someone, then bend it in from eighteen yards where the keeper can see it coming. If they go in, 'Great goal.' He'll do a person beautifully, but once you are in the box, you don't even have to beat someone, you just want to do enough to get a sight of goal and then it's 'Bang!' It's not a question of scoring pretty goals, but of getting inside the eighteen-yard line, which is where you score goals from, and he is not doing it. And he keeps talking to reporters and saying how close he is coming to scoring, but until he starts getting in there he is not going to score. Don has been pointing this out to him. In fact Don said something yesterday which I take as a great compliment, coming from him. He said to Charlie, 'Just do what Tony does. Try and learn from him. Watch what he does and learn from him. He likes the ball to his feet, but if it is not on, he's away. He's moved. But you want everything to feet, which is easy for defenders.'

Don has been telling him he is too static, because he has been standing still a lot, wanting balls played to him. And if they haven't come he has stood still. When they eventually do come he's been kicked or knocked off the ball. So Don has been saying, 'Look Charlie, you can't just stand up there. You've got to make little angled runs, you've got to create the space so they can give you the ball. You aren't going to get the kind of room you had in Scotland down here.'

Our partnership is not the best at the moment either, because sometimes he'll take one defender too many. He'll have the ball and they'll go to him, and then he should release it, but he hasn't been doing so. And he is not the type of player who will come short then spin and go for the ball over the top, because he is not that quick. I had a word with him because I also felt that on some occasions when he has gone for the ball and has not got it, he stands there looking while I'm behind him. What he should do then, if he hasn't got it, is clear away and leave the space for someone else.

I said to him that if he sees me in a position, and he thinks he is in a better one, he should just shout to me to get out of the way, and I'll go, without thinking. If he shouts, 'Out of the way', or 'Go left', I'll move to create that bit of space for him. He's got to start thinking that way.

He's got all these things to learn. Hopefully he will, and it will make him a better player in the end. I imagine that at Celtic everything came easy to him because he was in a good team, and he didn't have to work that hard to create chances. In the first division it's not like that – particularly at Arsenal at the moment; you have got to fight for everything.

He wants to do well, he listens to Don and accepts that it is down to him. Of course it isn't *just* down to him, which was what I said last year when I was struggling to integrate. We would all like better service from midfield; Don accepts that there is not much coming from there at the moment. But determination comes into it too. If you are determined enough to want to do it then you are going to do it.

There was a quote in one paper this morning from David O'Leary saying he was only going to play on Wednesday if he was completely fit. It made Graham Rix and I raise our eyebrows a bit when we read it; Graham has got a bad heel; I've got a bad ankle. There are probably four or five people playing at the moment who are not one hundred per cent fit.

Graham and I always meet for a drink on Sunday at lunchtime. We go to the Beehive in Enfield. It's a real man's pub, full of cabbies and barrow-boys, people who work in the market. We daren't go in before one p.m., we stagger out at two p.m. as it is, and if we got there before one o'clock we'd never make it.

I think that we should up our quota of nightclub visits. The cut-down obviously hasn't worked, we aren't playing any better now than we did last year, so I've suggested that instead of going to Stringfellows three times a week we should go several times. And if Don or Terry are reading this, that's a joke. . . .

Don was quoted in the paper as saying that Rixy is like a gambler who loses a tenner, so then puts on twenty pounds and so on, that if he gives the ball away trying to make a really difficult pass he'll try and make this an even more difficult one next time. I've told him that he tries to force things. Away from home he's fine – he plays it simple, there's more space and we carve teams up. But at home he tries to force it, whacking these ambitious long balls. The sign of a good player is knowing when to do it, and when not to do it. He is not having the best of seasons really, but he is definitely a good player.

He's not frightened to keep doing it though, I'll say that for him. But Rixy doesn't follow Cloughie's advice of 'Just give it to a red shirt, and if you are having a bad time make doubly sure you give it to a colleague.'

If he is having a bad time he wants to get out of it so badly that he wants to do something exceptional to lift himself. But it's not just one bad ball: he'll then think, 'I've got to make up for that one', and you get another, then another, instead of him thinking, 'It's one of those days', and playing it simple. But there is a lot resting on him, because we haven't got anyone else to open things up.

Graham finds having a friend who is a director a little strange. He is not quite sure how to relate to him, he feels a bit uncomfortable about it. We still go out with him with our wives, but Graham is not too sure about it. I couldn't care less. I treat him as a friend and that's that. Obviously we still talk about football; now he knows one side of it, and I know the other. But I don't ask him what's going on in the boardroom.

Jon Holmes doesn't approve either. He thinks you can't have a friend who is a director. He says, 'What about when you come to discuss your contract?' I don't see that as a problem. If he says, 'We don't want you at Arsenal', that's fair enough. And it certainly wouldn't embarrass me to go and ask him for a fortune. If he doesn't give it to me, he doesn't, but once we are away from Highbury and negotiations I'll still go and have a drink with him. I'm sure I can separate the two.

It is sometimes a bit funny though when we see him with the other directors. Usually we call him Dixie – Dixie Dein. We used to have games of football on his lawn; the Dein family v Arsenal. But if he's standing with the other directors you can't say, 'Hello, Dixie.'

8 NOVEMBER

Dave Madden is in the squad for tomorrow. I think he'll play if Davo is not fit. Obviously I don't want Paul to be injured, but I'd like to see Madden given his chance because I think he'll do well. He's a good player, and I think he'll sort them out. Hoddle will be jumping a bit if he's around. But if Roberts moves into midfield – which the papers say he might – there will be some clash between those two. Madden's a hard player, even in training when he is not trying to, he catches you.

I hope Roberts does play in midfield. I like him. I think he is a good player. I'd play him for England at the back, especially against continental teams who don't play with a typical centre-forward. If he misses the ball he makes sure he gets the man. I'd much rather play against Price. Against Roberts and Miller last time round there was a lot of off-the-ball stuff. I thought I did all right, but I didn't get much joy out of it.

I think our main problem is going to be if they can get the ball up to us. It's going to be interesting. Charlie has played in Celtic v Rangers, but this is going to be a battle. He is not going to be able to do his fancy footwork. It will certainly be working at hundred m.p.h. to start with. I'm hoping that will suit us. After the 5–0 thumping we got last time we've got to be keyed up for this match. If we are not we don't deserve to be playing for Arsenal. We've got to get something back. That was partly why they beat us 5–0 – because they were so keyed up after we'd beaten them at Christmas at Highbury. It's a game where you have to put everything in. Even if you've no chance of getting a ball, or only a one per cent chance, you've got to *try* and get it. You are fighting for every inch really. That's how it has been in the past, and this time it is a cup-tie.

I'm really looking forward to it. I've got two sore ankles – I got a kick on the other one this morning – and a sore knee. I got a kick on that, on the inside, and it takes me ages to get it moving and warmed up. But it'll be a great atmosphere. And I think Roberts is a good player and I like playing against good players – it's nice to go at them and test yourself against them.

Sometimes when I'm feeling tired and need to lift myself, I say to myself, 'C'mon, you're fit, you're fast, you've got good ball control, you're aggressive, you've got all that going for you, what has the other fellow got? If you can get over this tiredness and keep going you'll do him. Your recovery rate is good, and if you've got all that going for you before we start, the bloke who is marking you can't live with you.' I started doing this about six months ago, and I've done it a couple of times. When I make a run and I'm tired I think I'll just have a look at whoever's run with me and say, 'I'll run him again now and see what he is like after this.'

And you do find that if you start off tired and you battle through it you just get stronger and stronger. Sometimes after ten minutes in a game you think, 'God, another eighty minutes', and then by the end you feel so strong you don't want it to finish.

The other thing this season is that I've really followed Sundy's line. Before every game he says, 'Whatever you do, get your first touch right.' I think he uses that as a prod to himself as well, but he says it to me just before we go out, and I go out with that in mind now, whereas last season I'd maybe take the first ball a little bit easy, and not get it quite right. Now, whatever's happening, I make sure I do it properly when the first ball arrives, whether I've got to challenge for it or just lay it off. Then I say I've got to make sure I do the next one right too and just take it one step at a time. What I'm trying to do on the park at the moment is make sure that everything I do I do the way it should be done.

David O'Leary is playing. He doesn't seem too happy about it. I asked him this morning, 'Are you fit, Dave?' He said, 'Well, they tell me I'm fit, but I don't know if I shall last the game.'

I'm in the squad for Luxembourg. I hope I shall play. I like to think I would have played against Denmark and Hungary if I'd been fit, and there are stories that Trevor Francis is injured again. The team did well against Hungary. But you've got to pick what you think is your best team, whether you've won or not.

Rixy has been left out again. I'd play him on the left-hand side. He's naturally left-footed, he's a grafter as well. It's all against him at the moment, because at Arsenal he knows he has got to do it himself, there's no one else in our midfield going to create anything, but for England he wouldn't think that. He'd be able to relax and play naturally. And I think you've got to play four in midfield. Last time I think Bobby Robson played Mabbutt, who isn't fit now, there, because he wasn't sure about Hoddle. He picked Mabbutt to do Glenn's grafting for him.

After training I went in Lee Chapman's car, and in his paper there was a piece about the young Fulham full-back Parker. I've only seen him once and he didn't really impress me that day, but people at Fulham have said he is one to watch. But in the paper Malcolm Macdonald was saying that he would be an England player in a couple of years. And I remembered meeting Malcolm at a Pony function last year and he was saying then, 'I've got Dean Coney at centre-forward. Best player I've seen in years. No way he's not going to play for England.' And Coney's not even in their team now.

So I said to Lee, 'What an idiot saying that. How can he say that?'

And Lee came back with, 'Yes, but it must be good for the player to have a manager saying that when they do well.'

I could see that. I don't need it now, but it would have encouraged me as a young player. Even now I still like to hear and read nice things about my game. Probably if Terry said to Lee, 'Come on, Lee, you can do it for me. Keep scoring goals and you'll play for England', it would give him a boost. And I do think that's an area where Terry and Don fall down.

Cloughie went the other way when I was a young player. He was playing me left-sided midfield or left-wing in the reserves; and he'd come along to reserve games sometimes. He'd turn up late, and I'd have started off quite well. Then he'd come into the main stand and you'd hear this voice. 'WOODCOCK, do this. Do that', or 'WOOD-COCK, you're useless. Get hold of the ball.' And I'd be shaking, literally. I was a bag of nerves, and as soon as I knew he was watching a game I didn't want to play. It got so bad that I screwed up my courage and went to see him. I said, 'You're driving me crazy. Every time you come to a match you start shouting at me and I can't play.'

He said, 'I thought if I gave you a bit of stick it would put a bit of fight into you, encourage you to prove me wrong.'

So I said, 'I think you are right with some players, but not with me. Other players need different types of encouragement.'

And he just said, 'Well, you can't win 'em all', and walked off, leaving me standing there – which was a bit overwhelming for an eighteen-year-old after you had plucked up courage to go and see him.

10 NOVEMBER
Tottenham 1 Arsenal 2 Milk Cup Third Round
What a night. It was marvellous, the best I've had since I've been at Arsenal. It was undoubtedly the best game, and it was fantastic to beat Tottenham. The atmosphere was incredible, there were 52,000 there apparently, and when we went two up all you could hear was the Arsenal chants, which at White Hart Lane is a fantastic feeling. And to cap it all it was Pat Jennings's *This is Your Life* afterwards, the perfect day for it.

I didn't discover about *This is Your Life* until after training in the morning. We had a light session, and I'd just got out of the bath when Kenny said:

'Great about tonight, isn't it?'

'What are you talking about, Ken?'

'Oh,' he said, 'I've let it out of the bag.' Then he told me about it. 'I've got to make a million phone calls this afternoon to cancel

200

everything for this evening because we've got to go to the studios,' he added.

We were all in the same boat; I told a few of the others, and it was a bit of a rush job cancelling our arrangements.

I had even more of a rush job than most of us, because just as we were leaving Highbury a friend called me and said, 'Gemma rang me and said you were leaving two tickets for her.' And I said, 'No, she didn't ring me.' I'd been to see *Blondel* on Monday evening; afterwards we'd bumped into Gemma Craven in a restaurant, and she'd asked if she could come to the match. So I'd said, 'Yes, sure. Ring me up tomorrow and I'll get you two tickets.' But I didn't hear from her so I assumed she didn't want to go. But at Tottenham I had to search out two tickets for her because she was already on her way to the game. I managed it somehow, but then after all the hassle she didn't get in. There were so many people outside waiting that the police thought there would be a riot if they didn't allow them in, so they opened the gates and let them pay to get in to get them off the streets. Then when it was full they locked the gates and turned away people with tickets, so Gemma was walking around the ground for half an hour and they wouldn't let her in. She finally got into the players' lounge at half-time, and she and her friend watched the second half on their video. But she never really got the atmosphere or anything like that.

It was a great game. We played really, really well. Everyone gave well over a hundred per cent, probably because of the 5–0 thrashing in the spring. Charlie got a goal – a really good finish, even though it was sticking it into an empty net, because he had to loft it over a defender. That sent us in 1–0 up at half-time. And we'd been saying beforehand that if we could hold on until then we'd fancy our chances because Spurs have been fading in the second half, so we really thought we could do it.

Terry said beforehand that he had spoken to a couple of the Tottenham players, and they were feeling that they faded in the second half. They had had a strange pre-season with not training hard but playing a lot of games. Whether Terry was just saying that to boost us I don't know, but it certainly made us confident at half-time, and when we went two up three minutes into the second half that set us on our way. Then they came back into it from a penalty, so we were clinging on, but catching them on the break, and we could have scored a couple more.

Robbo did brilliantly. Glenn never had a kick against him. And whether it was Robbo or just how Glenn is now – there's been a bit of publicity about him being harder – but Glenn started putting it about. He whacked Rixy, caught me late on in the second half, and had a go at someone else. Rixy turned to him in the second half and said, 'Come on, Hod, leave it out a bit.' Glenn just gave him a cold stare, and carried on.

Roberts was different. We'd had a quiet giggle to ourselves at lunchtime when we heard he was playing in midfield. It was a real boost for us. Charlie and I said, 'Well, at least we are not going to be kicked all over the pitch.' They moved him back late in the second half and I felt him a couple of times after that. But it was Rixy who got the early onslaught. He caught Graham in the first five minutes. If he had caught him properly it would have broken his leg, but Rixy just managed to get out of his way. There was a bit of a shouting match about it, but he apologized during the match, and he couldn't stop apologizing after the game, so perhaps he isn't as vicious as some people think. I'd sooner play with him than against him though.

The first goal was down to Clem. A long ball was knocked up from right-back, trying to give it to me while I was going behind a defender. It was a very good ball and I thought I was in. It was coming across the face of me and I could see Clem coming out of the corner of my left eye, and I thought if I can just get to it I can knock it round him, and if it is a good enough touch I'll be able to put it in. I couldn't quite reach it, but my foot stabbing out at it seemed to put him off and he lent back at a crucial time. The ball bounced off him to the right of the penalty area where Charlie was standing. Then everything seemed to happen in slow motion. I said to Charlie afterwards, 'Usually I follow everything in. Whenever anyone is having a shot I'll be in there. But I was just rooted to the spot.' There was a defender on the goal-line, and Charlie floated it over him; and it went so slowly everyone just seemed to stop and watch, even their players. We were all watching and thinking, is it going to go in, or hit the bar, or just go over? And it just drifted in under the bar.

It was always going to be difficult for Price. He hadn't been playing, and then they pitched him into a big match like that. He was bound to be a bit nervous, and it was the same for Stevens. We tried

202

to rush him on a few occasions and you could see he was a bag of nerves.

The second goal came that way. I chased a ball and he had quite a bit of time to knock it back to Clem, but he just took that extra stride, then I was in on him, took it off him and got through. There was still a bit to do, but eventually I ended up putting it in. Again it was something we'd hoped beforehand would work out, because we'd said that Stevens does like to dwell on the ball a bit.

We were on the coach by twenty past ten to go to the TV studio. Steve Perryman came with us. It was a bit strange us all sitting on the coach laughing and joking when he came walking on. You could imagine how he felt.

It was nice being able to honour Pat, particularly on a night like that. There was a bit of a reception afterwards, then Charlie, Kenny, Rixy and I went on to a nightclub. We left the TV studios at about one a.m., and we couldn't find a taxi, so we got Bob, the Arsenal coach driver, to take us along in the coach. He wasn't too keen on the idea, but he was happy about the night in general, so we shouted him into it. We could see he was a bit nervous about it, but we persuaded him, jumped on the coach and went into the West End. He took us down a couple of really tight side streets, and we pulled up outside this club in the Arsenal coach. The four of us jumped out, and I swear, on my life, that the bouncer actually said, 'You can't park that there.'

11 NOVEMBER
Everyone is still high from Wednesday. We went on the pitch today and did shadow play, knocking the ball around without any opposition. Then we practised free-kicks and corners. Don is changing things around this year, as I said before.

Beating Tottenham means we can now hold our heads up until Christmas, at least. And even if we lost to them there in the League, we would still have knocked them out of the cup. It's better this way, because if you beat them in the League, they can still come top of the first division. But we've actually knocked them out of the competition, which one-off on the night was fantastic. Now we have got Walsall which is the perfect draw for us. We couldn't have wished for anything better. I'm sure we will beat them. And if we apply ourselves the way we did against Tottenham and then get a nice little draw in the next round, we'll be in the semi-finals.

Then of course you've got to expect to face the best teams, but we must have every chance. We're not the greatest team in the League, but we are better than we were last year. I'm convinced of that. We're scoring more goals for a start, and at least we know now with certain moves that a cross is going to come in and we can get on the end of things. Whereas last year we couldn't. Yet even then we got to two semi-finals, so with a bit of luck we might be able to go all the way this year.

12 NOVEMBER
Ipswich 1 Arsenal 0
We didn't create a chance the whole game. We did play some good football in the first half, but we never looked like scoring. I think Tottenham took a lot out of us, mentally and physically. We put so much effort into that game. You can't use that as a real excuse, because the really good sides produce week in, week out, but it did have an effect.

I wasn't really involved against Ipswich, I didn't see much of the ball. I was just relieved at the end to come off the field in one piece, thinking, 'Well, at least I can report fit tomorrow.' The England party gets together tomorrow for the game in Luxembourg and I was a bit nervous before today's game because having missed the last two England games I thought, 'I can't possibly get another injury, can I?'

13 NOVEMBER
We reported at Luton at six p.m., so at least there was no Sunday training to worry about.

It was good to see everyone again. The spirit among the squad is very good. They are all nice people, and you get a lot of jokes flying around. Before home matches I usually have a drink on the Saturday night with Paul Mariner; the two of us, Terry Butcher and the other Arsenal lads, Kenny, Rixy when he is with us, usually go out together before or after a game.

We caught up on the latest gossip. Graham Roberts was still apologizing for the tackle on Rixy. 'Tell Rixy I'm sorry about that tackle', he said to Kenny and me.

14 NOVEMBER

We flew out to Luxembourg and did a little training in the evening, which suited me fine. It was absolutely freezing. The pitch was bone hard and frozen, not exactly ideal for football.

15 NOVEMBER

Bobby Robson named the team, and then we had a practice game. Butch, who had been captain two matches ago, wasn't even on the bench, but he was fantastic in the game. I kept giving him the ball just to watch him. He was knocking it about everywhere and everything he did came off – oh, he did get one thing wrong. Right at the end he tried a back-heel flick over his head, and that didn't work. Even then it was a near miss – the ball hit him on the back of the head. It was one of those days – he was quite outstanding. I know it was only a training knock-about, but he has been playing like this all season. He was brilliant at Highbury, and you've got to say that on current form he is probably the best midfield player in England. And when he wasn't even down as sub I had to feel a little bit sorry for him.

We had to give our boot sizes, because they've decided to try and get those special astroturf boots over for us to play in because it is freezing underfoot.

We're stuck out in the middle of nowhere. It's pretty boring, there's not much to do except sit around and chat. There was one funny incident in the hotel bar. Phil Neal and Sammy Lee were sitting on high stools, and then Phil got down. 'Just hang on a minute Sammy, I'll just go and get you a ladder so you can get down.'

That provoked another story about Sammy Lee's height. It was typical of the Liverpool players' humour. Sammy opened this bar or restaurant recently, and was doing a bit of serving. All the lads had gone along, and every time one of them went to the bar they asked for a drink off the top shelf – which Sammy of course couldn't reach.

I had a chat with Bryan Robson, who said that they are looking desperately for a centre-half; both their two are having a torrid time at the moment. I've always felt they were vulnerable on the ground, but I'd settle for McQueen at Arsenal at the moment just to head the ball away. We could take him in part exchange for me!

More seriously, Graham Roberts's contract comes to an end at the end of this season, and he isn't too happy with things at the moment. I think he feels that them having such a big squad means you are on edge the whole time. He said he wouldn't object to playing for Arsenal, so I'm thinking of having a word with Terry and Don about him when I get back. I like him. You are going to get kicked nearly every time you get the ball, it won't necessarily be a foul, but every time you get it it's 'Bang!' And when you get that for ninety minutes, you do start looking over your shoulder.

Before the Hungary game I didn't think that having an extra weekend together would have made much difference. But a lot of the lads who were there did, and thought it was beneficial for the whole team. Kenny said, 'At the moment you feel you have to have a good match every time, or you are going to be out. And in training it is not very relaxed. But for the Hungary game every one was very relaxed.' And he said they could only put it down to being with each other for the extra two days, and getting used to each other that bit more.

A journalist asked me how I would approach the game if we had heard that Greece had lost. Bobby Robson had evidently said that he had to watch for any complacency setting in once we'd heard the result. I couldn't see that. It's an international match, and even if we are going to get knocked out you are still playing for a place in the side. There are friendlies coming up, and in six months' time we are going to start preparing for the World Cup. So I felt that if we did get knocked out I'd try even harder if anything. There will certainly be people just waiting to jump on us if we don't give a hundred per cent.

I was also asked if I was worried about us sneaking in through the back door again if we make it. I said, 'I don't mind how we get there so long as we do. In fact I'd pay to go, because I think we would have a great chance if we get there.' Qualifying is the most difficult thing. Once you are there it's just a question of who comes good in that three weeks, because there aren't any outstanding teams.

16 NOVEMBER
Luxembourg 0 England 4

I was on for ten minutes. I can't believe the luck I'm having. I was feeling really sharp. In the first five minutes I came close to scoring twice, and I thought, 'There's no way I'm not going to score tonight.' Then I went for a ball. I got into the penalty box and I slowed up suddenly to try and get the defender to tackle me because I thought, 'As he comes in a change of pace will do him.' But somehow I twisted and he caught me as well. I think I was twisting across his body and he knocked me the other way quickly, and I pulled a muscle. Obviously I wasn't that warm. I keep using the excuse that I'm too finely tuned this year. Maybe I need to slow down a bit, because I am feeling quick.

As we were leaving the hotel this journalist asked me if we were planning to listen to the Greece v Denmark match, whether they were going to get the commentary relayed to the changing rooms. I said I wasn't interested – I just wanted to know the result, nothing more.

Then when we got to the ground there were a lot of England fans there, and they were all shouting that Greece were winning 1–0. Someone asked them, 'Are you serious?' and they all replied, 'Yes. Greece are winning 1–0.' So we walked into the stadium thinking that they couldn't all be wrong, and we were really feeling quite good, a bit excited. But as we walked into the changing rooms someone shouted that it was 1–0 to Denmark. And then by the time we got across the changing room the shout came in that it was '2–0 Denmark'. So that really put us down.

They had got a radio down there. It was wired up in the medical room next door to the changing room. A few of the lads and Bobby Robson went in there and listened to the match. As far as I was concerned they could have switched it off there and then. Okay, if it looks like we are out, then we are out, but I found it a bit depressing listening to the commentary. I would have switched it off if I'd been the manager.

One of the United lads asked me if I fancied playing for them. They thought my contract was up in the summer, and to put it diplomatically there have been rumours that they are interested. But my contract doesn't expire until the following year. If it had come up this year, I'd have to be interested, because I'd like to play with Frank Stapleton. I'd certainly like to play in front of their mid-field.

As it is, if we finish in mid-table this year I will have to go in and let Don and Terry know I'm not happy with the situation, because I won't be. I'm not going to be content settling for a mediocre team, I want to be with the best. And if Arsenal aren't going to do anything about it, I'll have to let them know I'm not happy with it. They'll have had two seasons to do something by then.

We watched the Germany v Northern Ireland match on TV; Germany never really threatened. It just convinces me that if we had made it, we would have stood a great chance of going all the way. There's such a levelling off in international football. Italy, the World Champions, aren't even going. They just hit a peak during the World Cup Finals, and if you do that you've got a great chance. There aren't many outstanding teams.

17 NOVEMBER

In the footballers' autobiographies I used to read as a boy, after an important defeat it always used to say, 'It was a subdued party which returned to Luton Airport. . .'. It wasn't quite like that for us, though. We were all disappointed, but no one really showed it. We had a drink on the plane, and after we got to Luton we all went out – or at least a dozen of us did. Paul Mariner and Peter Withe joked that it was a farewell evening out because we'd never see each other again. All the papers have been talking about bringing in fresh faces in preparation for the next World Cup.

There's been a lot of talk about Paul Mariner being left out. I don't think he will be. But if he is, there's no big centre-forward, no other Paul Mariner or Peter Withe type coming through – certainly no one who is as good as them. That might suit me in a sense, because we will have to start playing in a certain way if we don't have a big centre-forward. And I think Denmark might help that along a little bit, because people have been impressed with them and their game, and they don't have a big centre. Their two goals against Greece were the product of being mobile; Simonsen made a fantastic run to get the second goal. And they certainly haven't got people stuck up there to toss high balls in to. So I hope that is a good sign.

But there are so many names being bandied about, and it really makes me angry. John Barnes didn't look that comfortable against Luxembourg. He has been getting great reports, everyone is raving about him, but I'm not too sure yet. He does things instinctively: he'll get the ball and run and beat someone and shoot. That's all well and good if you are in a settled side and things are going smoothly, (it's the same with Charlie Nicholas) but at international level you have to have some discipline in your game. He didn't appear to know what he was doing yesterday, and they were poor opposition. Yet people are talking about him coming in for the next World Cup.

I think I'll still be playing then; I'll be thirty, at my peak. I'm just hoping I can get a run in the team. I really can't see that the people they are talking about as coming prospects will give me anything to worry about as long as I can get into the team to start with.

If they really think that someone should play they should stick by him and say, 'Yes, this is my player.' But they'll tip someone, and then if he has a bad game he'll be out and they will tip someone else. I'd like to go back through the papers over the last few years and see some of the names who have been floated and then ask, 'Why not now?' A classic example was Paul Goddard. A year ago people were pressing his claims. I read in one paper that he was 'the next Rummenigge'. He can't even get in the West Ham team now, and he never gets a mention. And it is when they tip someone so strongly and then drop him as quickly that I despair – or get angry. Someone like Kevin Keegan played at the top and stayed there, and when he was knocked down he bounced back.

Players like Paul Goddard may bounce back too, I don't know. He has had bad luck with injuries, but talking to the West Ham lads they think it's partly psychological. It is unfair to select him, but he is the one who springs to mind. Recently Brian Stein of Luton was being mentioned. Why? He's a good player, but so is every regular first division player. I can't see that he is particularly special.

Then you get someone like Cyrille Regis. People spent seasons pushing his claims, then all of a sudden he disappeared completely. He battled hard against West Germany – that's the least you can do, and he did it. He worked hard. I thought he was a bit unlucky, but obviously the manager didn't fancy him. And none of the papers are pushing his cause now. He will probably be revived when they start on the search for a big centre-forward. But Cyrille is not someone to feed off; he is a bit like Luther, he wants to run at players all the time. But in home games in international football you can't do that, because teams are going to sit back, and there is nowhere to run. That's especially true in qualifying matches for the World Cup or European Championship, where they know it is like a two-leg game, so that they want the away draw.

19 NOVEMBER
Arsenal 2 Everton 1

I didn't play because of my injury. It was quite a good game. Andy Gray played well, he won everything in the air, so much so that the lads were talking about it afterwards. In fact I said it to Kenny and he jumped in. 'All but one. All but one.' Kenny had out-jumped him near the end when Andy didn't realize he was coming. I had to laugh because Kenny was the smallest player on the field, and he'd beaten him in the air.

But during the game Andy won everything. He was getting up there and knocking balls down into space, creating havoc. If he'd had someone clever enough playing off him. . . . As it was he laid on two or three chances which they should have done better with. I thought at the time I'd score hundreds playing alongside him. But, in case anyone thinks I'm contradicting myself, that's not because he's a big centre-forward. On another day I could have thought that about Crooks, or Walsh or Whiteside. But I must admit I did think, 'Crikey, if I was playing off him. . .'.

I'm more and more convinced, from what I've seen of him, that Charlie is not a striker. He doesn't get in the box enough, and he lacks a bit of pace. I must have a word with Don and suggest he plays him in behind me and Sundy. We would then have to have someone to give us width, but it would be better than what we have at the moment. Charlie needs someone to play off, and I'm not the type of player who is going to be knocking everything down for him all the time and saying, 'Go on, put this in.' I'm going to be turning with it myself or saying, 'Slip it in here for me.'

Over the last three weeks I've been reading constantly that Charlie's team mates are treating him like a social outcast and won't give him the ball. That's ridiculous. Okay, he doesn't get the ball enough. I don't get the ball enough either, but the thing is if you aren't being given the ball you've got to get it yourself, and Charlie doesn't do enough in that direction.

I make sure that on every occasion we have got the ball I say, 'Give it me here.' If Paul Davis gets the ball on some occasions you've really got to shout at him, while Charlie will just show himself, as much as to say, 'I'm here if you want me,' and if he doesn't get it he just turns away. But you've got to demand the ball off players, and I've told him two or three times now that when someone's got the ball he has got to make them give it to him. He doesn't do enough to help himself.

It has been a bit of a week for Sundy, he was taken off again for the third game running. He did go out of the game a couple of times, but to be fair he was the only forward who looked like he was going to score and with Robbo getting the other, he was the only forward who did score. But he is out of favour at the moment, and I think there's going to be trouble.

In mid-week they had a cross-country in which the best time was eighteen minutes. Terry Neill came in in twenty-one minutes and Sundy and John Lukic came in in twenty-eight. Those two were told to go in the next day and do some half laps. I was lucky I wasn't there, because I run with Sundy, so I'd probably have come in in twenty-eight minutes as well. But in mid-season, with all the games we are playing, I don't see the point of having cross-countries.

21 NOVEMBER

I'm on shift work at the moment. I'm in for treatment from ten a.m. to twelve; one p.m. to two; and 5.30 to seven p.m., which is a new thing Roy Johnson has brought in for people with minor injuries. I asked Roy if it was being done just for inconvenience by the management. I've heard they do that at Liverpool, which some people have said is one of the reasons they have so few injuries. And Tony Donnelly, our kit man, chipped in that years ago one of Arsenal's trainers used to have people in for treatment at eight a.m. He said that soon cut the injuries down. But Roy said it was nothing to do with the management, it was his idea; and although it is a bit inconvenient if it means you are going to get fit for Saturday it's worth it.

I've never had a pulled muscle in my life before, and now I've had two in a few weeks, both with England. I told Roy the trouble is I'm too finely tuned at the moment, like a sports car. But obviously I'm going to have to think more seriously about warming up properly. In the past I've never needed to, I can just go out and play cold. (Fortunately this is not a bad injury. It isn't in the groin area, so it isn't in a complicated position. And the Doc says there isn't one definite spot, which is a good thing according to him).

I'm also wondering whether not training but then getting off the table to play, which is what I've been doing for the past month, has something to do with it. The muscles aren't being used during the week, so perhaps that makes them more vulnerable when you go out and start going at full stretch in a match. I wondered because David O'Leary came back from Ireland with the same injury as I have, and he spends a lot of time on the table and gets a lot of knocks, so it seems like it is a continuing circle.

The *Sunday People* has been doing a series about injuries and their after-affects; most players have got something wrong with them. Someone pulled my leg (literally) the other day and there was this 'crack' from my knee, and he said, 'You're going to have arthritis there.' Rixy laughed. 'He won't worry about that when he's floating in his swimming pool.' That's a joke I always have with Carole when she complains that I'm just sitting around the house doing nothing. 'Do you realize the punishment I put my body through on a Saturday afternoon for you?' and she always replies something along the lines of, 'Don't worry, you are earning the money. We'll be able to afford a motorized wheelchair.'

22 NOVEMBER

The Wembley five-a-sides are tomorrow; I won't play, which doesn't particularly bother me. Tony Donnelly said that years ago players used to be queueing up to play in them. On the whole they don't seem bothered now, although Kenny Sansom is keen to play.

There is talk about Pat not retiring at the end of the season after all. He has had a couple of very good games, and he isn't really training seriously now, so he isn't feeling his age in aching limbs so much. I think if he is not being asked to train hard but just turn out for matches he could carry on playing for a couple more years.

I remember reading somewhere Bobby Charlton saying he retired too early, and the mistake he made was trying to beat the young players in training, feeling he had to train twice as hard as them. I think that's right. I think as you get older the thing to do is to pace yourself.

Too much is made of age in this country. You look at players like Van Moer, who was running the Belgium midfield at thirty-eight in the European Championships. Perhaps you can't run around as much, but I don't think you lose your sharpness over ten or twenty ysrds. I was a great fan of Jimmy Greenhoff's; I don't know how old he was when he was playing for United, but he had incredible sharpness in the box – a great player.

And there was Frank Clark at Nottingham Forest. I remember him when he first came, and I thought in our first practice game, 'Old feller, I'll just knock it past him and run after it,' because I was known for having a bit of pace. I tried it: he turned so quickly, and picked it up, so that I was left standing looking astonished.

My source (and it isn't David Dein, it is someone totally unconnected with the club), tells me that we are signing Tommy Caton. We do need a centre-half badly, so I hope he is right as usual.

24 NOVEMBER

Bad news: the Caton signing is off, I'm told, because of some hitch over money.

25 NOVEMBER

I did my first proper day's training today. I still felt the injury a little, but I said, 'I'm going to play at Leicester.' I just don't want to get weaker and weaker – I want to get back.

While I was out training they sent out to say that the Supporters' Club chairman was on the phone, did I want to talk to him. I thought he wanted to ask me to go and see someone or do a talk at a dinner, so I said, 'No, I can't, I'm training. Ask him to get in touch later,' and thought no more about it. But then Don phoned this evening to tell me I'd been chosen as their player of the year. It was typical of Don, he'd been told to tell me at the ground and had forgotten, but he wouldn't let it slide and had phoned me at home. That was very nice of him.

There's been talk for a few weeks now that we are going to have a winter break in Marbella; today it became official. A notice was put up saying that we are going after the West Brom game a week tomorrow for a four-day golfing holiday.

There was another notice too. Usually the club give the staff a Christmas turkey, but they aren't going to this year. It said at the bottom in inverted commas 'due to the trip to Marbella'. I don't really believe that, because they must have to order earlier than this – I think it is just a result of cut-backs. But if it is due to the Marbella trip, it's a bit unfortunate for the reserves and apprentices. They are losing out on a turkey, which is probably useful to them, while the first team squad are getting a nice few days away.

The Marbella notice said that we were definitely going, unless a replay with Walsall was necessary. So of course everyone was joking about that: 'Does that mean that if it's 0–0 with a minute to go we have to let them score?'

26 NOVEMBER
Leicester City 3 Arsenal 0

A shameful performance. In the team talk before the game, Don's theme was 'Do we want it badly enough?' He said, 'It's not about having a nice car, a nice house, it's about what you do inside the game, it's about winning medals, about playing as well as you can play.' And he said that he didn't want players who, when they got to thirty-five, said, 'Nobody ever told me', or thought back and said, 'We had a good team then but we didn't quite apply ourselves, didn't pull all we could have done out of ourselves. If we had done that we would have won something.' He didn't want players to get to that age and not have been told. And he said we could do it if we really wanted.

He kept saying, 'Do we really want to win?' He kept throwing John McEnroe at everyone, saying that McEnroe has got all this money in the bank but he keeps on winning. He fights everyone, fights the linesmen, the spectators, the umpires, but he keeps on winning. He has got this winner's streak in him. And he said we had got to have that. It was a brilliant talk but he might as well have saved his breath, because it just made the performance even more unforgivable.

It was all down to attitude. They aren't a good team, they just out-fought us and out-battled us. They just had more determination.

I was disgusted with it. I was playing not completely fit. I haven't got full range of movement, and I was a little bit wary of doing certain things because of the injury and because I haven't been training, so the muscles weren't toned up fully. I thought I had to go out and play and get back in the swing of things again, and I felt I did reasonably well without getting any chances. And Graham got injured so he could be excused, but generally people were just avoiding their responsibilities. I had a go at David O'Leary during the game. He's an international and he should be taking responsibility, but he's not playing with any confidence or authority at all. We were attacking, and this ball was knocked out to him, and it was coming down on his chest; he could have taken it there and got it down and played it, but he volleyed it wildly and it went into touch. I said, 'Show some confidence. If you are not going to what are young John Kay and Chrissie Whyte going to think?'

Don blew a fuse afterwards; he went crazy. We were in the changing room for nearly an hour. He had every right to do so after that pre-game talk. I think he was as hurt that that had been wasted as by the performance itself. He laid into David, into Chrissie, into Charlie. He had a go at just about everyone – I was about the only person to escape. He said I showed them the way and that I had battled.*

I think we all felt bad afterwards. We thought we didn't deserve the trip to Marbella after that, and with Walsall on Tuesday it means we've only got a few days to put it right. But that might be a good thing I think. We'll be that much more determined; and if we win we'll be in the quarter-finals, which will be a boost.

27 NOVEMBER

Charlie came with Graham and me to the Beehive. Graham said he thought he was almost certain to miss Tuesday's game, which is a blow. Looking on the bright side, I said, 'Oh, that must mean I've got a chance to be captain.' They both fell about. Charlie said, 'You must be joking. I've got more chance than you have.' And it got silly. But I was a bit surprised by their reaction – I really think I have got a chance. I wouldn't want the job permanently, but for a few weeks I quite fancy leading them out.

28 NOVEMBER

Don gave us a talk today, said it was disgusting that we should be out-fought, and that, 'We've got good lives, a good salary, we only work for a few hours a day. We should really want to go out and do it.' He's right. No one could say a word against anything he said.

Usually Wilf gives his chat on the opposition the day before, but they put it off so that we didn't get any of his gems.

A lot of people had watched the West Ham v Manchester United

* *Editor's note.* Don Howe's reaction after this game suggests that an article on the sacking of Terry Neill which appeared in the *Sunday Express* Colour Magazine in January does the author, Anthony Holden, little credit. Holden, who was on the coach for the Leicester game, quoted Neill as saying bitterly that players who gambled their weekly £1,500 salary away on cards were not motivated by win-bonuses of £200, and didn't care. Tony had been named as one of the card school – in fact the one-pound stakes mean that five or ten pounds is the maximum win or loss on a trip – and identified as one of the club's most highly paid players. Holden concluded his piece by suggesting that those who blamed over-paid players for the club's plight might be right. Howe's comments that same afternoon suggest that Holden's analysis was wrong, if not defamatory.

game on TV yesterday, or read in the papers this morning about Clive Thomas's latest about ushering people quickly back to the half-way line when a goal has been scored, and threatening to book them. It really put people's backs up. A lot of people say the sign of a good referee is when you don't notice him. You always notice Clive Thomas.

Generally, though, I never notice referees, unless they have an awful game, and even then I usually don't remember them. Often on a Friday someone will say, 'Oh, we've got so-and-so tomorrow', and it never means anything to me. And afterwards sometimes people will say, 'The referee had a good game', and I can't comment. It's an awful job though, with twenty-two people shouting at you the whole time, and whatever you do eleven are going to be upset.

29 NOVEMBER
Arsenal 1 Walsall 2

30 NOVEMBER
It's incredible how much things can change in three weeks. Tottenham was the best day I've had at Arsenal, the best feeling. Yesterday was the worst day ever.

I remember looking at the clock at 9.05. There was no way we were going to get a goal. I normally like to go out after a game, but I thought, 'I can't go out tonight, I just can't. I'm not going to have a drink, nothing.'

After the game I went into the players' lounge, and I still didn't intend to go out; I had a beer. Carole had arranged things with friends though, and in the end I was persuaded. We went out with them and Graham Rix and Tommy Caton, who had signed earlier in the day. But we just couldn't stop talking about it all night, and that's unusual for me. Usually within an hour after the game I am okay. I can say, 'It's only a game. We've lost. We'll get it right for the next one.' But this time I couldn't stop thinking about it. We went out for a meal and then on to a club. Carole took two friends home and left me there with a few other people. I just sat there. They ended up throwing us out of the place. I just didn't want to go home. I finally got back at about five a.m.

Graham, who had been watching, said that he thought some people hadn't given everything, and David Dein said the same thing. He came down into the changing room afterwards. He was the only

216

director to do so, although I think they should do that. He was speaking to me, but loudly enough so that the rest could hear. He said, 'That's terrible. That's disgraceful. I feel that two or three players aren't really trying.'

I talked to him later, during the night. He really feels for the club, and he wanted to shout at some of the players, but he didn't. He did it by speaking loudly to me, trying to voice his opinion. He is definitely not happy, and he is right not to be.

They taught us a lesson: showing confidence, getting the ball and making angles off one another. Whenever one of their players got the ball he had two or three options, which is the sign of a good side. They played it simple, their control was good. They were so impressive, and kept it up for ninety minutes. Even when they'd got the equalizer they didn't sit back and say, 'We'll take them back to Walsall', they thought they could win it. I thought they could too. I never got a glimpse of the ball at that stage. I was virtually a spectator watching the game from the half-way line. We were lucky to get away with 2–1. It could easily have been 5–1.

Although we were outclassed, we did have our chances. I missed one, a header; I didn't quite catch it right. I took my eye off the ball for a moment to see if there was anyone across goal I could head it to, because I was at an angle. It nearly went in anyway because the keeper had gambled the wrong way and he just fumbled it on to the post. If it had had more power it would have gone in.

And Colin Hill tried a header from an impossible angle when there were two of us unmarked in front of goal. I go crackers at that sort of thing. I had to apologize to him afterwards, but all it takes is a little bit of composure in the box.

The pitch did us on one occasion. How my Dad could say that the pitch must be the best in the country is beyond me. The grass is too long, and the goal-mouth in front of the North Bank is like a beach. I tried to take the ball round the goalkeeper, but it stuck in the sand.

In contrast we had nothing: no one wanting the ball in midfield, demanding it off the back four, giving it to the front players and saying, 'If you can't do anything I'll have it back.' Nothing.

'I'd expected changes after Leicester. But Colin Hill came back for John Kay, Ian Allinson came in for Rixy, and that was all. Allinson did all right. He's still got to learn when to run at people and when to release the ball, but in the circumstances he did quite well. When he came I remember saying I didn't think he would make it at Arsenal. But he has done well in the reserves and looks very sharp in training. So I put it down to him being nervous about coming to a new club, and he says he wasn't properly fit when he arrived. But at Colchester he was playing on the right side, and getting goals. We've been looking for someone to do that all season, but they've been playing him on the left in the reserves.

There were people outside afterwards chanting for Terry's head. Terry didn't play. All right, you can say it's up to him to pick and motivate the team, so it is his ultimate responsibility, but Terry didn't play. And we've all got to remember that.

1 DECEMBER

I just keep turning it over in my mind. I've only been at Arsenal a year, but I feel the club is special. There is something different about being an Arsenal player. I enjoyed being at Nottingham Forest because it was my home club, and I enjoyed Cologne, but this defeat seems much worse happening to Arsenal than it would elsewhere.

Do the other players feel that? David Dein and Graham Rix both said they thought some people weren't giving everything. It's hard to say that. I think everyone tried. People didn't go out there not to try. We were beaten by a better footballing side, and that's condemnation enough.

If only we could put it all together. Everyone keeps saying we did it against Tottenham, we did it against Aston Villa. If we could maintain those performances. . . . Well, Villa probably had a bad day themselves. But at Tottenham with the atmosphere and everything at stake it was a fantastic performance. So everyone keeps asking, 'Why can't we maintain it?'

'If it happens over a short period when you have generally been playing well and then you hit a bad patch I think you can ask that question. But this has been going on now for over a year, ever since I've been at the club. And I think you just have to say we are not good enough, not look for reasons why we do it in one game and not others but say, 'We are not good enough, let's get some new faces in.'

Sometimes Don and Terry think if players say that they are opting out. They think it is just an excuse, the easy way out. In many ways it is. But I'm looking at the team and we need some good, experienced international players in my opinion.

Now people look at the team and say we should be in the top three with the players we've got; they've been doing so in the papers today. We've got six internationals, half the team. But look at the other half. We have got a hell of a young team. And if you look at Manchester United, they've got twelve internationals on their books. So have Tottenham. I'm not knocking our young players, I'm certainly not saying, 'He shouldn't be in, and he shouldn't, and he shouldn't.' Everyone has opinions about that, and there may be some people who think I shouldn't be in the team. I think we've got some good young players and it is right they should be pushing for places, but as I've said, I think that to be up there challenging we need better, experienced, international players.

Obviously Don and Terry are on the line now. But I think the failure to get in new players is the main area where you can really ask questions about them. It's easy to be wise after the event, but I've said all along they should have snatched up Wilkins when he was available. He was there to be had, and they should have taken the chance. It's the same sort of economics as me trying to decide about a new shirt: if one is ten or twenty pounds more than another, but I like it better and am going to get more pleasure out of it, then I'll buy the more expensive one. I do think Arsenal are right in refusing to go badly into debt. Cologne used to have that policy too. But in football you have to back your judgement at some stage at a club like this. Bryan Robson must have cost two million pounds when it is all taken into account. But no one ever mentions him when they are talking about inflationary fees and over-paid and over-priced footballers, because he is doing the business. Against that you pay £500,000 for Lee Chapman and there's a comeback because he doesn't do it. If you buy players with that extra quality you aren't taking that much of a risk.

I think they could do more to motivate players too. That instance in the car with Lee Chapman when we saw that thing by Malcolm Macdonald was symptomatic. But when it comes down to it they can only work with the players they've got. There is also a lot of rubbish being written about it all. The papers are having a field day. There is all this stuff about Don's failings as a coach: 'He's a negative coach, always has been', and other remarks like that. And you can't judge Don by looking at Arsenal's record this season, and dismiss him as a failure as some people are doing. The way to judge him as a coach is to find out how he is regarded. If you ask Liam Brady, Frank Stapleton, Alan Ball or people like me and Graham Rix now, top players who have worked with him, we all respect him. That's the basis on which he should be judged. When Arsenal won the double he had great players to work with, and good characters, people who wanted to win even if they weren't the most skilful players – like Pat Rice and Sammy Nelson.

One of our problems is that we don't have anyone who will play well when the team is playing badly, except I think I do. I'm not saying that to blow my own trumpet, but I feel I have done well this season. There is a lack in defence in particular. When a defence is having a bad day all round, with some teams you can still read, 'If it hadn't been for X, such and such a team would have lost.' But we don't have a defender who will say, 'Well, it's not really on today, but I'm going to make sure no one goes past me', and stems the tide that way. When our defence starts to crumble, everything goes.

2 DECEMBER

Having West Bromwich tomorrow has at last given me something else to think about. I'm looking forward to it – it's a chance to go out and start putting things right. It is going to be a real test for us. I've got to psych myself up so much now. I know I've got to work for ninety minutes, give 110 per cent, even if I'm having one of those days when I can't kick the ball. I hope the rest are thinking that, not going into their shells and thinking, 'God, if I have a bad game tomorrow the crowd are really going to get onto my back.' Everyone really has to show their worth tomorrow. My injury feels a bit better now. I feel I'm probably over it, because I've played the two games I needed to go through to get back to match fitness. After half an hour it started to ache because I haven't been training and the muscle is not toned properly. But it should be all right tomorrow.

We aren't a very well equipped army for a do-or-die struggle. We are in the situation where I'd have to run and chase and get stuck in if I was playing with a team of internationals, and when you look at the team we've got. . . . I'm the oldest outfield player. Sundy's been dropped, which I don't agree with, along with Chrissie Whyte; David O'Leary is out injured, which might have saved them having to decide to drop him anyway; Graham Rix is injured. So we've got a back four of Hill, Adams, Caton, Sansom: a centre-forward converted to centre-half playing at right-back; a seventeen-year-old centre-half coming in with a new signing; and Kenny, who is our makeshift captain. (They gave him the ball to lead us out against Walsall. I was a bit disappointed.) In midfield we have Madden, Robson, Davis, Allinson: a player making his debut; a teenager; a player who is in a crisis himself; and a wide player in only his second game. And up front there are me, and Charlie, who is in a crisis. He hasn't scored a goal for 900 minutes at Highbury according to one of the papers.

The silly thing is that we've had a disastrous season, but if you look at the first division, with another six points we would be right up there. It's wide open at the moment. If we had another couple of players. . . . I've been saying that for a year now. Even if we had a run of six straight victories now, I'd still think we needed a better type of player.

The trip to Marbella is off. When it was announced Sundy said quietly, 'Does that mean we're going to get the turkey now?' He didn't ask Terry. You can imagine how that would have gone down – I think he'd have been sold the same day.

I think being dropped is a bit hard on Sundy. He has been made the scapegoat, because one or two reports suggested he didn't try. He didn't have the best of games, but I think he tried. And he is out of position; he wants to play up front. He thinks he is being pushed out of the club because of all his ups-and-downs with Terry, and being fined and appealing against it, and being stuck out on the right makes him feel that. It is hard to keep yourself going when you don't feel wanted.

That was one of the things I said in a long chat to Don before I left Highbury today. It started because I'm a couple of pounds overweight at the moment – mainly because I haven't been training. Don said, 'I've got to tell you. I've let it go for three weeks now and I don't want it creeping up without someone telling you.'

I said, 'I don't mind you telling me, but I am aware of it, and I'm aware I've got to keep in shape because when you get older you have to watch your weight. But it's mainly because I haven't been training. Once I start training properly I will be down to twelve stone or even less.' Then he asked me what I thought was wrong. I'd been meaning to go and have a chat with him, but every time I'd been going to there was a crisis meeting, and it would look like I'd gone in for one specific thing. I wanted to go in when we had a clear week.

So I said, 'There's no confidence in the team. People aren't demanding the ball and wanting it.'

Then he asked about specific players, and I told him what I thought. He asked about Charlie so I said, 'Well, I don't think he's really a front player.' And he tended to agree with me that Charlie lacks a bit of pace and doesn't get into the box enough. In fact that morning Don told him he is never in there for ricochets or to pick things up. Then Sundy came up, and I said I could see both sides of it. Sometimes his attitude hadn't been right in the past, and if they thought it wasn't right then he shouldn't be in.

But I said to Don, 'I think he tries. But he feels he is being pushed out, and he must be looking at Charlie and thinking, "I could do a better job as a front player," ' and I suggested it might be better to play him there with me and put Charlie in behind us.

'I've thought about that,' said Don.

'I should have said that last week, it's a little bit late now because Sundy is out of the team,' I answered.

But they could have done that. Then with Dave Madden in midfield they could have played Stewart Robson at right back or at centre-half. As it is we've got Tony Adams and Tommy Caton in the middle, and they are probably a bit similar in style.

We had a pep talk from the Chairman today, reminding us of our responsibilities, and saying it is down to us, not just Terry and Don. That is all very well but you wonder whether him stepping in isn't undermining the manager's position. And when he says that Terry's position is not being considered at the moment, and 'no one has a divine right to be employed by Arsenal', you start drawing conclusions.

We were agog for Wilf Dixon's chat today. Amid the gloom I didn't mention it earlier, but on Tuesday before the Walsall game he had added a new dimension. As well as the player's name and height, there was his weight. So it was right-half 'Joe Bloggs; five feet ten, ten stone eight pounds'; we were waiting to see if it had got star signs and favourite movie stars too – it hadn't.

The weight gave us a few giggles though. One of the Walsall players was down as six feet; ten and a half stone. So we were all saying, 'He needs a bit of weight on.' There was some irony in his Walsall talk. I said earlier we worried too much about the opposition

222

at Arsenal. On this occasion they put Wilf's chat off until the Tuesday, and when he was going through it Terry said, 'Oh, we don't want to know about them anyway. It's what we do on the night which counts.'

There was another meeting on Tuesday. Brian Talbot is our PFA representative, and on Monday he had gone to a meeting about the threat to black-out televised cup-ties if they tried to cut the amount of money paid to the PFA. On Tuesday Brian brought the recommendation back to us. It was pretty straightforward, because everyone has a lot of respect for Gordon Taylor and followed his lead; so if it comes down to it, which seems very unlikely, we would refuse to play.

3 DECEMBER
Arsenal 0 West Bromwich Albion 1
It is just desperate at the moment. Everyone tried, but confidence is so low things just aren't happening. You can say that it is only to be expected with the team we had out, but they had several players missing too. The difference is that their confidence and expectations are stronger than ours. It was just very depressing.

There were even bigger crowds outside this time afterwards, calling for Terry's head. The pressure is really on.

7 DECEMBER
Every day there is another piece in one of the papers about Terry's future. It's like a black cloud over Highbury at the moment. Terry is handling himself very well, keeping up a brave front. He is trying to keep us away from it all, coming into the changing room in the morning and cracking jokes, trying to lighten the atmosphere, but you are aware of it all the time; it is not a very nice situation to work in. It never is when you are losing. Training becomes harder, you don't want to get up and go in in the mornings, and you don't look forward to the game.

And on Saturday we have to go to West Ham. The way they are going at the moment, it would be hard if we were in a good patch. Now you think, 'We've got to give everything to stand a chance of getting a point.'

10 DECEMBER
West Ham 3 Arsenal 1

There seems no escape. We are at the stage where you wonder if you will ever win a game again. All you can do is just battle as hard as you can. I raced around, got tackles in, gave everything, but it couldn't alter the course of things.

I said in the dressing room beforehand, 'Come on, we've really got to fight today, let's go out and give everything.' Young John Kay took me a bit too literally. He got sent off for this lunging tackle on Swindlehurst. They lost Swindlehurst because he retaliated violently, which was a bit unfortunate for them, but it didn't make much difference.

We gave goals away again too. The first was bad marking, the second an own goal, so there was no possibility of hanging on for a point.

13 DECEMBER

Something has got to give. They've either got to make an unequivocal statement of support for Terry and Don, or change things. But at the moment everything is in an unpleasant limbo. Every morning when you go in, everyone is saying, 'What's happening? Has anything happened?' and it just can't go on like this. They've either got to say to Don and Terry go out and get some new players in and we'll support you, or they've got to make a change in the management. The current set-up just won't see us out of the rut. All the talking has been done really. You can't go on and on asking the players to go out and do it and to give everything. We've reached the point where diminishing returns have almost totally disappeared. It is not working, although everyone is trying, but there's no confidence and we need something to break the pattern. It is such a hard slog, and losing is a difficult habit to get out of.

We've had good and bad patches consistently for two seasons now. And I think every time we got out of a bad patch and had a good one it blinded them a little to the need for changes in the team. We'd go into a good patch and they would think, 'We're out of it, we're seeing the light and now we have a basis to build on,' and they could come in and say, 'Right, now let's really get it together.' Five weeks ago we had that great win at Tottenham, and they thought we were on our way. But now we are back in a bad patch again, and this time it is that much more desperate.

16 DECEMBER

Terry Neill was sacked today. I suppose it was inevitable, because we haven't been successful, and at Arsenal being in mid-table is failure. And in the end it comes down on the manager's head. You don't know what goes on in the boardroom, but if he has been given support, money basically, to strengthen the team, you have got to say he didn't do that well. Since Liam Brady left we've been short in midfield. And there are stories that even when Brady was here the players felt that the club needed a couple more players, and then could really have challenged Liverpool for the Championship. Instead it has been allowed to get weaker. But the results haven't been down to Terry: the players have to take responsibility too.

I think everyone was a bit sad when they heard. Years ago there was a lot of hostility towards Terry from players, but I think that's mainly gone now. Some of the players who have been here a long time weren't very keen; some felt he'd let them down over contracts and things. No one had great respect for him as far as the football went, but he left most of that to Don. Some people used to complain that he said silly things before a game and at half-time, and he did. But I used to ignore them, not let them get to me. I think you should be able to motivate yourself and sort out your own game rather than let things like that affect you.

I thought that if Terry was going, Don should go too. There should be a clean break, and Don was the man we dealt with on the playing side. He's the dominant figure there. With Terry's personality you couldn't say he was a shadowy figure exactly, but we felt we were much more Don's team than Terry's. It's Don we've dealt with every day, Don is much the more powerful personality, Don who did the serious pre-match talks, Don who did the coaching.

Typical of this club. No one called the players together and told them that Terry had been sacked; by the end of training every player knew it. We knew that the directors were around and something was afoot when we came in in the morning. But we heard from the switchboard operator and the doorman and the office. It was passed on by word of mouth, so everyone knew.

It's not going right for Sundy at the moment. Raph went into him in the five-a-side and gave him a dead leg. Sundy went down and hobbled off, so he is out tomorrow. It was a total accident but it looks as if Raph is the beneficiary: he's in.

We had a session in the gym lining up the wall at free-kicks. We started with Paul Davis lining it up, and you could have scored in three or four different places. Then Raph had a go, which was a bit better. Then I had a go, and it was much better. So I'm doing it tomorrow. They said, though, 'Clive Thomas is referee, so whatever you do don't stand on the ball while you are doing it. He always books people for that.'

17 DECEMBER
Arsenal 3 Watford 1
What an eventful afternoon; what a start for Don, proving how important luck is sometimes.

Getting a result like that is always on under a new manager, because players are keyed up. There was a lot of shouting on the pitch, which had been noticeably absent in previous games. People wanted to impress. But it could have gone either way. They were down to ten men from early on, yet they still could easily have scored a few. When it was 2–1 they were right in it.

Raph got a hat-trick, which was quite a comeback for someone who had been right out of things this season, and for someone who was only playing because of Sundy's injury yesterday. They were basically easy goals, but he got them. The change in formation helped, and he changes things a bit anyway, because he isn't someone you really play with – he's a head down and run man, a bit like Luther Blissett. Raph's quick, but he isn't what I would call sharp. I don't think he sees things that second early. It'll be interesting to see what happens now, an interesting test for Don, because I'm sure in the long term Sundy would be the better player. But the only manager I know who would say, 'Meade scored a hat-trick but Sundy is fit and he is my player,' is Cloughie.

Having Clive Thomas in charge is a problem. He sent this Watford boy, Price, off for a tackle on me. He'd already been booked for a tackle on Charlie, which was fair enough, but with me it was terrible. I was just too good, too quick for him. I turned quickly, sold him completely and he caught me. I turned him so well he had no chance. It wasn't a bad foul at all. And I saw Clive sending him off and I went up to him and said, 'You must be joking. I was just too quick for him.' And he said, 'No, that's it. He's off.' I said, 'You must be crackers,' and he went for his top pocket so I had to shut up. I didn't like it though.

Then he booked me anyway. I was lining up the wall. And they'd said beforehand, 'Clive's in charge so don't stand on the ball.' I stood behind it, so I wasn't interfering with play. And he was pushing them back and threatening. Then I walked past the ball and he booked me. I couldn't believe it.

So when Raph got his hat-trick I remembered his thing about hurrying players back from the West Ham TV game. So I gave Raph a wave and said, 'Well done Raph, but I'm not coming over. He might send me off.'

Don was very positive. He walked into the changing room before the game and was really definite. 'Now I'm in charge, anyone who doesn't do it is out.' It'll be interesting to see if he carries that out.

The country club where Terry, Charlie, Tommy Caton and John Lukic are staying is only a couple of minutes from my house, so I sometimes go over for a drink in the evenings. John Lukic is never there though. He isn't a drinker – and if he doesn't like it that's fair enough. But you would think that even if he was only going to have an orange juice he would be in the bar sometimes just to be sociable. But he is a bit on the outside, doesn't really mix with the lads. Virtually every opportunity he gets he's on the motorway back up to Leeds, and when his girlfriend comes down, one still doesn't see much of him.

20 DECEMBER

The stuff in the papers about David Dein and his relationships with players has provoked some comeback in the dressing room. Graham and I are getting a few snide comments. 'Who's going to be the next manager, Tony?' and things like that. It doesn't matter to me, but I think it is getting to Graham.

Don asked me about Paul Mariner and Viv Anderson. I said, 'Buy them!' He was a bit worried about Anderson's knee, but I told him that as far as I knew there was no long-term problem. And I said, 'If Paul has looked after himself, as I am sure he does, the next couple of years will be his best.' I think at the moment we should just buy any quality players who come up, and they would both be very good for us.

Don said, 'For me, Charlie's not a front runner, and I know you've been on your own for a few weeks.'

It was the first time I'd been asked my opinion about players they are thinking of going for. Whether it is because he is getting to know me better now, or because he is now in charge, I don't know. He certainly seems to think that if he can get it together he will get the job.

Last week I wouldn't have approved of that, but he is undoubtedly a changed man. When we had that chat before the Tottenham game at Easter it became clear that he had less influence on the England team than I had thought, and it is also beginning to look as if he had less here than we all thought. He did all the coaching, but obviously he had less say in the team and the formation than we knew. I think the fact that he moved Charlie back behind the front two as soon as he took over, when it was something we'd talked about weeks ago, was indicative. And if he does carry out his promise that if people aren't doing it they will be out, I shall be convinced. Because that's been a constant theme throughout the time I've been at the club, but nothing was ever done about it.

We're having our Christmas lunch on Friday at 'Bedside Manners'. It's a bit like the place where they serve school dinners – we couldn't get in there – with the waitresses dressed as nurses. I'm the organizer – it was handed over to me by the skipper along with the title 'vice captain and entertainments officer'. It seems like almost everyone is going to come, which is good.

I would like us to sign Paul Mariner. He is a very, very good player. He battles for you, and he has got a good touch on the ball. He isn't a great goal-scorer, but he does score. He is mobile; although he is not a runner with the ball, and won't beat that many people, you can knock it up to him and he can handle it. He can shield it and lay it off, and his passing is good. And from the few times we've played together I think we work pretty well together. I know where to go to feed off him, I know where he is going to put it. I thought that first game against Greece was a good illustration of what we could do as a partnership.

I get on very well with him personally too. We always have a night out together before or after England get-togethers, and when Cologne played Ipswich in the UEFA Cup I stayed over for a couple of days because I had been sent off the week before and so was suspended for four League matches. And when they came back for the second leg, although they went back straight after the match, Paul's wife came out and stayed with us.

21 DECEMBER

Training has been given a buzz again. It comes from Don, he really winds people up. I was running with Colin Hill, and he yelled, 'Hilly, go on, run him into the ground, he's easy.' So of course I left Colin trailing, which was just what Don was trying to achieve.

Then we played this match in torrential rain.

22 DECEMBER

We are playing a lot more football now. It's all very competitive because Don says things like, 'C'mon. You've got to play to win.' He really likes the competition. This morning we had a five-a-side competition. He put all the names in the hat and drew the teams. And we all had to put in a pound as stake money. He got hold of one of the apprentices who was in my team, and pointed at me and said, 'You going to give him a rollicking if he makes a mistake? He might not fancy it this morning' – he really likes an edge on things. In fact he is always telling us about how many fights the double team used to have in training. He thinks that's a good sign.

I can imagine it though with the people they had in that side. Early last season we had a five-a-side match against the double team for the opening of our sponsors' centre, the JVC centre. People thought Sammy Nelson and I had something between us because we were going at each other hammer and tongs, pushing and kicking. And I'm not that type of player, it was only because he started it. He whacked me in this exhibition match, and I thought, 'He's not getting away with that', so I started. But that was the type of player Don had to work with then.

It looks like Lee Chapman will be on his way. He is talking to Sunderland. There were stories that Don had never fancied him and that he was Terry's signing. I had a chat with him last week. He was really despondent, because he has been getting a lot of goals in the reserves – he got two at Fulham last night to make fifteen in ten games, but it doesn't seem to be getting him anywhere. I said, 'Well, all you can do is keep on doing it and someone will come in for you.'

This afternoon we went to a Junior Gunners – the club for our young supporters – party and then made hospital visits. It's a good thing to do.

23 DECEMBER

The Christmas lunch ended badly. Sundy got stabbed. There had been talk that we might meet up with the Tottenham players after the lunch, but instead we met up with their fans during it.

It all started so well. We were having a really good time, when this bunch came in. And they made a few comments, but it was all good-humoured. We were having a drink and enjoying ourselves, and setting up various people to go to the examination couch for examination by one of the 'nurses', and it was all fine.

Then I went to the loo. And this guy from the other table was in there. And he said, 'Enjoying yourself?' and I said, 'Yes, it's a really good do', and it all seemed perfectly amicable. But then he went to the basins to wash his hands, and when he had finished he snapped the glass shelf below the mirror and went out with it. I went out to discover he'd just gone up behind Sundy and stabbed him in the neck with the glass and run out. And one of the others in that group had got his nose splattered by one of the lads and was protesting violently because he said it was unprovoked assault, nothing to do with him and his shirt was ruined by the blood spattered all over it. He was threatening to sue, so we had a quick whip round to pay for the damage to his clothes, which we shouldn't have done, because we then heard that he had been one of the people involved. Then we took Sundy off to the hospital for stitches. Fortunately it wasn't too serious, although he had to have seven stitches in it.

24 DECEMBER

We went in half expecting trouble. Don had been trying to get hold of people because the press had got on to the story last night, and David Dein also rang Carole and Graham Rix's wife. He wasn't very happy about it, so we thought that they might use us being out a couple of days before a big game as a stick to beat us with, even though we were quite confident in our own minds that we hadn't been out of order.

But when Don came in he went up to Sundy and said, 'Are you all right, Al?' Sundy said, 'Yes,' so Don just said, 'There are some real lunatics about aren't there?' then turned and asked Rixy and myself what happened. We told him and he said, 'Right, let's go training,' and nothing more was said.

We've trained every day leading up to the Christmas period, but it has been good. We have gone in, done an hour of very sharp work and then finished. It has kept us sharp, and I think everyone has enjoyed it.

25 DECEMBER

We had a typical footballer's Christmas Day, although it could have been a lot worse. There was no chance of over-indulging, because we go back to White Hart Lane tomorrow, but at least we had lunch at home. Before Terry got sacked he had put up our Christmas itinerary, which had us training this morning, but Don changed that. He said come in to Highbury at seven p.m., and we'll do half an hour then go to West Lodge Park, and that was what we did.

26 DECEMBER
Tottenham Hotspur 2 Arsenal 4
We did it again.

It all began so inauspiciously too. A few weeks ago I did something to my back playing squash. My partner had had a good lunch and was trying to sweat it off, but he wasn't playing very well as a result, so I was serving virtually the whole game, and I think I pulled a muscle in my back. It stiffened up last night, so when I got up I walked to the bathroom virtually bent double. And Charlie was lying on his bed with his arm stuck up in the air, because he'd gone in goal in last night's five-a-side and had got his hand bent back. He had hardly slept because of the pain and the awkwardness of the position he was in. We looked at each other and just started laughing. 'Some strike force eh?' I said. 'If they could see us now.'

We got up at 8.30 a.m. and left at 9.15, because it was a morning kick-off. It felt very strange. We travel in tracksuits now, which is another of Don's innovations, so we were nice and comfortable, and didn't have to shave. We used to do that at Cologne as well. I think it's good provided you are smart. I do think it is important that teams are properly turned out, it's a psychological boost. One of the big talking points in Italy during the European Championships was the clothes the Italians had, they looked so good.

The coach journey was a little strange too. It must be the only one where we have a van load of police behind us as well as the usual motor bike escort in front. They had done it for the Cup game too. Obviously they don't want to take any chances, but it seemed a bit strange.

In the changing room before the game we were ever so relaxed, which I don't really like. Before the Cup game we were so determined and serious, we all meant business. This time there were a few jokes flying around, and I thought back to the Cup match and was a bit worried. But then we went out for a warm-up and we all got keyed up. The conditions were not ideal for a derby – the wind was swirling fiercely.

We had to survive some early pressure. They had two headers which looped onto the bar, but then Charlie scored and we thought, 'We're going to do it again.' But then they equalized just before half-time. It was another goal given away from a free-kick just outside the box, which we've done so often this season. This time Paul Davis couldn't get high enough to head it away, and Roberts came in round the back. Don thinks we are giving these goals away because we don't push out. We are standing on the six-yard line instead of rushing out, and making them rush out with us.

So that was a bad goal to give away, and it came at a bad time. And we haven't reacted well to having a lead pulled back this season, we've tended to go to pieces a bit. But recently we've shown a bit more determination when it happens, and we did this time. We went in at half-time and said, 'Come on, it's only the same as being 0–0', because if it had been 0–0 there would have been a lot of determination there.

We went out with that attitude and got an early goal. Then they pulled it back again and I thought, 'We're going to be up against it now.' But then we went to 3–2 ahead while I was off the field and then, with them throwing men forward we got it to 4–2.

Ardiles caught me. When it was 2–2 I turned past Roberts and Ardiles came in and hit me with this very heavy tackle from the side. He knocked my ankle sideways, and I went over on it. I lay there and I really thought he had damaged it pretty badly. I couldn't move it at all. But Stewart Robson had already gone off, so they wanted me back out there, and after five minutes it started coming round again. I was on the touchline having it strapped up and while they were doing it we got the third goal.

I couldn't believe my eyes. It was obviously an extra incentive to go back, so I said, 'Come on, get it strapped up a bit tighter, I'm back on here.' And although I could feel it I was all right and pulled the ball back for the fourth.

Tottenham were very shaky at the back. Roberts puts it in, but Stevens is having a bad time. You've always got a chance with him, and when forwards know they have got a chance with a defender they don't give him a second. I said to Raph before the game, 'Just rush at him. Shout at him even. Really. He is that nervous at the moment and under so much pressure from the Tottenham fans that even shouting will make him jumpy. Something like, "I'm going to get you this time," when you rush at him.'

For Charlie's second goal there was this gaping hole in the middle of their defence. He ran right through the middle, and a good ball by Ian Allinson put him through, but there was just no one on him. I couldn't believe it. Then Clem sold himself a bit, making it easy for Charlie to lob him, but he deserved better protection than he got.

I went from the half-way line on one run with three of them chasing me. I gave Roberts a few yards start. My main idea was to get to the penalty area as quickly as possible; I left the three of them for dead, and I was the one running with the ball. Roberts just got back to get a tackle in at the last minute, so I must be a little bit quicker than I thought. It is encouraging. I've been aware since I came back to England that I haven't been running at players and taking them on, which was an important part of my game at Forest. I lost it in Germany a bit, because it wasn't so much part of the game over there, but I've been thinking I should do it more for the past month or so.

Pat made one of his famous one-handed catches – the best I've ever seen him do. The ball came in and he came sailing out really high and went thud! He caught it one handed, stood there and threw it out without his other hand touching it. It was brilliant, and we all knew then it was going for us. We've been winding Pat up a bit recently, because although Clem has been having a bad time lately, he has been given a new three-year contract. So we've been saying to Pat, 'What's happening here? You've been playing well and you can't even get a new one-year one, can you?'

I had a bit of fun with the crowd near the end, which I enjoyed. When we had been beaten 5–0 last Easter the Tottenham fans had given me some terrible stick – nothing malicious, just singing, 'If

Woodcock can play for England so can we,' things like that. So when we were winning 4–2 I was over near their fans and one big lad was yelling at me, and I just pointed at him, shook my head and burst out laughing.

It was a great Christmas present to win at Tottenham again, and we were all happy on the coach afterwards. We thought Don might give us a couple of hours off in the afternoon to go home if we wanted to, but when we got back to the hotel we went in for our meal and he said, 'Right, you can have a few glasses of wine or beers, you're quite welcome, but this afternoon I want you all in bed with your feet up.' I think that is right after a hard game with another one tomorrow. You could argue that you could go home and relax, but it wouldn't be the same as being in bed. So that was what we did. We got up for a meal and then went back to bed again.

Lee left tonight. He has gone to Sunderland. He collected his stuff, said his goodbyes, and went. I hope he has got the right move this time. He has been getting a lot of goals in the reserves.

27 DECEMBER
Arsenal 1 Birmingham City 1
My ankle had swelled up like a balloon. I did well to start, let alone get through the game. It wasn't very satisfying anyway, although Charlie at least got his first Highbury goal, even if it was from the spot. But when teams come down to pack the midfield, and are kicking and biting and not trying to play, if you don't get an early goal it goes from bad to worse.

The most pleasing thing was that a year ago we were getting beaten in games like this. Here we battled and got a goal back after going behind.

Raph didn't score, but his run continued in a way, because he made the penalty. He is not the type of big front player some people think I need. He is strong, but he is not that strong at holding the ball up and laying it off. He's more the Luther type, very fast and with a knack of being in the right place at the right time.

He's been in and out of the team over the last couple of years. When he has come in, he's tended to get a goal and do quite well, but he hasn't been able to maintain it in the past. After three or four games he isn't doing much, and he's been out of the side again.

I had a chat with him at the Christmas lunch and told him that he has got to be a bit more determined if he wants to stay in, because Sundy is going to be fit soon and I think he only got in because Sundy wasn't available. But so far Raph's been given his chance and has taken it. I said to him just take any ball as it comes, concentrate fully on the first ball, then on the second and so on. And I think he has taken that advice. He is certainly putting himself about more and being more consistent. I think he realizes that if he is going to stay in the team he has got to give everything in every game.

Probably the most remarkable thing about the game was that afterwards Don had a go at Pat, said he should have come for the ball for their goal. That's never happened before while I've been at the club.

28 DECEMBER

The lads have got two days off now, but I'm in for treatment. I'm not the worst off though. It really hasn't been Sundy's month. He went to see a specialist because he couldn't tense the muscle in the leg which Raph knocked the day Don took over. The specialist looked at it and sent him home to get some clothes and booked him in for an operation tomorrow. He has a blood clot in the leg.

John Robertson came down today to take his daughter to hospital, and we had an evening out. He is in a terrible situation and is understandably not very happy. He's gone to Derby, they are bottom of the second division and they owe him some money, and all the while he is still living in Nottingham so he can see how well Forest are doing. And he is a great player. Carole said afterwards she felt sorry for him. You have to to some extent, but at the same time it is his own responsibility. He made mistakes in the past when he came to the end of his contract. He should have realized it was an important decision for him at thirty, and he should have made sure the move was right. He could have taken the decision to go down to Derby or a club like that in three years time. We could certainly have done with him.

We had quite a laugh today. There was a story that the manager of a Ladbrokes betting shop was sacked because he had quoted odds of a million to one against Arsenal winning the League, and this punter put fifty pence on. 'A Mr Neill,' said Sundy.

30 DECEMBER

We were chatting about contracts today, specifically because Rixy's ends this season. People say that situation puts players under pressure, but I always enjoy it in a way, and I said I certainly always play better when the contract is coming to an end, especially if I know I'm moving at the end of the contract. People sometimes say that you won't be committed to a club if you have already got someone else lined up, but both at Forest and Cologne when I knew I was leaving I did very well for them because I wanted to go out on a high note.

The main difference is that foreign clubs tell you what is going on. No one has said a word to Rixy, and at the same time, which I also can't understand, he hasn't gone in and said, 'Let's get it sorted out now.'

It is a gamble for the player, because if he is in demand he is in a stronger position at the end of the season. But then again if there is no one after him when he becomes a free agent he is in a weaker position. But he could go in and say, 'I want to sort it out now, but as that means I'm forgoing opportunities which might come up at the end of the season, it'll cost you.'

I think for the club, who want to have their team together, there's even more incentive for them to say to him now, 'We want you to stay, let's settle it now', but it just doesn't happen.

It was very different in Germany. I'd only been there six months when I was sitting at dinner one night and Weisweiler said to me, with all the other players around, 'Barcelona want to buy you. I've told them no at the moment, but perhaps soon, are you interested?' So I said, 'Yes.'

'You can't go while I'm here, but when I go to Cosmos, you can.' Nothing came of that, but then a year later there was speculation that they had offered Simonssen and cash for me. And then in my last season at Cologne we played a pre-season tournament there, and Cologne told me that they had had another approach. Barcelona wanted to buy me and then loan me to an English club, so that I was available if Schuster and Maradonna didn't work out. It was strange that they could think that way. I've had fantasies about coming off the field at Arsenal to be told there was a plane waiting to take me to play for Barcelona the next day. It didn't happen, and I'm not sure I'd want to go to Spain anyway. It is vicious out there, particularly it seems for foreign players. I was talking to Johan Cruyff during the World Cup and he was saying that no foreign player goes

236

to Spain without ending up in hospital for an operation. And when you think of the list: Cruyff himself, Schuster, Laurie Cunningham, and now Maradonna, that seems true. I don't know whether it is coincidence or not, but I don't think so from what I've seen. What seemed strange, though, to English players, was that Cologne would keep me informed like they did. Liverpool made an approach for me when I was there.

It was again while we were in Barcelona for that tournament. I was in my hotel room when the phone went. I picked it up and it was Peter Robinson. He introduced himself then said, 'Mr Paisley wants to speak to you.' I was a bit taken aback, and I'd had that argument with John Robertson just that summer when I'd said I didn't really fancy playing for Liverpool, I'd always wanted to play for Arsenal. So I said, 'Oh, yes. Hullo, Mr Paisley how are you?' and he asked if I was interested in going to Liverpool. And I said, 'Well, yes. I don't know what the situation is with Cologne, but yes, I'm interested.' And after all I'd said to Robbo, it was such a boost to be wanted by Liverpool. I had a great tournament.

I spoke to Bob on three or four occasions after that. He kept asking, 'What's the situation?' and it was when Cologne were playing two out of Fischer, Allofs, Littbarski and me, so there was the chance they'd have let me go if I hadn't been in the team. But I kept saying, 'Well, I'm playing, and I'm playing well, but obviously I'm interested.'

So eventually they said they wanted to do things properly and would talk to Cologne, and I told Cologne that I wanted to speak to Liverpool. Liverpool rang them then and asked permission to speak to me, and they said, 'Yes, of course you can.' But they added, 'Speak to whom you like, but you aren't going anywhere. You are our player and you are staying here until the end of the season at least.'

I rang Bob Paisley. And he said, 'We're coming over. We've a flight to Dusseldorf tomorrow.' So I said, 'You know they won't let me go?' and he was astonished. 'But they've just said I could speak to you.' So I told him that I'd got to stay to the end of the season and he said, 'I didn't realize that. We'll have to cancel it then.' So I said I'd speak to them at the end of the season and see what the situation was, but by then Ian Rush was in the team and scoring goals, and they said they were worried about meeting my personal terms.

But that whole approach is different, and I think better.

31 DECEMBER
Arsenal 2 Southampton 2

People said afterwards it was a great game. I couldn't really tell, but we tried to play, and did knock it about a bit which was pleasing, especially as the conditions were bad – a high wind; and of course the pitch. Shilts said afterwards the North Bank goal-mouth was the worst he has played on, there were holes everywhere and he said his feet kept just sinking in.

But it probably cost us the game. Raph had two chances down there in the second half, and the pitch was probably responsible for the misses.

Steve Williams had a good game for them. I think Don fancies him, and Strachan, and there are rumours that Strachan will come at the end of the season.

I feel more optimistic than I would have thought possible a few weeks ago.

We have now had a four-game run unbeaten, probably the best since I arrived at the club. And although two of them were draws, it is something to build on, which we haven't had since I came to Arsenal.

I hope now that Don gets the job. My first reaction when they sacked Terry was that Don should have gone too, and I would have liked to see Terry Venables getting the job. But if he comes it will take him a few months to get the team the way he wants it, and I could be at the end of my contract by the time things have settled down. And seeing the way things are going, Don is earning the job. I'm sure we will qualify for Europe, and we are talking about putting a bet on ourselves to win the FA Cup.

Everyone has noticed the change in Don. He is doing really well, and everyone is behind him. He doesn't go on about opponents now, it is much more, 'C'mon, let's get out there and do it', before the games. And he is more relaxed. But he is still hard. He had a go at Pat after the Birmingham game, so he is not being a nice guy so the players will like him. He is having a go at other people too. I think he feels that if the players put it in for him, he has got every chance of getting the job, and they are doing so at the moment.

My other hope for 1984 is to get a decent run in the England team. So far Bobby Robson has had fifteen games as manager, and

I've only started in four of them. Some of that was due to injuries, but I still suspect that he is not sure about me. I think he should be. I can't honestly believe that some of the players being put forward are as good as I am. A year ago I was convinced that 1983 would see my acceptance as a regular. Instead I seem to have gone back. I hope 1984 will see a change.

POSTSCRIPT

Looking back, just over a year after that final diary entry, so much has happened that in some ways it is impossible to believe it all took place only the year before last. By the time you read this I might have played my last game for Arsenal, for my contract expires in the summer, and at the time of writing it is by no means certain that I shall re-sign for the club. Real Madrid and my old club Cologne have both been mentioned as being interested in signing me. Both have their attractions to say the least, but I like living in London so much that staying here, although not necessarily with Arsenal, cannot be ruled out.

Unfortunately, as Peter Ball remarked in his introduction, this book is not the story of success which we hoped it would be, yet the fact that we caught the club at a moment of crisis I hope makes it interesting. And I hope people will take that into account when they are reading some of my judgements. Some of them now make me cringe, and I thought hard about watering several down, and omitting others altogether. But in the end I didn't because they were true at the time. If you are in a crisis, whether in a relationship or at a business or a football club, things look different to outside observers, or when looking back with hindsight. This book was my view as a *participant* in Arsenal's crisis.

My judgements on players, both colleagues and opponents, has erred on the side of being critical. What I didn't say in some cases, and perhaps should have, was that I take it for granted that people playing for Arsenal, and even more for England, are very good players: they wouldn't be there if they weren't. So what I've done has been sometimes to dwell on their faults – I hope in a constructive way – rather than just saying what good players they are. Charlie Nicholas, David O'Leary and Stewart Robson in particular might feel they get bad treatment in the book. Charlie is obviously a fine player, but he was being judged by the highest standards, and that was why I was perhaps over-critical.

With David O'Leary that is even more true. He is undoubtedly one of the best centre-halves in Europe. That goes without saying. But he still annoys me sometimes because he is an easy-going man, and with his ability he doesn't demand as much from himself as he could, coasting through games instead.

Stewart has certainly matured in the last year, and is now on the fringe of the England squad. But he is still a bit headstrong, and as he gets more experienced he will become an even better player. Of opponents, probably Remi Moses came in for the most criticism. We did feel that he deserved it at the time. I think that was a phase he was going through too – whether he was being told at United to get stuck in I don't know, but he was obviously having to do something special to claim a place in that team. He has shown since that he can also play; his disciplinary record is much better, and I wouldn't be at all surprised if he had established himself on the right side of midfield in the England team by the time this appears.

If some of the judgements on people were harsh, I think on the whole the judgements on events stand up quite well. The optimism of that last diary entry was not totally misplaced. Obviously we didn't win the F.A. Cup, and we just missed out on qualifying for the UEFA Cup. But I don't think there was any doubt that we turned the corner in 1984, and although there were the inevitable ups and downs, the situation at Arsenal has definitely improved.

Don certainly continued his impressive start as manager. His first signing, to my pleasure and approval, was Paul Mariner. It was probably his best signing too. I've always said that you can't go wrong if you sign quality players, and Paul proved the point, as I expected he would. I was delighted to be able to play with him in club matches as well as internationals, because I think we have a good partnership. But even more than on the field, Paul made an immediate impact in the dressing room, and I think that was a major factor in our run in the second half of that season. I thought he should have been made captain straight away, because all the players respect him. He had done it all, and was known to be a forceful character.

Even without the captaincy Paul made his presence felt. He is a very loud character, very funny. From the moment he puts his head round the dressing-room door you start laughing, and he brought one or two other people out of their shell. But he is also very straight and doesn't mind saying what he thinks, so that our team meetings became much more open. We began to criticize one another more openly under his influence, and it had a good effect on team spirit. Of course Don made his contributions to straight talking as well, particularly after our one really bad performance at Stoke after he had taken over. He went through the whole team from Pat to Rixy – I think I was the only one to escape being torn to pieces.

It was actually quite embarrassing at the time, because he had really let everyone else have it. When he got to me he said 'I can't say anything, because you're doing it.' And he said to the group 'Tony deserves his big house and his nice car, because he goes out and does it on a Saturday.' Which made his comment when I was dropped, that I'd been messing him about for two years, look slightly inconsistent to say the least.

Paul's signing of course was the final sign that Sundy's career at Highbury was coming to an end. He went to Ipswich, initially on loan, but he knew he was getting a free transfer at the end of the season, and he eventually joined them. I think he had become a little bitter, and it was sad to see a player who had done so well for the club during their years of success leave on that note. After all, he had had a very successful partnership with Frank Stapleton, and had been considered to be near an England cap at that time.

I ended the season with twenty-one League goals; Paul got seven in fifteen matches, and I think we did really well to finish sixth; it gave us confidence for the next season. And when Viv Anderson, who is another good buy, the type you can't go wrong with, was signed, we really felt we could win the championship.

For the first couple of months we played some fantastic football, scoring some great goals. Charlie proved what an outstanding player he is. With Paul and Viv we had suddenly become a team in every sense of the word. We all fitted together. I'd been very pleased with my own performance the previous season – I'd got twenty-three goals in all, and I think my general play had been good too – but I think as the 1984–85 season got under way I became a bit less single-minded. Perhaps I lost too much of my selfishness. Because Paul, Charlie and I are such good friends and work so well together I'd sometimes look to put them in when I was in a position where I should really have had a shot myself.

But it was all going so well, and then we suddenly had this bad week, partly through the power of television. It was hard enough anyway: West Ham, Oxford and Manchester United all away in the course of eight days. Because of television requirements we had to play them in seven days; and Oxford and Manchester United over three days because Oxford wanted coverage for the Milk Cup match. That meant we had to play on Wednesday rather than Tuesday. To crown it all our league match at Old Trafford was a live Friday-night match. So that made it even more difficult. We went to West Ham as leaders, but Paul didn't play, nor did Tommy Caton or I, and our squad couldn't cope with that, although we had our moments.

Tommy and I were fit for the game at Oxford. And we began as we had been playing all season. For the first forty minutes we pulverized them, and how we didn't get a lead of three or four goals in that spell I will never know. But Pat was playing with an injury and he let in a goal which he would normally have saved, and we ended up losing. Had we won that game I am sure we would just have carried on as we were.

But we didn't, so we had then lost two on the trot, and we had to play United at Old Trafford forty-eight hours later. We were doing great, 2-1 up at half-time, but then we let it slip. So in seven days we'd gone from being on top of the world to questioning ourselves again, asking 'Are we good enough?' And we just slipped further and further out of it for a time, because when you fall into a rut it is difficult to get out of it, and we weren't helped by a series of injuries.

I wondered if Don lost his way slightly about this time too. We had had a tricky start to the season, drawing at home to Chelsea and then losing at Forest, and it didn't faze him at all. We came back and beat Watford and Liverpool and we were just going out to play our football. But this time, when we had this bad run away from home, I thought maybe he was looking too hard for the reasons. Instead of being calm and saying, 'It'll come back,' he began to question things. We began to change to accommodate the opposition again, which I don't agree with. I'd always say, 'Get out there and play, let them worry about us.' Against Tottenham at new year, with Kenny Sansom injured, he put David O'Leary at left-back to counteract Chiedozie. I thought that was completely wrong. Tommy Caton had played there at Newcastle where we had won, and he had done brilliantly. He's naturally a left-sided player, and he was hitting great balls forward for us. I'd have told him to get stuck into Chiedozie, and left him to get on with it, rather than unbalancing the team to put David over there.

As well as making that kind of specific change – because, at least until Steve Williams arrived, we were still a bit short at times in midfield – I think he tried to compromise our style of play. We were hustling people, cutting down space and generally getting on top of them, not allowing them to settle. Sometimes, of course, it worked perfectly – we beat West Brom 4-0 with those tactics, they never had a second to settle – but it meant that we lost a bit from our own game in consequence, and we do have some very skilful players. When things are on a down, I think that is the time to be restoring your confidence and getting back to your basic structure, rather than fiddling about with tactics.

Also, harping back to my days at Forest, I thought we felt too desperate to go out and win to get us back up there. It was something which again draws attention to how wrong the idea of Don as a defensive coach is. He was saying, 'C'mon. We can take these. Play your football and you'll win.' He was also saying, 'Three points today and then we've got a home game next week, which is another three. That's six, which should take us back to the top.' I think that was wrong. We should have said, 'Let's get things back on the right road again. Let's get a point. Anything more is a bonus, but let's make sure we don't get beaten. Let's dig in, get a point and get ourselves back on the right lines.' That's what Cloughy would have said. That's what Liverpool do – get a point here, a point there, take the strain when they need to. And I think Don should have said, 'Hold it. Don't get too excited and go over the top,' instead of us chasing helter-skelter after three points, and ending up with none.

Things weren't helped by off-the-field events. I had been breath-alysed, and lost my licence early in the year. Raphael Meade and Charlie were both done as well, and when stories about Charlie's batch of girlfriends began to hit the headlines, suddenly Arsenal was being presented as an undisciplined, degenerate bunch. Other clubs, including other London first division clubs, have had players lose their driving licences, but because of Arsenal's prim and proper image it made news with us in a way it wouldn't at other places.

Charlie was actually left out for a couple of games. Pat, who had staggered on with an injury because John Lukic was also injured, was left out too. But while Charlie was brought back, Pat wasn't. And suddenly we hardly ever saw him, because he wasn't travelling with us, and the goalkeepers train separately. But I got the impression he had suddenly become the forgotten man, and was being ignored. After all those years of being the man everyone relied on, it didn't seem the right way to treat him.

Things steadied down eventually, and we began to put some results together. We won at Newcastle, we did well against Norwich. The signing of Steve Williams for midfield, the area where we had still been a bit short, made a difference. I thought it was going to help Charlie get back to his form of the start of the season.

So as 1985 began I felt that things were really going to go well – we'd got something to build on. I'd begun the season with a virus infection, and although it hadn't kept me out for long, I was still feeling the effects of it until Christmas. There were games when I felt I could scarcely put one leg in front of the other. But at last I began to feel really strong again. I scored the goal which got us a draw at Hereford in the third round of the cup, and when we hammered them in the replay we really seemed to be picking up the threads again.

Instead the wheels fell off as we lost at York in the next round to a penalty in the last couple of minutes. It was a terrible pitch. We didn't really create anything, but we had done the hard job, and then Steve Williams pulled this guy down off the ball.

Then of course all the criticism started again, and I think Don reacted the wrong way to it. We had, inevitably, the 'Where-are-we-going-wrong?' meeting on the Monday morning – one of Don's monthly 'sort-outs'. He went on and on about whether we competed enough. I said we'd been knocked out of two cups because of individual mistakes: at Oxford because Pat was playing with an injury and tried to protect it; and at York because Steve had made that silly foul. It wasn't because we weren't competing. Don wouldn't accept that. 'Is that an easy way out? Do teams think we are an easy touch?'

I had to admit that sometimes that might be true, and that we might not be competitive enough. But I felt Don was overstressing the point, that it wasn't why we had lost at York, and nor was it the only reason for some of our other defeats away from home.

Then we went training. And we trained really hard on Monday, and Tuesday . . . and Wednesday . . . and Thursday – it was like pre-season. I asked, 'Would we have trained this hard if we'd won at York or got a draw there?' It was clear that it was a punishment for losing. I'd said in the meeting, 'If Steve hadn't done that we'd have got them back to Highbury and everyone would have said, "Arsenal gave a really professional performance",' but Don jumped down my throat for saying that.

On Friday we were weighed. I'd been out for a late meal on the Thursday, and I knew before I'd got on the scales what was going to happen. I was four pounds overweight. Terry Burton immediately went into see Don. Nothing was said at the time, and the sheet went up for the Saturday's match against Coventry.

Then on Saturday Don said he was leaving me out of the team. I went to see him, and he said I'd been messing him around for two years. I'd got away with it last season because I'd been playing well, but I'd been inconsistent. I said it was the wrong time. If he'd left me out before Christmas because I wasn't playing to my full potential I'd have had no argument. As it was things got quite heated. I said I'd still got him thirteen goals in twenty-nine games, and it was just as well I had because no one else was going to. He said goals aren't everything – which I agree with – and he also said that I didn't want to chase after full-backs or tackle centre-halves and win the ball back, I just wanted to play around the penalty area and put the ball in the net. And that he hadn't seen what he wanted to see from me in training during the week. But I don't think I've ever cheated on the team. I do moan in training, but I put it in when I need to. As for not working, and tackling back, I do think I work hard as a forward. And he said that he knew I went out on Thursday and Friday nights. I told him that I sometimes went out for a meal on a Thursday, but that was all, and that I never went out on a Friday. He said there were stories that I did. I wanted to know why he hadn't said at the beginning of the week that he was going to leave me out. Don's answer was that he'd been looking at me in training, and hadn't seen what he was looking for, so I ended up assuming that I'd been dropped for going in overweight on Friday, even though I would have been my normal weight again on Saturday. So I went and asked the office to order me a taxi and left the ground, because I was furious and didn't want to see anyone in case I said something I would later regret. But of course that provoked some bad press. On Monday I saw Don and he said that according to the Arsenal rule book, which he was holding, there was nothing that he could fine me for, and we patched things up quite amicably.

But I was not happy about my position. I was bitterly disappointed with the reasons I was given for being left out. I felt that if Don had wanted to give me a kick up the backside, which he did, a warning that he would drop me if I didn't pull my finger out would have been all that was necessary; I felt I deserved a warning first. But I thought that he had done it at the wrong time. Before Christmas I could have understood it. I had been having an inconsistent season. But I didn't think it should have happened at this stage, and I couldn't accept the contradictory reasons for it. The press asked if it would influence my decision about whether I'd re-sign or not. I said that all I wanted to do was think about the rest of the season, and play well for the rest of the existing contract, but clearly it wasn't going to make me rush to re-sign.

I was also slightly concerned because of its effect on my international career if I wasn't back in the Arsenal team. For the first time, with the wins over Finland and Turkey, I'd begun to feel an established part of the England team. For unlike at the club, 1984 had begun badly and ended well for me with England. The first game of the year was the friendly with France. Paul Mariner had joined us by then, and was playing well; he and I were hoping for the chance to revive our international partnership, which had been hindered by my injuries the previous year. But as we had been knocked out of the European Championships, Bobby Robson decided to pick an experimental team. When he named the team, Walsh and Stein of Luton were the two strikers. Paul stormed out, and I wasn't happy either. I thought he should at least have told us beforehand what he was going to do. Obviously we wanted to play in that match, and against France in Paris, against the team which had reached the World Cup semi-finals and was going to win the European Championships that summer. I thought we should have played, rather than two inexperienced players. To throw them into a match like that he must have thought a lot of them, but neither is on the scene a year later, although in Walsh's case that is partly because he has had injuries.

But perhaps we were lucky to miss it after all. For the last home international championship I was back in; I got the goal against Northern Ireland, which we won 1-0, survived a poor team performance against Wales at Wrexham, which we lost 1-0, and then scored a very satisfactory goal against Scotland.

Unfortunately my hamstring went as I jumped to celebrate that goal. In the second half I felt it go again as I ran and jumped for a ball, jumping putting extra pressure on it. That kept me out of the Russia match – again, perhaps a fortunate miss – and I shouldn't have gone on the South America tour, but I hoped that with a week's rest beforehand it would clear up. It seemed to go away for a bit, but then it came back. I played against Brazil, and with the hard ground I was feeling my achilles tendon as well; it went again, and in the second half it was hopeless. I had to come off even though the injury wasn't visible.

After that I thought there was no point my staying on the tour, and I asked to go home. But Robson said, 'I'd rather have you playing seventy per cent fit than not at all. I want you here.' So I stayed. But I couldn't train. And in Uruguay, which was our next destination, the only thing to look forward to is training! So while the rest were playing five-a-sides, I was standing on the sidelines doing nothing. I felt like I was wasting away.

I said to Robson, 'It's not right. But why don't you make me sub and put me on with twenty minutes to go, then we'll know one way or the other, and it'll save me going to Chile if it's no good.' So he did. I could run around okay, so people on TV were saying, 'He's all right, can't see anything wrong with him.' But it wasn't right. It stiffened up, and I thought, 'I've got to get this cleared up for next season.' There was no point playing on a tour of South America, and then not being available when the World Cup qualifiers start. So I said that was it.

We began with a friendly against East Germany. Mark Hateley, who had come in almost as a last resort on the tour of South America and done well, wasn't picked. Paul and I were. I thought we played well, but the goal wouldn't come, Paul took some terrible stick, and late into the match Trevor Francis and Mark replaced Paul and I. Paul and Trevor were both injured for the next game against Finland, so Mark and I played, and at last it came together. I missed half a dozen, but I thought I contributed well in other areas, and we won really well. And at last everyone was pleased with the team. Interestingly, apart from Mark Wright, John Barnes and Hateley, it was the team Robson had when he began, so after all the experiments he had come back to it.

As Hateley was injured, Peter Withe came back in for the match with Turkey, but otherwise it was the same team: so at last we had a settled side. And you could really see the benefits. I know people were quick to say how bad Turkey were afterwards, but I think that result must have reverberated round Europe. For a start I can imagine what the West Germans thought when they saw us getting eight goals there, because they think Turkey is the worst place to have to go. They think getting a point is a good result there. Of course that is partly because of other factors. The Turks are second class citizens in Germany, so their teams tend to be fired up to show the Germans how good they can be, but even so German players are respectful of Turkey.

I was disappointed not to get a hat-trick. I had three chances and got two goals. I might have had another, but after Steve Williams hit the post, I was stretching to turn the rebound in when I heard Bryan Robson shout, 'Leave it,' so he got it. I'm sure I would have got a third if I'd played the full ninety minutes, but Bobby Robson wanted to give Trevor a run, and he wanted Peter Withe to get a goal, so he took me off and left Withe on.

But at last I really felt I was in possession as a permanent member of the team. The team spirit in the squad is so good at the moment, and we are looking such a good team, that I'm convinced we can do really well in the World Cup – even in South America.

ARSENAL PLAYERS 1982–3 SEASON

Player	Position
Pat Jennings	Goalkeeper
George Wood	Goalkeeper
Rhys Wilmot	Goalkeeper
David O'Leary	Central defender
Chris Whyte	Central defender
John Kay	Full-back/Central defender
Colin Hill	Full-back/Central defender
Kenny Sansom	Full-back
Danny O'Shea	Full-back
John Devine	Full-back
John Hollins	Defender/Midfield
Stewart Robson (Robbo)	Defender/Midfield
Graham Rix	Midfield
Brian Talbot (Noddy)	Midfield
Peter Nicholas (Nico)	Midfield
Paul Gorman	Midfield
David Cork (Corky)	Midfield
Paul Davis (Davo)	Midfield
Brian McDermott	Winger
Tony Woodcock	Striker
Lee Chapman	Striker
John Hawley	Striker
Alan Sunderland	Striker
Raphael Meade	Striker

Signed in mid-season

Vladimir Petrovic	Midfield

ARSENAL PLAYERS 1983–4 SEASON

Player	Position
Pat Jennings	Goalkeeper
John Lukic	Goalkeeper
Rhys Wilmot	Goalkeeper
David O'Leary	Central defender
Chris Whyte	Central defender
Colin Hill	Full-back/Central defender
Tony Adams	Full-back/Central defender
Danny O'Shea	Full-back
Kenny Sansom	Full-back
John Kay	Full-back
Graham Rix	Midfield
Brian Talbot	Midfield
Stewart Robson	Defender/Midfield
Peter Nicholas*	Midfield
Paul Gorman	Midfield
Paul Davis	Midfield
David Cork	Midfield
Charlie Nicholas	Striker
Alan Sunderland	Striker
Tony Woodcock	Striker
Lee Chapman	Striker
Ian Allinson (Ally)	Winger
Brian McDermott	Winger
Raphael Meade	Striker

Signed in mid-season

Tommy Caton	Central defender
Paul Mariner	Striker

transferred to Crystal Palace in mid-season

INDEX

254